CHOREOGRAPHING
HISTORY

Unnatural Acts: Theorizing the Performative

SUE-ELLEN CASE
PHILIP BRETT
SUSAN LEIGH FOSTER

The partitioning of performance into obligatory appearances and strict disallowances is a complex social code assumed to be "natural" until recent notions of performativity unmasked its operations. Performance partitions, strictly enforced within traditional conceptions of the arts, foreground the gestures of the dancer, but ignore those of the orchestra player, assign significance to the elocution of the actor, but not to the utterances of the audience. The critical notion of performativity both reveals these partitions as unnatural and opens the way for the consideration of all cultural intercourse as performance. It also exposes the compulsory nature of some orders of performance. The oppressive requirements of systems that organize gender and sexual practices mark who may wear the dress and who may perform the kiss. Further, the fashion of the dress and the colorizing of the skin that dons it are disciplined by systems of class and "race." These cultural performances are critical sites for study.

The series Unnatural Acts encourages further interrogations of all varieties of performance both in the traditional sense of the term and from the broader perspective provided by performativity.

Choreographing
HISTORY

Edited by
Susan Leigh Foster

Indiana University Press

BLOOMINGTON AND INDIANAPOLIS

Library of Congress Cataloging-in-Publication Data

Choreographing history / edited by Susan Leigh Foster.
    p.   cm. — (Unnatural acts)
    Includes bibliographical references and index.
    ISBN 0-253-32411-4 (cl : alk. paper). — ISBN 0-253-20935-8
(pa : alk. paper)
    1. Body, Human—Social aspects.   2. Body, Human—Symbolic aspects.
3. Historiography.   4. Dance—Social aspects.   I. Foster, Susan
Leigh.   II. Series.
GN298.C48   1995
306.4—dc20   94-3622

1 2 3 4 5 00 99 98 97 96 95

CONTENTS

Historians as Bodies in Motion

Embodying Theory

Corpologue

ACKNOWLEDGMENTS

Careening through time at breathtaking speed, the two-headed figure of this moment's motion points toward its future while gazing back at its history. It rushes past (or is it through?) the slower-moving, primitive-looking figure of motion-past, itself in motion. The vaporous traces of motion-present permeate the condensated inscriptions of motion-past—those blood-blisters on the skin of time produced by the scarification of many moving bodies. In that interdisciplinary moment of contact between these two temporal bodies, a new discursive space opens up.

Such an interdisciplinary moment came to pass at the conference titled Choreographing History, held at the University of California/Riverside in February 1992, out of which the essays in this volume were generated. The conference brought together historians of the arts, science, sexuality, and history to discuss the project of writing about the body and its movement. Focus on body as an analytic category, in the organization of this conference and in current critical theory, brings into sharp relief theoretical concerns in the writing of history. Body as a subject of scholarly inquiry also invites participation across disciplines and from various constituencies who previously have found little common ground.

For initiating the idea of an interdisciplinary forum to address the body's motion past and present, we wish to acknowledge the visionary influence of Christena L. Schlundt. For their support in turning motion's movement into dialogue and, subsequently, into writing, we thank the University of California Humanities Research Institute and its director, Mark Rose; the UC/Riverside Center for Ideas and Society and its director, Bernd Magnus; dean of the College of Humanities and Social Sciences at UC/Riverside, Brian Copenhaver; the staff of the Department of Dance, Darline Starling, Karen Bain, and Laurie Hall; research assistants Richard Kiovsky, Jennifer Fisher, and Anne Dunkin-Willis; and dance faculty Sally A. Ness, Susan Rose, Fred Strickler, and most especially Linda J. Tomko.

An Introduction to
Moving Bodies

SUSAN LEIGH FOSTER

Choreographing History

Manifesto for Dead and Moving Bodies

*Sitting in this chair, squirming away from the glitches, aches, low-grade tensions rever-
berating in neck and hip, staring unfocused at some space between here and the nearest
objects, shifting again, listening to my stomach growl, to the clock ticking, shifting, stretching, settling, turning—I am a body writing. I am a bodily writing.*[1] **We used to
pretend the body was uninvolved, that it remained mute and still while the
mind thought. We even imagined that thought, once conceived, transferred
itself effortlessly onto the page via a body whose natural role as instrument facilitated the pen. Now we know that the caffeine we imbibe mutates into the
acid of thought which the body then excretes, thereby etching ideas across the
page. Now we know that the body cannot be taken for granted, cannot be
taken seriously, cannot be taken.**

A body, whether sitting writing or standing thinking or walking talking
or running screaming, is a bodily writing. Its habits and stances, gestures
and demonstrations, every action of its various regions, areas, and parts—all
these emerge out of cultural practices, verbal or not, that construct corporeal
meaning. Each of the body's moves, as with all writings, traces the physical fact
of movement and also an array of references to conceptual entities and events.
Constructed from endless and repeated encounters with other bodies, each
body's writing maintains a nonnatural relation between its physicality and
referentiality. Each body establishes this relation between physicality and
meaning in concert with the physical actions and verbal descriptions of bodies
that move alongside it. Not only is this relation between the physical and conceptual nonnatural, it is also impermanent. It mutates, transforms, reinstantiates
with each new encounter.

Today's creaking knee is not yesterday's knee jogging up the hill. The way
one reaches toward that knee, as much a metaphor as any attempt to name or
describe the knee, already presumes identities for hand and knee. But during
their interaction identities for hand and knee become modified. Together they
discover that the knee feels or sounds different, that the hand looks older or
drier than yesterday. Comparisons between past and present knees provide some

sense of continuity, but the memory is also unreliable. Was it a year ago that the knee started creaking that way? Did it cease to make that noise during running, or after stretching? Why did it hurt yesterday and feel fine today?

The body is never only what we think it is (*dancers pay attention to this difference*). Illusive, always on the move, the body is at best *like* something, but it never *is* that something. Thus, the metaphors, enunciated in speech or in movement, that allude to it are what give the body the most tangible substance it has.

Organized collections of these metaphors, established as the various disciplines that scrutinize, discipline, instruct, and cultivate the body, pretend permanence of and for the body.[2] Their highly repetitive regimens of observation and exercise attempt to instantiate physical constants. Thousands of push-ups, pliés, or Pap smears later, the body appears to have consistent features, a clear structure, identifiable functions. If one is willing to ignore all subtle discrepancies and to uphold the statistical averages, one can almost believe in a body that obeys nature's laws. But then it suddenly does something marvelously aberrant: it gives out, comes through, or somehow turns up outside the bounds of what was conceivable.

This is not to say that the body's latest unanticipated gestures occur beyond the world of writing. On the contrary, the body's newest pronouncements can only be apprehended as *bricolages* of extant moves. A sudden facility at physical feats figures as the product of past disciplinary efforts to render the body faster, stronger, longer, more dextrous. The onset of illness signals deleterious habits, psychological repression, a cleansing process. Any new sensation of sex issues out of an expanded, but not alternative, sensorium. These new writings, even as they jar perceptions with their arresting inventiveness, recalibrate, rather than raze, bodily semiosis.

How to write a history of this bodily writing, this body we can only know through its writing. How to discover what it has done and then describe its actions in words. **Impossible. Too wild, too chaotic, too insignificant. Vanished, disappeared, evaporated into thinnest air, the body's habits and idiosyncrasies, even the practices that codify and regiment it, leave only the most disparate residual traces. And any residue left behind rests in fragmented forms within adjacent discursive domains.** *Still, it may be easier to write the history of this writing body than of the pen-pushing body. The pen-pushing body, after all, bears only the thinnest significance as an inadequate robotics, the apparatus that fails to execute the mind's will.*

What markers of its movement might a bodily writing have left behind? But first, which writing bodies? empowered bodies? enslaved bodies? docile bodies? rebellious bodies? dark bodies? pale bodies? exotic bodies? virtuoso bodies? feminine bodies? masculine bodies? triumphant bodies? disappeared bodies? All these genres of bodies first began moving through their days performing what they had learned how to do: carrying, climbing, standing, sitting, greeting, eating, dressing, sleeping, touching, laboring, fighting. . . . These quotidian activities— not just the signing of a decree, the waving of the battalion into action, the posing for a painting, not just the body on the rack, oozing with puss, foaming at the mouth—these bodies' mundane habits and minuscule gestures mattered. These "techniques of the body," as named by Marcel Mauss and John Bulwer before him, bore significance in the way they were patterned and the way they related with one another. Each body performed these actions in a style both shared and unique. Each body's movement evidenced a certain force, tension, weight, shape, tempo, and phrasing. Each manifested a distinct physical structure, some attributes of which were reiterated in other bodies. All a body's characteristic ways of moving resonated with aesthetic and political values. The intensity of those resonances are what permit genres of bodies to coalesce.

Yet each body's movements all day long form part of the skeleton of meaning that also gives any aberrant or spectacular bodily action its luster. Those everyday patterns of movement make seduction or incarceration, hysteria or slaughter, routinization or recreation matter more distinctively. The writing body in the constant outpouring of its signification offers up nuances of meaning that make a difference. The writing body helps to explicate the blank stare of the black man in the white police station, the raised shoulders and pursed lips of the rich woman walking past the homeless family, the swishing hips and arched eyebrows of gay men as a straight couple enters their bar, the rigid stance and frowning forehead of the single woman waiting at the bus stop next to the construction site. Or put differently: the writing body helps to explicate the blank stare of the black man in the white police station, the blank stare of the rich woman walking past the homeless family, the blank stare of gay men as a straight couple enters their bar, the blank stare of the single woman waiting at the bus stop next to the construction site. Each body's distinctive pronouncements at a given moment must be read against the inscription, along with others, it continuously produces. A blank stare does not mean the same thing for all bodies in all contexts.

How to get at this skeleton of movement's meaning for any given past and place? Some bodies' quotidian movements may have been variously recorded in manuals—ceremonial, religious, educational, social, amorous, remedial, martial—that instruct the body, or in pictures that portray it, or in literary or mythological references to its constitution and habits.[3] In their movements, past bodies also rubbed up against or moved alongside geological and architectural constructions, music, clothing, interior decorations . . . whose material remains leave further indications of those bodies' dispositions. Insofar as any body's writings invited measurement, there endure documents from the disciplines of calculation addressing the body's grammatical makeup—its size, structure, composition, and chemistry—that tell us something about what shape a body was in.

These partial records of varying kinds remain. They document the encounter between bodies and some of the discursive and institutional frameworks that touched them, operated on and through them, in different ways. These documents delineate idealized versions of bodies—what a body was supposed to look like, how it was supposed to perform, how it was required to submit. Or they record that which was nonobvious, those details of bodily comportment construed as necessary to specify rather than those deemed self-evident. Occasionally, they reflect patterns of bodily deviance, whether ironic, inflammatory, inverted, or perverted, from the expected. Whatever their take on bodies, these documents never produce an isolable and integral single physical figure, but instead stock an antiquarium storeroom with the sharded traces of bodily movement across the cultural landscape.

A historian of bodies approaches these fragmented traces sternum leading, a sign (*in the West since, say, the eighteenth century*) that his or her own body is seeking, longing to find, the vanished body whose motions produced them. Yes, the historian also has a body, has a sex, gender, sexuality, skin color. And this body has a past, more or less privileged, more or less restricted. This historian's body wants to consort with dead bodies, wants to know from them: What must it have felt like to move among those things, in those patterns, desiring those proficiencies, being beheld from those vantage points? Moving or being moved by those other bodies? A historian's body wants to inhabit these vanished bodies for specific reasons. It wants to know where it stands, how it came to stand there, what its options for moving might be. It wants those dead bodies to lend a hand in deciphering its own present predicaments and in staging some future possibilities.

To that end historians' bodies amble down the corridors of documentation, inclining toward certain discursive domains and veering away from others. Yes, the production of history is a physical endeavor. It requires a high tolerance for sitting and for reading, for moving slowly and quietly among other bodies who likewise sit patiently, staring alternately at the archival evidence and the fantasies it generates. This physical practice cramps fingers, spawns sneezes and squinting.

Throughout this process historians' own techniques of the body—past practices of viewing or participating in body-centered endeavors—nurture the framework of motivations that guide the selection of specific documents. One historian's body is drawn toward domestic labor and the panoply of sexual practices. Another responds to etiquette, fashion, and dance, but ignores training for sports and the military. Another frames questions around physical education, anatomy, and medicine, but avoids representations of the body in painting; another looks to hunting or the crafting of musical instruments alongside the practices of pornographic publishing. Another looks for excessive gestures in highly contained places. One looks for physical repetitions; another for exaggerations; another for defiant actions. Whatever the kinds and amounts of bodily references in any given constellation of practices, they will yield versions of historical bodies whose relation to one another is determined as much by the historian's body history as by the times they represent.

In evaluating all these fragments of past bodies, a historian's own bodily experience and conceptions of body continue to intervene. Those bodies of the past were "plumper," "less expansive in space," "more constricted by dress" than our own. They tolerated "more pain," lived with "more dirt." The "ankle was sexier," the "face less demonstrative," the "preference for vertical equilibrium more pronounced," than in our time. They "smelled," or "shaved," or "covered themselves" in a different way. They "endured more," "strained harder," "held on more tenaciously." Even the space "between" bodies and the codes for "touching" and "being touched" signaled differently from today.

These comparisons reflect not only a familiarity with corpo-realities but also a historian's interpretation of their political, social, sexual, and aesthetic significance. Any of the body's features and movements—the space it occupies, its size and dispositions, the slowness, quickness, or force with which it travels, a body's entire physicality—reverberate with this cultural significance twice over: Physical actions embodied these values when the body was alive and kicking, whatever documentary apparatus registered its actions then reevaluated as it reinscribed the body's semiotic impact.

But if those bodies of the past incorporate a historian's bodily predilections, its political and aesthetic values, they also take shape from the formal constraints imposed by the discipline of history.[4] Historians' bodies have been trained to write history. They have read widely among the volumes that compose the discourse of history and from them learned how to stand apart in order to select information, evaluate its facticity, and formulate its presentation in accordance with general expectations for historical research. From this more distant locale, they work to mold the overall shape of historical bodies by asking a certain consistency, logic, and continuity from the many and disparate inferences of which they are composed. They have also listened to authorial voices within histories that strive to solidify themselves so as to speak with transcendental certainty. From these voices they have learned that pronouncements about the past should issue in sure and impartial tones. They have deduced that historians' bodies should not affiliate with their subjects, nor with fellow historians who likewise labor over the secrets of the past. Instead, those voices within past histories teach the practice of stillness, a kind of stillness that spreads across time and space, a stillness that masquerades as omniscience. By bestilling themselves, modestly, historians accomplish the transformation into universal subject that can speak for all.

But dead bodies discourage this staticity. They create a stir out of the assimilated and projected images from which they are concocted, a kind of stirring that connects past and present bodies.[5] This affiliation, based on a kind of kinesthetic empathy between living and dead but imagined bodies, enjoys no primal status outside the world of writing.[6] It possesses no organic authority; it offers no ultimate validation for sentiment. But it is redolent with physical vitality and embraces a concern for beings that live and have lived. Once the historian's body recognizes value and meaning in kinesthesia, it cannot dis-animate the physical action of past bodies it has begun to sense.

Tensing slightly closed eyelids, some bodies dimly appear: glancing, grasping, running in fear, standing stoically, sitting disgraced, falling defiantly, gesturing enticingly. **In that dream-like space that collects filmed or performed reconstructions of the past, visual images from the past, and textual references to past bodies, historical bodies begin to solidify.** *The head tilts at an angle; the rib cage shifts to the side; the writing body listens and waits as fragments of past bodies shimmer and then vanish.*

If writing bodies demand a proprioceptive affiliation between past and present bodies, they also require interpretation of their role in the cultural production of meaning: their capacities for expression, the relationships between body and subjectivity they may articulate, the bodily discipline and regimentation of which they are capable, the notions of individuality and sociality they may purvey. The facts as documented in any recorded discourses, however, do not a body's meaning make. They substantiate the causal relationship between body and those cultural forces that prod, poke, and then measure its responsiveness. They substantiate only bodily reaction. They lie askew from a body's significance and in its wake. And even a historian's movements among them cannot draw them together so as to fashion meaning for a past body's candid stance or telling gesture. The construction of corporeal meaning depends on bodily theorics—armatures of relations through which bodies perform individual, gendered, ethnic, or communal identities.[7]

Bodily theorics already exist embedded in the physical practices with which any given historian's body is familiar. Each of his or her body's various pursuits elaborates notions of identity for body and person, and these conjoin with the values inscribed in other related activities to produce steadier scenarios of who the body is in secular, spectacular, sacred, or liminal contexts. Any standardized regimen of bodily training, for example, embodies, in the very organization of its exercises, the metaphors used to instruct the body, and in the criteria specified for physical competence, a coherent (or not so coherent) set of principles that govern the action of that regimen. These principles, reticulated with aesthetic, political, and gendered connotations, cast the body who enacts them into larger arenas of meaning where it moves alongside bodies bearing related signage.

Theorics of bodily significance likewise exist for any prior historical moment. Circulating around and through the partitions of any established practice and reverberating at the interstices among distinct practices, theorics of bodily practices, like images of the historical body, are deduced from acts of comparison between past and present, from rubbing one kind of historical document against others. In the frictive encounters between texts, such as those expressing aesthetic praise, medical insights, proscriptive conduct, and recreational pursuits, theorics of bodily significance begin to consolidate.

The first glimmerings of body theorics put meaning into motion. Like the shapes that pieces from a puzzle must fit, theorics contour bodily significance within and among different bodily practices. Theorics allow interpolation of evidence from one practice where meaning is specified to another where it has remained latent, thereby fleshing out an identity for bodies that informs a specific inquiry and also the larger array of cultural practices of which they are a part.[8] Theorics make palpable ways in which a body's movement can enact meaning.

Not all writing bodies, however, fit into the shapes that such theorics make for them. Some wiggle away or even lash out as the historian escorts them to their proper places, resisting and defying the sweep of significance that would contain them. In the making of the historical synthesis between past and present bodies, these bodies fall into a no-man's-land between the factual and the forgotten where they can only wait for subsequent generations of bodies to find them.

I gesture in the air, a certain tension, speed, and shape flowing through arm, wrist, and hand. I scrutinize this movement and then feel my torso lift and strain as I search for the words that would describe most accurately this gesture's quality and intent. I repeat the movement, then rock forward insistently, pressing for a conversion of movement into words. A sudden inhalation, I haven't taken a breath in many seconds. I am a body yearning toward a translation. Am I pinning the movement down, trapping it, through this search for words to attach to it? This is what we thought when we thought it was the subject doing the writing. We thought any attempt to specify more than dates, places, and names would result in mutilation or even desecration of the body's movement. We gave ourselves over to romantic eulogies of the body's evanescence, the ephemerality of its existence, and we reveled in the fantasy of its absolute untranslatability.[9] Or else, and this is merely the complementary posture, we patted the mute dumb thing on the head and explained to it in clearly enunciated, patronizing tones that we would speak for it, thereby eviscerating its authority and immobilizing its significance.

It is one thing to imagine those bodies of the past, and it is another to write about them. The sense of presence conveyed by a body in motion, the idiosyncrasies of a given physique, the smallest inclination of the head or gesture of the hand—all form part of a corporeal discourse whose power and intelligibility elude translation into words. Bodies' movements may create a kind of writing, but that writing has no facile verbal equivalence. In commencing to write a historical text, discrepancies between what can be moved and what can be written require of historians yet another form of bodily engagement and exertion. Yes, the act of writing is a physical labor, rendered more vividly so when the subject of that writing is bodily movement resurrected from the past by the imagination.

But to construe bodies' movements as varieties of corporeal writing is already a step in the right direction. Where bodily endeavors assume the status of forms of articulation and representation, their movements acquire a status and function equal to the words that describe them. The act of writing about bodies thereby originates in the assumption that verbal discourse cannot speak *for* bodily discourse, but must enter into "dialogue" *with* that bodily discourse.[10] The written discourse must acknowledge the grammatical, syntactical, and rhetorical capacities of the moved discourse. Writing the historical text, rather than an act of verbal explanation, must become a process of interpretation, translation, and rewriting of bodily texts.

How to transpose the moved in the direction of the written. Describing bodies' movements, the writing itself must move. It must put into play figures of speech and forms of phrase and sentence construction that evoke the texture and timing of bodies in motion. It must also become inhabited by all the different bodies that participate in the constructive process of determining historical bodily signification. How could the writing record these bodies' gestures toward one another, the giving and taking of weight, the coordinated or clashing momentum of their trajectories through space, the shaping or rhythmic patterning of their danced dialogue?

And what if the bodies I am writing about spring off the page or out of my imagination, I don't know which, and invite me to dance. And what if I follow and begin to imitate their movements. As we dance alongside one another—not the euphoric dance of the self-abandoned subject, not the deceptively effortless dance of hyper-disciplined bodies, but instead, the reflexive dance of self-critical bodies who nonetheless find in dancing the premise of bodily creativity and responsiveness—I'm not leading or following. It seems as though this dance we are doing is choreographing itself through me and also *that I am deciding what to do next.* **Dancers have often described this experience as the body taking over, as the body thinking its own thoughts . . . but this is as inaccurate as it is unhelpful; it is merely the inverse, again, of the pen-pushing body.**

At some point, historical bodies that have formed in the imagination and on the written page can seem to take on a life of their own. The historical inquiry takes on sufficient structure and energy to generate meaning and to narrate itself. Its representational and narrational determinants, infused with their author's energy and with the vibrancy of dead bodies, begin to perambulate on their own. When this transformation in the nature of the inquiry occurs, a corresponding redefinition of authorial function also takes place: The author loses identity as the guiding authority and finds him or herself immersed in the process of the project getting made. *This is not mystical; it's really quite bodily. Rather than a transcendence of the body, it's an awareness of moving with as well as in and through the body as one moves alongside other bodies.*

The transformation in authorial identity shares nothing in common with the appearance of modest objectivity that the universal subject works to achieve. The universalist voice, even as it strives not to contaminate the evidence, not to neglect any point of view, nonetheless treats the historical subject as a body of facts. Similarly, the partisan voice, fervently dedicated to rectifying some oversight and to actively exposing an area of deficiency in historical knowledge, approaches the past as fixed sets of elements whose relative visibility needs only an adjustment. If, instead, the past becomes embodied, then it can move in dialogue with historians, who likewise transit to an identity that makes such dialogue possible.

In this dancing out of all the parts that have been created, historians and historical subjects reflect upon as they reenact a kind of improvised choreographic process that occurs throughout the research and writing of history: As historians' bodies affiliate with documents about bodies of the past, both past and present bodies redefine their identities. As historians assimilate the theories of past bodily practices, those practices begin to designate their own progressions. As translations from moved event to written text occur, the practices of moving and writing partner each other. And as emerging accounts about past bodies encounter the body of constraints that shape the writing of history, new narrative forms present themselves.

To choreograph history, then, is first to grant that history is made by bodies, and then to acknowledge that all those bodies, in moving and in documenting their movements, in learning about past movement, continually conspire together and are conspired against. In the process of committing their actions to history, these past and present bodies transit to a mutually constructed semiosis. Together they configure a tradition of codes and conventions of bodily signification that allows bodies to represent and communicate with other bodies. To-gether they put pen to page. Together they dance with the words. Neither historian's body nor historical bodies nor the body of history become fixed during this choreographic process. Their edges do not harden; their feet do not stick. Their motions form a byway between their potential to act upon and be acted upon. In this middle ground they gesture toward one another, accumu-lating a corpus of guidelines for choreographic signification as they go, making the next moves out of their fantasies of the past and their memory of the present.

Ambulant Scholarship

In his essay "Lesson in Writing," Roland Barthes contrasts Western and Bunraku puppet traditions in order to imagine a bodily writing. Where the conventions of Western puppet performances hide the puppeteer backstage either above or below the puppet, the Bunraku puppeteers hover just behind the puppet, on-stage and in full view. Where Western puppets consist of glove-like sacks which the puppeteers' hands animate, or jiggling, jointed appendages strung up to the puppeteers' controlling hands, Bunraku puppets are propped up with sticks swiftly relocated by the puppeteers in order to shift their bodily positions. Para-doxically, Barthes observes, the physical presence of the puppeteers in Bunraku helps to give the puppets an uncanny corporeal power. The Western puppet re-mains an instrumentality, a simulacrum of the body, whereas the Bunraku puppet performs its concrete abstraction. In its corporeal writing we see "fragility, discre-tion, sumptuousness, extraordinary nuance, abandonment of all triviality, [and] melodic phrasing of gestures. . . ."[11]

The image of the Western puppet, in its causal dependence on the puppet-eer, succinctly summarizes the treatment of the body in Western scholarship since the Renaissance. Conceptualized as a natural object, the body has regis-tered, but never manufactured, psychic or social forces; it has conveyed, but never articulated, unknown or untamable realms of experience. As a mechanics, the body has constituted a topic of research insofar as it houses diseases, aberra-tions, and frailties, or as it decomposes into chemical or structural components, or as it demonstrates reflexive and instinctual responses, or as it reflects the re-sults of regimentary programs of training that transform it into athlete, actor, soldier, or dancer. As a metaphor for unknown and mysterious forces, the body has stood in for the unconscious, desire, libidinal or sexual impulses, or irra-tional, whimsical or perverse actions. As a bearer of cultural symbols, the body has been aligned with the feminine, the decorative, the pleasurable, or the fash-ionable. In each of these capacities, the body, like the Western puppet, is construed as an index of forces that act upon and through it. Its fascination as a topic of research resides in its responsiveness as an instrument of expression and in the degree to which it eludes precise verification of its instrumentality.

In this reification, the body shares with women, racial minorities and colo-nized peoples, gays and lesbians, and other marginalized groups the scorn and neglect of mainstream scholarship.[12] The canonical thrust of Western scholarship has worked at every turn to deny and repress or else to exoticize the experience of these peoples just as it has dismissed body-centered endeavors and the participation of the body in any endeavor. The critiques of canonical scholarship established in feminist and queer theory, postcolonial and minority discourses of inherent racial, class, and gendered biases have immediate relevance for a scholarship of the body. These critical inquiries explicate techniques of dismissal used in canonical scholarship that find direct analogues in scholarly approaches to body-centered endeavors. The unease felt by dancers, for example, working in the academy shares with the Native an exasperated sense of the skewed terms in which cultural exchange has typically occurred. Little wonder that dancers often retreat into recalcitrant muteness, insisting that they can only dance their responses to all curricular and research issues.

Critiques of traditional scholarship aid in understanding strategies of the body's neglect, but inquiries into bodiliness can, in turn, extend these critiques by elucidating new dimensions of patriarchal and logocentric value systems. A serious consideration of body can expose and contest such dichotomies as theory vs. practice or thought vs. action, distinctions that form part of the epistemic foundations of canonical scholarship. The Platonic fantasy of heads unencumbered by limbs or torso or by the "beast teathered just beneath the diaphragm" has persevered as a guiding image in academic research, one whose full power and influence come into sharp relief when bodily participation in endeavors is allowed to inform the inquiry.[13] Are not reading, speaking, and writing varieties of bodily action? Can theory attain definition apart from the medium in which it finds articulation? Critical focus on the body forces new conceptualizations of these fundamental relations and of the arguments addressing individual and collective action that depend on them.

Body stands along with Woman, Native, and Other as a neglected and misapprehended subject of inquiry, but it stands uniquely as a category that pivots inquiry easily into any of these marginalized domains. The questions "what bodies are being constructed here?" or "how do these values find embodiment?" or "how does the body figure in this discourse?" can be asked within each non-canonical field of study. To ask such questions is to establish a possible grounds on which to base coalitions among these various constituencies. Body thus constitutes both a subject area and also a mode of inquiry that can connect distinct fields. If bodily actions are allowed to carry their own inscriptive weight, if they are given more than just a sex or a set of regimented requisites, then they may empower us with a newly embodied sense of human agency. If body claims consideration as more than holding ground for unconscious desires, instincts, drives, or impulses, then it may point the way toward new kinds of coalitions and new forms of collective action.

The possibility of a scholarship that addresses a writing body as well as a body written upon can be traced to widespread aesthetic, technological, and political changes in the early decades of the twentieth century. At the beginning of the century, new regimentations of the relations between bodies and machines isolated the body's physical labor, giving it intrinsic interest while at the same time subjecting it to close analysis designed to yield the most efficient routinization of movement.[14] Cinematic representations of the body as well as its treatment in the emerging field of advertising enhanced the body's visibility but also imbued it with an objectified concreteness. Futurist artists, in their praise of the body as machine, reduced it to abstract measurements of velocity and force. Choreographers, from Nijinsky to Graham and Humphrey, working to develop a modernist aesthetic, treated the body's movement as a kind of material substance, capable of being shaped and manipulated, even as they attributed this corporeal reality to a manifestation of the psyche. Thus, the body attained a new autonomous existence as a collection of physical facts, even as this physicality was seen as resulting from individual subjectivity or from the political and economic forces shaping the individual.[15]

This new conception of the body is eloquently reflected in the work of choreographer and movement theorist Rudolph Laban, whose analyses of human movement focused on the positions of body parts, the temporal and tensile qualities of movement, and on the body's paths through space. Laban's work generated two distinct, mature notation systems, one that recorded the body's changes in position and the timing of those changes (Labanotation), and another that documented the effort and flow of movement and the body's shaped configurations in relation to its own parts and other surrounding objects (Effort-Shape). His systems of movement analysis also found application in a second generation of Tayloristic research on worker efficiency. Laban's pioneering studies elaborated, for the first time, multiple variables for observing movement and sophisticated structures to explain their combined physical effects. At the same time, he asserted that the preference for specific patterns of speed, flow, and directionality clearly indicated a given psychological orientation. In his work as a choreographer, he likewise coordinated large numbers of amateurs in performances, known as movement choirs, whose spatial configurations and simple movements would not only represent but also instill in performers and audience alike certain social values.[16]

The conception of body as tangible physicality transporting psychological and social values likewise registered in the scholarship on the body from that period. In the 1930s the idea of the body as a subject of historical research became more widespread, as seen in Norbert Elias's epic histories of bodily conduct and Mikhail Bakhtin's examination of bodies as represented in literature.[17] Elias and Bakhtin, both writing in response to the rise of fascism, focused critical attention on the body's relation to the state. Elias, highlighting the significance of daily patterns of behavior, saw in these compulsory routines the state's capacity to infuse the body with its controlling devices. His copious lists of prescriptions for proper comportment are designed to make manifest the increasing effort to discipline individuals by the progressive containment of social conduct, sexual relations, and affective life. Bakhtin, in search of a conception of body that admitted individual agency, examined the body's capacity for transgressive and rebellious resistance through participation in carnival and other rituals of excess. As analyzed by Bakhtin, however, the body's transgressive capacity remains contained by society's use of the carnival as the designated site at which transgression can occur. Furthermore, the body's power to function transgressively is never articulated in any detail, so that the body remains only an instrumentality through which the dark forces of rebellion and the menace of the uncontrollable are expressed.

This same decade witnessed a burgeoning of ethnographic research that elaborated distinct identities for the body as an intrinsic feature of culture. Accounts by Margaret Mead and Gregory Bateson, Maurice Leenhardt, Marcel Mauss, and Marcel Griaule among others gave sustained consideration to the cultural specificity of beliefs and attitudes toward the body that surfaced as part of their ethnographic inquiries.[18] In this ethnographic ouevre, the body assumes a kind of isolable existence as a category of cultural experience, as a bearer of cultural information and participant in the production of meaning. Yet these solicitous inquiries into bodily specificity are conducted as part of the larger anthropological project of rationalizing difference within an imperialist economic context. Thus Mead's profile of Balinese children—full of tacit comparisons with U.S. children, as in the Balinese "omission" of the crawl stage, their "meandering" tonus, "compliant" sitting, "greater eversion, extension, and rotation" of limbs, their bodily "dependence on supporting forms"—uses the body as mediator between individual and national character, and by extension, as the instrumentality that will both establish and transcend the relativities of cultures. Mauss, in his heroic attempt to remove techniques of the body from the anthropological category of "the cultural miscellaneous," does so in order to study the "whole man." Leenhardt, in his dual commitment to anthropology and the ministry, enacts the ability of a member of a dominant culture to understand and sensitively interpret a "primitive," and "pre-literate" one. In each of these ethnographic projects the cultural Other is resolved so as to rationalize a colonizing agenda that includes humanitarian "aid," cultural "exchange," and economic "development."[19]

If these corpora of historical and ethnographic scholarship generated a profusion of categories of bodily attributes, they did not exhaust the possibilities for showing how those attributes could generate meaning. The body, now a proliferation of physical characteristics, constituted a transparent conveyance of whatever meaning other cultural categories invested in it. Its naturalness remained unquestioned except insofar as cross-cultural comparison pointed up culturally specific treatments of it. In semiotic terms, the conception of the body forged in the 1930s presumed the body as a sign, consisting of cultural signifier and physical signified, yet the relation between the two was far from arbitrary.

Not until Barthes and Foucault, writing as part of the sweeping social upheavals of the 1960s, does the body begin to bear a nonnatural relation between signifier and signified. With the possibility that minority and colonized voices might register their protest and be heard, the relations between body and culture took on distinctive and multiple modes.[20] Foucault's histories track the conversion of publicly punished body into privately incarcerated body and of foolish body into mad body. His histories examine how the forces that draw bodies together lose their metaphoric magnetism and fracture into endless hierarchized taxonomies of sameness and difference that inscribe bodies in new ways.[21] In embodying these epistemically distinct structurings of meaning, the body is shown as able not merely to manifest new meanings, but to participate in the restructuring of meaning production. The body is represented as functioning among endless similitudinous attractions or in relation to a set of indexical vectors or as one of the organically organized microcosms of social processes.

Yet Foucault's aggressive interrogation of the workings of power, even as it elucidated the body's varying modes of representation, assigned little if any agency to individual bodies. Now only a set of arbitrary references, bodies after Foucault are capable of materializing in any form or format. But are they capable of making signs as well as embodying them? And is there some expanded conception of the transgressive bodily excesses proposed by Bahktin that could resist what Foucault has depicted as the hegemonic peregrinations of power?[22] What models of body cultivate physicality as a site for the invention of meaning?

To approach the body as capable of generating ideas, as a bodily writing, is to approach it as a choreographer might. Dance, perhaps more than any other body-centered endeavor, cultivates a body that initiates as well as responds. Even those dance-makers who see in the dancer's body a mere vehicle for aestheticized expression must, in their investigation of a new work's choreographic problematic, consult bodies, their own or the dancers'. During this playful probing of physical and semantic potential, choreographers' and dancers' bodies create new images, relationships, concepts, and reflections. Here, bodies are cast into a discursive framework where they can respond in kind to the moved queries initiated in the process of formulating a dance. Such bodies have, admittedly, been trained so as to accomplish this fluency, a disciplining that strongly shapes the quality of their interaction with dance-making. Nevertheless, they sustain a "conversation," throughout the rehearsal process and sometimes in performance, that imaginatively invents and then lucidly enunciates their specific corporeal identities.

Traditional dance studies, replete with the same logocentric values that have informed general scholarship on the body, have seldom allowed the body this agency. Instead, they have emphasized individual genius over the rehearsal process and the social networks and institutional frameworks that enable the production of the dance. They have glossed over the functionality of dance in a given time and place by using unexamined distinctions between artistic, popular, social, ritualized, and recreational forms of dancing. And they have privileged the thrill of the vanished performance over the enduring impact of the choreographic intent. Still, those who make and study dancing have developed certain knowledges of the body as a representational field and certain skills at viewing and interpreting human movement that offer crucial insights for a scholarship of the body. This expertise is reflected in recent studies that have begun to ask of dance the kinds of questions raised in contemporary critical theory about other cultural phenomena.[23]

The possibility of a body that is written upon but that also writes moves critical studies of the body in new directions. It asks scholars to approach the body's involvement in any activity with an assumption of potential agency to participate in or resist whatever forms of cultural production are underway. It also endows body-centered endeavors with an integrity as practices that establish their own lexicons of meaning, their own syntagmatic and paradigmatic axes of signification, their own capacity to reflect critically on themselves and on related practices. Dancemaking, for example, becomes a form of theorizing, one that informs and is informed by instantiations of bodily significance—athletic, sexual, fashionable, mediatized—that endure alongside it. The theoretical, rather than a contemplative stance achieved afterwards and at a distance, becomes embedded (embodied) within the practical decisions that build up, through the active engagement of bodies, any specific endeavor.

The act of translating such physical endeavors into verbal descriptions of them entails, first, a recognition of their distinctiveness, and then a series of tactical decisions that draw the moved and the written into an interdisciplinary parlance. Utilizing this parlance, the descriptive text can be fashioned so as to adhere to the moved example. The organization of the descriptive narrative can trace out the patterns and shapes that moving bodies make. The narrative voice can take on not only a positionality and a character but also a quality of engagement with and in the moving subject matter, the authorial presence thereby exuding both physicality and motionality.

As a body in motion, the writing-and-written body puts into motion the bodies of all those who would observe it. It demands a scholarship that detects and records movements of the writer as well as the written about, and it places at the center of investigation the changing positions of these two groups of bodies and the co-motion that orchestrates as it differentiates their identities. This ambulant form of scholarship thus acknowledges an object of study that is always in the making and also always vanishing. It claims for the body, in anxious anticipation of this decade's collapse of the real and the simulated into a global "informatics of domination," an intense physicality and a reflexive generativity.[24]

The essays in this volume undertake to reflect these possible new movements in a scholarship of the body. The products of an interdisciplinary concern with the body, they point toward a sustained critical inquiry into bodies past and present by responding to the following kinds of issues: first, how to elucidate a more detailed reconstruction of historical bodies, one that presents them as political, aesthetic, and also consummately physical entities; second, how such vivid reconstructions of bodies or even a sustained attention to the category of body might impact on the very structuring of knowledge as it is constituted in a given discipline; third, how an investigation of the bodily reveals resonances and intersections among disparate cultural practices and enables a more profound apprehension of the body's significance in any given practice; fourth, how a historian's body engages a historical subject, shaping its meaning and moving with it throughout the process of analysis; and finally, how the scholarly text can reflect and even embody the theoretical concerns that a consideration of bodies brings forward.

Heterogeneous in both subject matter and methodology, these essays expand, as did scholarship on the body from the 1930s, the range of bodily actions and endeavors that deserve our attention, for what they indicate about body and about related cultural practices. Unlike those earlier investigations of body, they treat corporeality as polyvalent in its forms of signification and as capable of generating its own significance. These essays also enact an awareness of the theoretical issues, concerning narrative position, form and voice, that are foregrounded by a consideration of the body. In the reflexive analytic structure that they elaborate, made of similar themes taken up at different moments and for complementary but not equivalent reasons, they gesture toward the kinds of multidisciplinary and multiconstituent coalitions that could become possible by giving the body serious critical attention.

Bodily Musings

I can see them now, Clio and Terpsichore, costumed in their combat boots and high-top sneakers, their lycra tights and baggy trousers, a leather jacket, a vest, under which can be glimpsed unshaven armpits, perhaps even a bow tie or some plastic bananas as a hairpiece. . . . I can feel them spinning, lurching, sidling and smashing up against one another, laughing knowingly as they wipe the sweat off foreheads and from the skin be-tween lips and nose; in a standoff, carefully calculating the other's weight and flexibility, careening toward one another, rolling as one body and then falling apart, only to circle around for a fast-paced repartee, trading impersonations of past historians and choreog-raphers they have inspired. Wickedly realistic details of one caricature set the other muse in motion. These simulated bodies pop out of theirs, a kinetic speaking-in-tongues, only to be displaced by other corporeal quiddities. Finally, they run out of steam, col-lapse on the ground, adjust a sock, scratch an ear. But these pedestrian gestures, infused with the natural reflexiveness of all muses, doubly theatricalized by the attentive gaze of the partner, commence yet another duet: the crossing of legs in response to the lean on an elbow, a tossing of hair in response to a sniffle. This duet rejuvenates itself endlessly. It has an insatiable appetite for motion.[25]

But where are they dancing, Clio and Terpsichore? in what landscape? on what occasion? and for whom? No longer capable of standing in contemplative and gracious poses, no longer content to serve as the inspiration for what others create, these two muses perspire to invent a new kind of performance, the coor-dinates of which must be determined by the intersection of historiographies of dance and of body. But what will they claim as their dance's origin? How will they justify their new choreographic/scholarly endeavor?

Sifting through images of originary bodies, Clio and Terpsichore stumble upon an account of the origins of dance and also of rhetoric, the discipline that, after all, spawned that of history, iterated in the introductions to several hand-books on rhetorical practices written after the third century A.D. and up until the Byzantine period.[26] These mytho-historic anecdotes focus on the city of Syracusae at a moment when the tyrants Gelon and Hieron rule with savage cruelty. In order to ensure total control over the populace, they forbid Syracusans to speak. Ini-tially, citizens communicate with the rudimentary gestures of hand and head that index their basic needs. Over time, however, their gestural language, now iden-tified as *orchestike,* or dance-pantomime, attains a communicative flexibility and sophistication that leads to the overthrow of the tyrants. In the elated confusion that follows, one citizen, a former adviser to the tyrants, steps forward to bring order to the crowd. Integrating gestural and spoken discourses, he organizes his arguments into an introduction, narration, argument, digression, and epilogue, the fundamental structural categories of rhetoric, the art of public persuasion.

In this account, the tyrant's eradication of speech—a leveling gesture that sweeps across public and private spaces—puts all citizens, male and female, those with expertise in logos and those who excel at chaos, on the same footing. From this common place, the rebellious bodies of the citizens slowly infuse movement with linguistic clout. They circulate around the tyrant, conspiring on a tacit and circumspect kinegraphy that not only indicates their expressive and physical needs but also a reflexive awareness of their predicament. Eventually, their collaborative subversion prevails, and the tyrant is overthrown. In this moment of political liminality *(and taking precisely the amount of time necessary to leap an epistemic fault)* the dancing body, forged in subversive communality, feeds/bleeds into the rhetorical body, a public and powerful figure. The reinstantiation of speech, however, does not return the community to speech as formerly practiced. Instead, the speaking body attains new eloquence, a new fascination, a new and seductive hold over its listeners.

What seems so promising about this story, beyond its delicious obscurity or its singular pairing of dance and rhetoric, as an originary pretext for Clio and Terpsichore's duet? They are not immediately sure, for it takes the two muses hours of negotiation (danced and spoken) to arrive at an interpretation they can agree upon: Clio initially refuses to believe that the rhetorical body, once originated, had retained any resonances of the dancing body. Terpsichore sulkily retreats into silence, gesturing with dignity and disdain the absolute untranslatability of her art. Clio, attempting to dialogue, praises the primordial status of dance, mother of all the arts. Terpsichore, infinitely bored by this guilt-ridden and misguided tribute, accuses Clio of inspiring only desiccated, static drivel. Now, they're mad: They stomp; they shout; they hyperbolize; they posture; they pinch their faces, hunch their shoulders, and spit out the most absurd and hurtful provocations, then feign distress, victims of their own drama. But in the ensuing silence, the choreography of their combat in its full rhetorical glory stands out. Embarrassed by their excesses, but intrigued by the aesthetics of their anger, they cannot resist a candid glance at one another. Biting their lips to keep from laughing, they determine to continue their deliberations.

Terpsichore senses the need to rationalize choreography as persuasive discourse, and Clio realizes the need to bring movement and fleshiness into historiography. They both agree that they cannot help but admire the immense power in the resistive wariness of those bodies that have tangled with the demonic character of a tyrant. And they sense the strength of a choreographic coalition composed of multiple constituencies. They desire bodies capable of troping, that can render or depict, or exaggerate, or fracture, or allude to the world, bodies that can ironize as well as metaphorize their existence.[27] Troping bodies do not merely carry a message or faithfully convey an idea, but also assert a physical presence, one that supports the capacity for producing meaning. Irresistibly, such bodies retain no authority over some transcendental definition of their being, but instead remain entirely dependent on their own deictic gestures to establish identity.

Clio and Terpsichore have watched this troping body emerge in their own collaborations. They believe in this body that fuses dance and rhetoric, but they also sense, just as the story predicts, its sinister potential. It can become powerful enough to sway other bodies, or even fix them in its hold. It cannot command such power if other bodies have learned the choreographic and rhetorical conventions through which meaning is conveyed. As long as every body works to renew and recalibrate these codes, power remains in many hands. But if any bodies allow this body of conventions to overtake them unawares, then the tyrannical body gains the upper hand.

Determined to keep such tyrants disembodied, *Clio and Terpsichore finish their coffee, roll up their sleeves, and begin to write (or is it dance?):*

Post-Script

The claim for a writing-dancing body, formulated in response to political exigencies of this specific moment, dates itself in the kind of inscription it undertakes to make apparent. At another moment and given different political circumstances, the metaphor of a bodily tropology might well prove reactionary rather than resistive. At such a time Clio and Terpsichore might agree instead to reinvent a separation between body and writing so as to preserve the powers of both rhetoric and dance. In a world, for example, beyond script, one consisting only of screens of simulacra that invite us to don virtual reality gear and dive through ever-unfolding windows of images, what could give the body's presence or its vanishing urgency over other visions?

NOTES

1. Roland Barthes opened up for consideration this approach to bodily writing most palpably through his attention to the physical circumstances surrounding his own profession as a writer—the organization of his desk, his daily routines, etc.—in his autobiography *Roland Barthes by Roland Barthes* and also in his brilliant analysis of the Bunraku puppet theater appearing both in *Image, Music, Text* and in *Empire of Signs*. In that essay, which I take up in the second section of this chapter, he argues that the dramatic gestures of the puppets, the pragmatic manipulations of the puppeteers, and the hyperbolic vociferations of the singer can each be considered as a form of writing.

2. Michel Foucault's studies of the body as inscribed by penal, medical, and sexual systems of meaning have generated a substantial literature investigating the cultural mechanisms through which the body is regulated.

3. See "Techniques of the Body" by Marcel Mauss and John Bulwer's *Chirologia and Chironomia* (1654), whose significance is addressed by Stephen Greenblatt in his chapter for this volume.

4. Natalie Zemon Davis introduces this issue in her article titled "History's Two Bodies," which served as an inspiration for this essay. In *The Writing of History,* Michel de Certeau provides an eloquent and far more detailed description of the disciplinary training of the historian. See especially his chapter titled "The Historiographical Operation," pp. 56–113.

5. My proposal here for a kind of empathic relationship between the historian's body and historical bodies is inspired by the complex use of the term "passion" in Marta Savigliano's *Tango and the Political Economy of Passion*. For Savigliano, passion is *both*

a culturally constructed event, susceptible to commodification and exportation, *and* a primal rousing of feeling in response to another.

6. The concept of kinesthetic empathy is inspired by dance critic John Martin's conception of inner mimicry elaborated in his *Introduction to Dance*. Martin argues that bodies respond proprioceptively to the shaping, rhythmic phrasing, and tensile efforts of other bodies. Martin proposed this empathic exchange among bodies in order to justify his conception of choreography as an essentialized or distilled version of feelings which, via inner mimicry, transfer into the viewer's body and psyche. I am clearly not interested in rationalizing essentialist theories of art, but I do believe that feeling another body's feelings is a highly significant (and under-valued) aspect of daily and artistic experience.

7. The *Oxford English Dictionary* identifies two meanings for the archaic word theoric, one pertaining to the theoretical and the other to the performative. In resurrecting this term, I am trying to gesture in both directions simultaneously.

8. One of the best examples of theory's ability to enable the historian to apprehend analogies among distinct cultural practices remains Raymond Williams's essay on the emergence of the monologue as a theatrical practice in *The Sociology of Culture*, pp. 119–47.

9. June Vail presents an informative critique of this typical posture in "Issues of Style: Four Modes of Journalistic Dance Criticism."

10. In "The Promises of Monsters: A Regenerative Politics for Inappropriate/d Others," Donna Haraway makes the distinction between "speaking with" and "speaking for" in her analysis of the debates over ecological issues in which certain constituencies claim to speak for species on the verge of extinction.

11. Barthes, "Lesson in Writing," in *Image, Music, Text*, p. 172.

12. Consider, for example, the relative prestige of the following academic subjects: anatomy and kinesiology, psychoanalysis and movement therapy, the history of law and the history of manners, literature and dance.

13. The reference here is to descriptions of the body found in Plato's *Timaeus*.

14. Of the many studies that take up this new conception of body in relation to technology Siegfried Giedion's *Mechanization Takes Command* (New York: Oxford University Press, 1948) remains a landmark and influential point of departure.

15. Much more needs to be said about this originary moment in the historiography of the body. In this brief sketch that assembles in one paragraph arts, commerce, and industry, I am merely trying to avoid the typical separation of art from politics and from labor that prevailed in early Marxist analyses that asserted the division between base and superstructure cultural activities.

16. Laban's theories of human movement are presented in his books *The Mastery of Movement, Choreutics*, and *Modern Educational Dance*. His early years as a choreographer are described in his autobiography *A Life for Dance*. Cogent overviews of his work are presented in Vera Maletic's *Body, Space, Expression: The Development of Rudolf Laban's Movement and Dance Concepts* and in Cecily Dell's *A Primer for Movement Description Using Effort-Shape Analysis*.

17. I am deeply indebted to Dorinda Outram's essay on the history of histories of the body that opens her book *The Body in the French Revolution*. She was the first to observe the intense proliferation of scholarly interest in the body during the 1930s, which she traces to the threat of fascist policies in Europe. She argues that Elias and subsequently Foucault focused critical attention on society's capacity to infuse the body with its controlling devices. To this scenario of bodily infiltration and cooptation, she opposes the unruly bodies delineated in Bakhtin's work. In search of a conception of body that admits individual agency, she privileges Bakhtin over Foucault in her inquiry into political conceptions of the body before and during the French Revolution.

18. Marcel Mauss's encyclopedic inventory of bodily endeavors "Techniques of the Body" was joined by Maurice Leenhardt's eloquent depiction of Melanesian conceptions of the body in *Do Kamo: Person and Myth in Melanesia;* Margaret Mead and Gregory Bateson's detailed inquiry into Balinese socialization practices *Balinese Character* and Mead's *Growth and Culture;* and Marcel Griaule's comprehensive studies of the Dogon, among

others. Antonin Artaud's manifestos on the body could also be listed here as a different sort of ethnography.

19. Space permits only the sketchiest of arguments concerning the role of the anthropological project in the imperialist agendas of First World cultures. For a fuller critique the reader is referred to Stanley Diamond, *In Search of the Primitive;* Talal Assad, ed., *Anthropology and the Colonial Encounter;* Genit Huizer and Bruce Mannheim, eds., *The Politics of Anthropology: From Colonialism and Sexism toward a View from Below;* and Trinh T. Minh-ha, *Woman, Native, Other: Writing Postcoloniality and Feminism.*

20. Fredric Jameson suggests this interpretation in "Periodizing the Sixties."

21. I refer to Foucault's *Discipline and Punish, Madness and Civilization* and *The Order of Things.*

22. Although I am about to argue that dance offers exemplary versions of bodies that can resist even a Foucauldian conception of power, another, equally persuasive model is provided in the final chapter of Jacques Attali's *Noise.* This political and economic history of music applies the epistemic structuring of knowledge proposed by Foucault to the development of Western music. Attali ends his analysis with the suggestion that new forms of composition and dissemination of music have the potential to disrupt and disperse the capitalist commodification of music and its production. Attali's version of composition shares with the analysis that follows the idea that individuals can compose alternatives to hegemonic cultural values that lie outside those value systems.

23. For example, Cynthia Novack, *Sharing the Dance: Contact Improvisation and American Culture;* Mark Franko, *Dance As Text: Ideologies of the Baroque Body;* Susan Manning, *Ecstasy and the Demon;* Sally Ness, *Body, Movement, and Culture: Kinesthetic and Visual Symbolism in a Philippine Community;* Lynn Garafola, *Diaghilev's Ballets Russes;* Sally Banes, *Greenwich Village 1963: Avant-Garde Performance and the Effervescent Body;* and Randy Martin, *Performance as Political Act.*

24. Donna Haraway's essay "Manifesto for Cyborgs" traces the shift from white capitalist patriarchy to what she calls "the informatics of domination," a shift that provides the political context for the notion of ambulant scholarship that I propose here. Ambulant scholarship as I develop it embraces the cyborg while also asking for a careful accounting of the body's physical participation in it.

25. Here the reader may recognize a reference to Carolyn Brown's exquisite essay on Merce Cunningham titled "An Appetite for Motion." Cunningham's influence on this duet between Clio and Terpsichore is explicated more fully in my book *Reading Dancing: Bodies and Subjects in Contemporary American Dance.*

26. Vincent Farenga brings this account to light in his insightful article "Periphrasis on the Origin of Rhetoric." His interest in the account is complementary to but differs from that of the muses in that he focuses on the inability of language whether spoken or gestured to address directly the functioning of rhetoric.

27. Remarkably, the late-eighteenth-century movement theorist Johan Jacob Engel outlined these rhetorical possibilities for the body in his extraordinary study of dramatic gesture titled *Idées sur le geste et l'action théâtrale.*

Resurrecting
Historical Bodies

STEPHEN GREENBLATT

Toward a Universal Language of Motion: Reflections on a Seventeenth-Century Muscle Man

In 1649, a little-known English savant, John Bulwer, published in London a book called *Pathomyotomia, or a Dissection of the Significative Muscles of the Affections of the Minde*.[1] The author was a physician, and the title might suggest a medical text, but Bulwer's "dissection" is figurative rather than literal. His concern is with somatic signification. How does the body convey meanings? How are commands conveyed from the spirit to the muscles? How do "affections"— passions, ideas, responses, projects—pass from the silent and inaccessible inner reaches of the mind to the world? The obvious passageways, of course, are speech and writing, but central to Bulwer's inquiry is his conviction that speech and writing are only part of the signifying resources of human beings, and not the most reliable part at that. For language is notoriously slippery, deceptive, and unstable—notoriously, from the point of view of both theology and science.

The Hebrew Bible relates the fall of language in the wake of the attempt to build a tower that would reach to heaven. "The whole earth was of one language, and of one speech," the Bible says, when the tower was undertaken; its builders proposed to "make us a name, lest we be scattered abroad upon the face of the whole earth" (Genesis 11:4). The human fear, then, appears to be a fear of fragmentation, of being lost in the vastness and diversity of the world, of ceasing to speak to one another as a single people. Making the tower and making a name are a single project, a project that deeply alarms God: "And the Lord said, Behold, the people is one, and they have all one language; and this they begin to do: and now nothing will be restrained from them, which they have imagined to do." In response to this threat—the threat of a unified humankind with a common project that promises to realize the dreams of the imagination—God confounds language so that humans no longer understand each other's speech.

He does then what the builders most feared and tried to prevent: He shatters humankind and scatters the fragments across the face of the Earth. The tower gets a name, but the name signifies the splits, gaps, opacities, and multiplicities in language and in human culture: "Therefore is the name of it called Babel; because the Lord did there confound the language of all the earth; and from thence did the Lord scatter them abroad upon the face of all the earth."

To this melancholy account of the fracturing of human unity through the confounding of language was added in the late sixteenth and early seventeenth centuries the searching epistemological skepticism of Montaigne and Bacon. The problem was not, Montaigne recognized, simply the multiplicity of languages; a single, familiar, apparently shared language is in fact deeply unreliable: "Our speech has its weaknesses and its defects, like all the rest," he writes in "The Apology for Raymond Sebond." "Most of the occasions for the troubles of the world are grammatical."[2] For Montaigne, the acknowledgment of the defects of language leads to an acceptance of human limitation, an awareness of all that will remain unstable, unresolved, imperfect, incomplete. To grasp the inherent weaknesses of speech is to give up the grand ambitions of the human mind, the dreams of perfection and certainty. For Bacon, by contrast, a skeptical critique of language is the necessary precondition of a programmatic advancement of learning. Only by liberating oneself from the fraudulence and sloppiness and myth-making of ordinary language can one begin to acquire a genuine and well-founded knowledge of things, a knowledge that will initiate the long road back to the unity and the power possessed fully in Eden and lost definitively at Babel.

With Bacon we return to the obscure John Bulwer. For Bulwer was a Baconian, not one of those followers who refined the experimental methods or who pondered the epistemological problems of the emerging science, but one who responded to the utopian element implicit in Bacon's program, the dream of recovering the primal power whose key was the primordial language spoken before the confounding of tongues. The revolutionary ferment of the mid-seventeenth century sparked many searchers for this ur-language or at least enabled their ambitious projects to surface in print. Often their hopes led them to Hebrew or to some version of Hebrew cleansed of its post-Babel corruptions. Hence, in 1655, Thomas (TheaurauJohn) Tany informed the world that he had received a revelation of "the pure language," which English was capable of rendering in utterances like the following: "obedient alma honasa hul; generati alvah ableuvisse insi locat amorvissem humanet rokoas salah axoret eltah alvah hon ono olephad in se mori melet eri neri meleare; okoriko olo ophaus narratus asa sadoas loboim olet amni Phikepeaa ebellrer elme bosai in re meal olike."[3] Others sought not only the primordial spoken language but also the root and origin of writing, the so-called "Real Characters" that would not merely represent things but express in direct and unmediated form the essence of reality itself.

Bulwer's project in the *Pathomyotomia* and other works is clearly related to this search, but there is a significant difference. Where Tany and others were searching for the universal language in writing and speech, Bulwer had the idea of looking elsewhere in what, following Aristotle, he takes to be the highest perfection of a living creature: *motion*. For a living creature, he writes, "is a living Creature by *moving*" (1). This is why, he reasons, God brought his creation of the world to a climax in the creation of sentient creatures capable of movement. In making "most Noble and necessarie and no way to be despised *motion*, especially its chiefest and neerest instruments, the *Muscles*" the Great Parent of Nature had reached the pinnacle of honor (2). Bulwer is aware that his celebration of muscles is leading him in a strange direction, for the human mind and soul were for millennia the virtually inevitable candidates for the place of honor in God's universe, but he insists on his radical revision of the traditional hierarchy: Take away the power to move, he argues, and a man "would degenerate into a Plant or Stock." The qualities and attainments that characterize human identity depend on the muscles; without them man "would be left destitute of the grace of elocution, and his mind would be enforced to dwel in perpetual silence, as in a wooden extasie or congelation; nay his Soul which is onely known by Action, being otherwise very obscure, would utterly lose the benefit of explaning it self, by the innumerable almost *motions* of the Affections & passions which outwardly appear by the operation of the *Muscles*" (3).

In the muscles, then, lies the key to human identity and, more particularly, to the link between the soul—"being otherwise very obscure"—and the known world. Human expression demands motion, and for Bulwer the principal sites of significant motion are the head and the hands. In 1644, he published *Chirologia; or the Naturall Language of the Hand*, an achievement that prompted him thereafter to wish to be known as "the Chirosopher." Words are conventional, slow, and often misleading, but the signs made by the hands are "part of the unalterable laws and institutes of nature" (16). The natural language of the hand, Bulwer writes, "had the happiness to escape the curse at the confusion of Babel" (19). And if we think that the hands are too limited a means of human communication compared with the tongue, Bulwer proposes to show us that their range of expressiveness is actually greater than that of words. In a flight of rhetorical enthusiasm that leads him to forget that he is himself, after all, using words, Bulwer offers his proof by launching into a list of what we do with our hands:

> Sue, entreat, beseech, solicit, call, allure, entice, dismiss, grant, deny, reprove, are suppliant, fear, threaten, abhor, repent, pray, instruct, witness, accuse, declare our silence, condemn, absolve, show our astonishment, proffer, refuse, respect, give honor, adore, worship, despise, prohibit, reject, challenge, bargain, vow, swear, imprecate, humor, allow, give warning, command, reconcile, submit, defy, affront, offer injury, complement, argue, dispute, explode, confute, exhort, admonish, affirm, distinguish, urge, doubt, reproach, mock, approve, dislike, encourage, recommend, flatter, applaud, exhalt, humble, insult, adjure, yield, confess, cherish, demand, crave, covet, bless, number, prove, confirm, congee, salute, congratulate, entertain, give thanks, welcome, bid farewell, chide, brawl, consent, upbraid, envy, reward, offer force, pacify, invite, justify, contemn, disdain, disallow, forgive, offer peace, promise, perform, reply, invoke, request, repell, charge, satisfy, deprecate, lament, condole, bemoan, put in mind, hinder, praise, commend, brag, boast, warrant, assure, inquire, direct, adopt, rejoice, show gladness, complain, despair, grieve, are sad and sorrowful, cry out, bewail, forbid, discomfort, ask, are angry, wonder, admire, pity, assent, order, rebuke, savor, slight, dispraise, disparage, are ear-

nest, importunate, refer, put to compromise, plight our faith, make a league
of friendship, strike one good luck, give handsel, take earnest, buy, barter,
exchange, show our agreement, express our liberality, show our benevolence,
are illiberal, ask mercy, exhibit grace, show our displeasure, fret, chafe, fume,
rage, revenge, crave audience, call for silence, prepare for an apology, give
liberty of speech, bid one take notice, warn one to forbear, keep off and
be gone; take acquaintance, confess ourselves deceived by a mistake, make
remonstrance of another's error, weep, give a pledge of aid, comfort, relieve,
demonstrate, redargue, persuade, resolve, speak to, appeal, profess a willing-
ness to strike, show ourselves convinced, say we know somewhat which yet
we will not tell, present a check for silence, promise secrecy, protect our innocence, manifest our love, enmity, hate, and despite; provoke, hyperbolically
extoll, enlarge our mirth with jollity and triumphant acclamations of de-
light, note and signify another's actions, the manner, place, and time, as how,
where, when, etc.[4]

This reminder that the Renaissance was the great age of lists is not likely to
persuade many readers that "postures of the hand" exceed "the numerical store
of words," but it is enough to license Bulwer's lengthy and painstaking analysis
of gestures, from scratching the head with one finger (an "*effeminate* gesture
bewraying a *close inclination to vice*" [130]) to putting forth the middle finger,
the rest drawn into a fist ("a natural expression of *scorn* and *contempt*" [132]).
And Bulwer's passionate interest in what he called "manual rhetoric" led him to
a singular achievement: In 1648, in a book called *Philocophus: Or, the Deafe and
Dumbe Mans Friend*, he published what appears to be the first hand-alphabet for
the deaf.

But if this accomplishment would seem from our vantage point to be the
triumph of Bulwer's career, he himself would no doubt have regarded it as a
minor bypath on the road to what the *Pathomyotomia* calls the "universall and
naturall Language" (55), now not of the hand but of the head. That is, Bulwer
does not consider facial expressions to be merely conventional; they are voluntary—that is, the product of muscular movements under the guidance of the
soul—but the expressive system they articulate is not bound by the particular
will of either individuals or cultures. After all, Bulwer observes, we do not actually think about most of our facial expressions, nor are we generally aware of
commanding them (though they are not, in his view, less voluntary for that).
But we are able to read those facial expressions; indeed, we count on doing so
as part of understanding our social interactions. A face condemned to one fixed
posture "would be like a Cabinet lockt up, whose key was lost" (40). There
would be no access then to the subjectivity of the other, "no certaine way of
entrance into his mind."

The *Pathomyotomia* intends to systematize this entrance by performing what
it calls "dissections"—isolating, analyzing, and naming the muscles of the head
that govern the range of human expressions. Hence, for example, "When we
would bow low, as in *assenting with reverence*, or to *adore, worship*, or *profess a
submissive respect*, the whole Neck with the Head is inclined and lowly bent
forward" (51–52). This motion is performed, Bulwer writes, by two pairs of

muscles, the first called *Longus* and the second called *Triangulare*. After describing these in some technical detail, he proposes to rename them in keeping with "the naturall Philosophy of Gesture": "The first long Muscles which so appeare active in these Declarations of the Mind might by our scope of Denomination be called *Par reverentiale*, the Reverentiall paire; The other commonly called *Triangulare*, for distinction, *Par adorans*, the Muscle of Worship or Adoration, or the Muscles of the yoke of submissive obedience" (53). This is the basic form for dozens of "dissections," from the "Muscles of Rejection," to the "Muscles of Supplication," to "the Arrogant paire or the Muscles of Disdainfull Confidence," which work in tandem with "the Insulting or Bragging paire or the Muscles of Insolent Pride, and fierce Audacity"—that is, the proud stiffening of the neck and elevation of the head produced "when all the hinder Muscles of the Neck and Head and that confused Chaos and heape of Muscles in the Back, which are like a Labyrinth of many waies, work together" (78).

As Bulwer is fascinated by the movements of the head, he is equally fascinated by the subtlety and range of facial expressions: "the pleasant Muscle of Loves pretty Dimple" (109), "the Severe and Threatning Muscles" (148) that cause the brows to contract, "the Muscles of Wonder or Admiration" that lift the eyebrows, "the Muscle of Staring Impudence" that "draws the superior Eye-lid upwards" (158), "the Dastard Muscle, or the Ranke cowards Sphincter" that causes "the affrighted *Eyes* to twinkle, that is to open and incontinently to shut more than is convenient" (159). No movement—the pursing of the lips, the twitching of the ears, the slight rounding of the eyes—is too small for his attention, but he is particularly taken with that exuberant, convulsive spectacle unique to humans, laughter. Bulwer conceives of laughter as a great "Dance of the Muscles performed . . . upon the Theater of Mirth, the Countenance" (106), and he analyzes its component parts for many pages. What particularly strikes him is the extent to which laughter is not only an effect of the mind or the heart or the body but "of *totius conjuncti*, of the whole man" (128). Accordingly, "in laughter the Face swells; for, the whole Countenance is powred out and spread with the Spirits that then swell the Muscles" (110).

If laughter is the very heart of the universal and natural language of the head, it is also the limit case of Bulwer's claim that this language is essentially voluntary. For Bulwer himself recognizes that by his own account laughter resembles the experience that had, at least since St. Augustine, been recognized as the very emblem of the involuntary, the male erection: "So that the Muscles of the Face are filled with Spirits after the same manner as a certaine member directly opposite unto it which importunately sometimes lookes us in the Face, which being filled with Spirits growes stiff and is extended" (110). Why then does he continue to insist on the principle of voluntary motion—not only in the case of laughter but even of sleepwalking? The answer seems to lie in the utopian impulse with which we began: Bulwer is determined to recover and to analyze the pure and unfallen communicative system of humankind, and this system must by definition enhance the power of the human will.

Bulwer's analysis of the signifying power of the muscles, then, is haunted by two demons that he must hold at bay. The first is the demon of involuntary or nonsignificant movement: all of the twitches, tics, swellings, and contractions that do not seem to express meanings or that cannot be performed at will. And the second is the demon of culture, the possibility that the expressive motions of the muscles are not primordial, pure, pre-Babel, but rather, like any other language, determined by the varied and changing customs of peoples. The possibility surfaces on occasion in his books on the hands and the head, as when he writes that the Cretans make the sign of refusal or denial by moving their heads straight backward "not as we *refuse* and *denie*, who drive the head about him in a circumduction" (*Pathomyotomia*, 54). But somehow such observations never compel Bulwer to abandon or even substantially to modify his conviction that the muscles speak the true language of nature. There is some indirect evidence, however, that he was aware of the problem and troubled by it. In 1653, he published yet another study of the body, but this time his point was not that the body did not lie. The work's full title sketches its principal argument: *Anthropometamorphosis: Man Transform'd: Or, the Artificial Changling Historically Presented, In the mad and cruell Gallantry, foolish Bravery, ridiculous Beauty, filthy Finenesse, and loathsome Lovelinesse of most Nations, fashioning and altering their Bodies from the mould intended by Natvre; With Figures of those Transfigurations To which artificiall and affected Deformations are added, all the Native and Nationall Monstrosities that have appeared to disfigure the Humane Fabrick. With a Vindication of the Regular Beauty and Honesty of Nature.* The body in its natural state is impeccably "honest," but as Bulwer makes clear, in more than five hundred pages of closely packed and often zany citations, there is virtually no culture in the world that does not fashion and alter the body "artificially."

Bulwer's obsession with the body's natural language has, in effect, generated a counterobsession with all of the things that cultures do to change the body from its natural state. In this extraordinary work—a strange precursor of ethnography written out of loathing and disgust—he comes close to imagining the virtually limitless malleability of the body: heads drastically change shape, the genitals are cut and resewn, the skin is made into a canvas, lips, ears, nose, and nipples are pierced, the thighs are artificially fattened or thinned, breasts are enlarged or reduced or removed altogether, feet are crushed or elongated. Nothing is but what is not. And in an appendix, Bulwer has the tremendous perception that contemporary English clothing actually reproduces many of the transformations that are carried out in other cultures on the flesh itself. He has then one of the first anthropological accounts of the body: He doesn't think of the body's transformations in the mythic terms encouraged by Ovid and his followers or in the closely related mythic terms specified in the trials of witches. Rather, he wants to understand what is actually done systematically and culture by culture to change the body's shapes. But he can only have this perception in the mode of horror: After all, he longs for the body in its natural state, a state he imagines precisely as a single, universal norm from which virtually all cultures have fallen away. He stands, then, in some sense for a turning away from the multiplicity of the languages of the body, even at the moment that this multiplicity is first powerfully acknowledged, precisely *because* it is the moment in which it is first powerfully acknowledged.

NOTES

1. Subtitle: *Being an essay to a new method of observing the most important movings of the muscles of the head, as they are the neerest and immediate organs of the voluntarie and impetuous motions of the mind. With the proposall of a new nomenclature of the muscles.*

2. Montaigne, *Complete Works*, p. 392.

3. Tany, Thomas, *TheauraùJohn His Aurora*, pp. 54–55. I owe this passage to Luxon, "The Place of Displacement."

4. Bulwer, *Chirologia*, p. 20.

JOHN J. MacALOON

Interval Training

There is a specter haunting semiotics. It is the body.
—J. KRISTEVA

We feel in one world; we think, we give names in another.
Between the two we can establish a correspondence,
but we cannot overcome the interval.
—A. ARTAUD

For any dedicated observer of the Olympic Games, that is, for any *theorist* in the original Greek meaning of the term, the body can scarcely be treated as some haunting specter.[1] Academic discourses may cycle as they like between rescuing embodiment from its representations and semiotic representation from its disembodiments. The body may be conceived as an undifferentiated, foundational thing, or as a historically complex and culturally diverse production. "Reflects," "reproduces," "reverses," "represses," or "rebels"—or "disciplines"—may be claimed as the critically liberating predicate lying between the body and social history, or else be dismissed as sterilely mythological in Roland Barthes's sense.[2] But in its own institutionalized practices and everyday speech, the Olympic movement only winks and nods at such academic dichotomies and problematics. Since Olympic practice flourishes so spectacularly, enough is being said; or rather, in Wittgensteinian terms, what really needs to be said when everything is being clearly shown?

After all, so the reasoning goes, half the world's population attends with some degree of intensity to at least some bits of a summer Games. Even in the United States, where awareness of the Olympics as a social movement scarcely appears in public culture and insular professional and school sports dominate cognition and speech, Olympic television broadcasts draw the only audiences for scheduled programming ever measured as exactly mapping American demography. Moreover, these masses of American body-persons arrange themselves around the television in a distinctive living room choreography.[3] Cohabiting with such facts, most Olympic authorities and participants seem to have a difficult time imagining any mysterious conflict, any tragic poverty of mere correspondence between the body, signification, and history. Let the academic theorists and text-capitalists play with one another in their schoolyard contest to distinguish themselves from the masses of theorizers more corporeally engaged with the big Games. This is the practical attitude in Olympic circles toward the transformation of performance into verbal explication. However, while it is certainly laughable to think that any texts might substitute for the global performances that they write, even the ancient theorists had only words with which to report what they saw going on at Olympia.

Bodies and the World System

Though it has and is creating conditions for such performances, modernism (including pre- and post-) has difficulty grasping the logic of world commonality and diversity that Olympic bodies have come to embody. In the Games, a few simple forms of physical movement incarnate and organize a nearly global diversity of meanings into a common space-time, though a transient, performance-bound, and—as I will go on to suggest—an interculturally unknowing one. The Olympics are a paradigmatic instance of the general law of cultural production in the contemporary "world system": the simultaneous, reciprocal, and codependent production of interconnection and diversification, integration and differentiation, homo- and heterogeneity through transnational (or paranational or postnational) forms increasingly emptied of all but genealogical ties to particular civilizations.[4]

Take, for example, Olympic national bodies. Marching in the Olympic opening ceremony—that is, being connected into the world system through what for many, particularly Southern Hemisphere nations, is its master ritual performance—requires acceptance of certain forms. A people must have a name, a recognized National Olympic Committee (NOC), some athletes, a flag, an anthem, and a parade costume. To be defined, recognized, and interconnected as a national particularity requires demonstration of transnational sameness through the agency of these forms. At the same time, commonality entails, indeed requires, differentiation. National emblems must be recognizably different to outsiders and plausibly indigenized to insiders. They must articulate valued cultural differences, or differences capable of taking on cultural values through political contestation.

The social compositions of NOCs, their adaptations to local institutions, and their modes of doing business vary radically among countries, as do their degrees of success in placing the creation of Olympic athletes on local sociopolitical agendas. Successes are invariably accompanied (most often after the fact) by a marking out and naturalizing of putatively special connections between local cultural traditions and one or more of the thirty-odd Olympic sports. Appearance in the opening parade of nations is by definition a particularized globalization. Anyone anywhere who has listened to media commentary or spectator reaction or their own internal dialogue during an Olympic opening knows full well that the interest lies in making out how national groups are, or interestedly represent themselves as, particular and peculiar. This popular ethnology is in turn dependent upon a temporary taking for granted of those things we all are. Each cycle and extension of these processes further deracinates the forms through which the simultaneous expansion of global homogeneity and local diversity is accomplished, rendering the forms yet more fit to do their work.

The main forms of conception and movement that organize Olympic practice are genealogically European. The "emptying out" of these forms proceeds in three dimensions. The first is historical, in highly varying and rivalrous popular-cultural, class-status group, national, and scientific histories. It is asserted, for example, that Olympic ritual and ideological forms chiefly derive from the French Revolution and Olympic sport forms from nineteenth-century Britain. But, no, others counter, they're really artifacts of the German Enlightenment, or rather of Christianity and the Holy Roman Empire. Then again, of course, they're ancient Greek, though there are strong precedents in Egypt and Persia. And in the Han Chinese courts, contesting acrobats and martial artists seem to have been identified as representatives of the various subject peoples, so. . . .

The second dimension is social and cultural indigenization and naturalization, in which the foreign, frequently imperial and colonial origin of forms is forgotten, neutralized, or actively conquered through various modes of reappropriation. Certainly cricket was British, but they didn't know how to play the game. It's ours now: for symbolic raiding and exchange, if we're Trobriand, or to show the world real art and style (and beat the hell out of the British), if we're West or East Indian. As for football if we're Brazilian, or boxing if we're Thai or Korean, or gymnastics if we're Japanese. . . .

The third dimension involves the kind of mixing occasioned by Olympic forms that are not identified as European in popular histories and by European or formerly European forms being radically infused and transformed by non-European conceptions and practices. Europeans now resist or struggle to appropriate for themselves this conglomerate. Examples include: East Asian martial arts, cosmologization of Olympic ritual, and plutocratic capitalization of Olympic institutions; North American sports marketing and conceptions of excellence; African psychologies of athletic success and recastings of humanist Olympism as human rights.

Needless to say, the relative degree of emptiness of intercultural forms depends on whom, in which context, and under which conditions of relative power one talks to. But for purposes of defining the concept, the aggregate result can be evoked in a set of fairly straightforward questions. Which nation, culture, class, or ethnicity any longer owns or is directly indexed by the parade of nations, the 200-meter backstroke, target archery, the soccer match, or the Olympic victory ceremony? Will the same answer have to be given soon for the basketball game, judo, and the doping test? Will the International Olympic Committee session, the television contract negotiation, and the gender test indefinitely resist evacuation of their European social substance? Or will they too one day be hollowed out sufficiently to permit highly particularizing and differentiating appropriations in worldwide localities?

The paradigm for this sort of analysis is of course Marx's of the commodity form, but the relationship is also a highly ironic one. At a few shimmering moments, Marx grasped the mutual constitution of the local and the global through the instrument of empty forms. In *The German Ideology*, he averred that the philosophers of "Criticism," "Man," and "the Unique," who "imagine themselves infinitely exalted above all national prejudices," are "in practice far more national than the beer-quaffing philistines who dream of a united Germany." But confined to satire and polemic, this logic of intercultural relations could not be imagined as systematic. It was suffocated under the Marxian version of universal history and theory, in which the active differentiations of nationality, language, religion, ethnicity, and the rest of the cultural "muck of the ages" were to be swept aside. Such verities of nineteenth-century social science may have passed, but the effects of this missed chance are very much with us.

"Commodification," as the term is often used in contemporary critical discourse on the cosmopolitan left and right, upon inspection turns out to be a name for the general process of simultaneous production of transsocial interconnection and cultural differentiation, misrecognized as an exclusive logic of homogenization of values particular to capitalist political economy. To commodify means in the first instance to disconnect values from their indigenous cultural contexts, to turn them into empty forms suited for travel abroad or back into their original places to be reappropriated through novel local meanings or traditionalisms created for the task. Difference is regained through difference lost, but across a wider sphere of communication. Sale on the market is a principal but neither the only nor the necessary motive and consequence of this very general process. Selling and selling out are key figures in Euro-American and much cosmopolitan discourse about Olympic practices. But in this performative world where money so obviously follows meaning, these verbs depend for their impact on abstract, universalistic nouns: the Body, Nations, Internationalism, Victory, Humanity. Like the Market, Anticapitalism, Liberalism, Social Science, and Criticism, these are empty transcultural forms, barriers to meaning and at the same time the common boundaries within which meanings are articulated and experienced in movement.[5]

In butting up against them, bodies hypostasize these semantic and social walls, while simultaneously constituting the generative spaces amidst them, spaces that bodies then cross in desire or on the rebound. It is not a question of overcoming intervals, but rather of filling them in. Perhaps the body is the only means we have of crossing any interval; perhaps the body is the *intervallum*, the space between the semiotic ramparts. Since professional theory requires strange locutions to distinguish and value itself against other speech, a new predicate in this case, why not be as playful and obscene in training for articulation as is the phenomenon itself: Bodies and histories intervalate each other.[6]

Choreographing the historical anthropology of any globalizing body practice—or rather, for an unreconstructed ethnographer and that sort of body-person, being choreographed in writing by it—begins with recognition that the interconnected world of human variety is simultaneously shrinking (as we are pleased to say) and immeasurably expanding (as we find it difficult to grasp). Analysis must therefore consist in further specification of the genetic codes of signification—the interlacing ramparts of forms—that delimit intramural spaces for multicultural intervalation. In what follows, I further specify this process with respect to the categories of modern social identity most globally relevant to Olympic sport and ritual practice.

But the analysis must equally demonstrate that the phenotypic diversities of meaning thus generated can scarcely be imagined as a whole, much less written out. If there is any specter haunting the subject of the intercultural body, surely it is this. Precisely because localization and difference are what is being produced in common, any rhetorically successful *exemplum* should generate a specific set of cries: maybe them, but not those others, and not us, and not me, at least not in that way. The example I have chosen for the purpose here—choreography of the opening ceremonies of the Albertville winter Games—invokes two further issues of globally localizing and locally globalizing forms: Dance and Sport as categories of body practice and the panoptical/myopic characteristics of Mass Media.

Finally, the critical issue on which the analysis demands judgment turns out to be somewhat unexpected and uncomfortable, alike for popular and professional theorists, universal humanists and liberal relativists, Olympiasts and their critics. Cooperation and harmony sufficient to permit the twin process of interconnection and diversification to proceed depend as absolutely on restricted knowledge, miscommunication, and intercultural invisibility and inaudibility as they do on International Communication. The infamous silences of the body have their intervalating uses too.

Embodiment of Identities

In the dominant logic of the Olympic Games, a holy trinity of modern identity is performatively materialized and set into motion—turned from nouns through verbs into nouns again—through the symbolic operator of the athletic (but also the dancing, processing, queuing, singing, ambling, viewing, cheering) body. The individual body is repeatedly *nationalized* and the incarnated nation *individualized*, and both are *humanized*, that is to say, presented as ontological features of a shared humanity. The game—or rather, the performative genres of game, rite, festival, and spectacle in complex relations, whose verbs are to contest, consecrate, enjoy, wonder and fear[7]—is deployed as a dramatic demonstration of this sociologic. (Political demonstrations against it can, of course, interrupt the game.) Individuality, nationality, and humanity are rhetorically represented—rendered here and now once again—as natural entailments of being alive, as socially inevitable, logically noncontradictory, and ideologically desirable features of modern identity (or as variously becoming so, that's the universalizing history part). The evidence for so-saying lies in so-showing, in the moving athletes and the Olympic movement, in the global audiences who attend to their performances *no matter what anyone says about them*. Academics and other spoilsports can, will, and should argue all they like—athletic individuality is cyborgism, nationality is nationalist evil, humanity is imperialist illusion, esprit de corps is an alienated commodity—but since the terms of resistance are the same ones constituting the object itself, resistance too must be an ontic sign of a common world. From the standpoint of official Olympic practice and ideology: Q.E.D.

The emptiness of these identity categories exemplifies on a global scale Durkheim's law of the progressive abstraction of collective representations as social units grow larger, denser, more plural and stratified. What other identities could today permit 185 nation-state cultures and uncountable sub- and post-national formations to attend to and participate in the same performances to a greater or lesser degree and more or less peaceably? For the Olympic symbol to have become recognized by every person in some places and some persons in every place, it has had to consist of five empty rings. The remarkable thing is that such abstractions could move anyone to identify themselves at all. This magic is accomplished through marriage of the identity calculus with high-performance athletic bodies. These most particular, and yet, because "human limits" are defined by them, these most generic bodies are created by an apparatus of simple movement forms (running, jumping, throwing, sliding) and complex institutions existing to distinguish, measure, rank, and enshrine named Olympic champions as *differentiae* of world history.

This grand oxymoronic field of incarnate abstractions and generic particulars is the ground of possibility for transforming into normalized common sense all manner of strange speech about nationalized persons and personalized nations, humanized individuals and individuated humanity, nationalized humanity and humanized nationality. "The Swiss won the downhill." "China is delirious over Wen." "The human will to triumph over adversity shined through in Greg." "The Brazilians have the flair, the Germans have the precision." "Kipchoge Keino embodied that typical Kenyan courage." "The Canadian runner expanded the limits of human possibility today."

These categories alone are sufficient to generate a ripe international and intercultural politics of identity. It seems hardly disputable that every culture marks off individual persons from one another in some way, that few persons are left in the world who elude the claims of nation-states upon them, and that some sort of notion of generic humanity is at least emergent everywhere. But this is hardly to say that dynamic predications among these general categories, much less their substantive realizations, are the same in other civilizations as they are for the sorts of Western Europeans who invented the forms, installed their hegemonic logics, and continue to dominate the institutions of the modern Olympic movement. Neither is it to say that Europeans or North Americans necessarily have any idea of how others in the world are filling in the meanings of these events and practices, any more than that non-Europeans are perfectly familiar with Western interpretations.

For example, in a four-year ethnography of Korean speech about the Olympics, my colleagues and I heard next to no doubt, embarrassment, suspicion, or rejection of nationality as a marked category of identity in the Games. In contemporary Korea, as in other states completing the decolonization process, there is little of that discourse on the evils of nationalism so familiar in Europe and America, particularly among intellectuals and related status-elites.[8] There is little interest in the Korean *uri nara* ("our place") in categorically delineating state from civil society in the mode of the West, with its consequent Us/Them crabdance between patriotism and nationalism. Instead, vexations produced in South Korea by the core Olympic code lay chiefly in what content should be given to humanity, or rather "Human Being," "Man," and "World" in Kor-glish idioms. The official slogan of the Korean Olympics was "Seoul comes/goes to the World, the World comes/goes to Seoul": translatable general categories, fundamentally different cultural grammars and ontologics. South Korea devoted some 5 percent of their gross national product over five years to the Asian Games and the Olympics and got a new domestic political regime, diplomatic and trade relations with the then-socialist countries, and the makings of a superpower deal on reunification into the bargain. But the arrival of "the World" in Korea was not automatically good or pleasant for elites or the general populace. As stunningly dramatized in the Seoul opening ceremony, with its mad invasion of masked figures from the cultures of the world, the question of what relation contemporary Korea should take up with the foreigners (*mikukin*, literally, "Americans") haunted Korean Olympic discourse. Mediated in great measure by the subject and the subjects of Korean Christianity, the issue was handled in very different fashion than by other Olympic host cultures in the West, or for that matter in Japan.

An equally heavy interpretive burden fell upon Koreans in supplying indigenous flesh to the Olympic categorical Individual. In the sports contests, individual Korean body-persons won medals, young (junior) ones, not old (senior) ones, and from low-status families besides. That such bodies could accomplish what their corporate elders had failed so long to do—among other things, to defeat the Japanese and the Chinese before a maximum global audience—was a challenge to frame in Korean cultural idioms. When interviewed for the newspapers, every Korean contender said roughly the same thing: "I will sincerely struggle to listen to my coaches and to do my best at this so important moment for *uri nara*." In most cases, Korean journalists never spoke at all with the individual athlete they "quoted." What need was there to do so? The English "I" in the quotation does not exist in the original. Linguistically and pragmatically speaking, my body is an our body in Korean. Only with effort can things be imagined otherwise, just as it requires extreme circumstances for a Western individual to imagine that his or her body is many bodies (not the same as anybody's). Korean team-sport successes were rather easier to interpret within the Korean inflection of humanized nationality in the core Olympic code, except perhaps for the matter of their gender. "We are wondering," said the chief of the Seoul Olympics to a group of foreign anthropologists at the height of the Games, "why our women do so much better than our men."

Any symbolic construction of the body depends on a logic of distinctions. Maintaining the trinitarian core of Olympic socio-logical *somantics* requires formally unmarking, masking, or suppressing other identities. Where suppression is impossible, diffusing their identity-bearing features in performance and leaving their meanings exclusively to multicultural audiences multiculturally to fill in become the key defenses. Olympic somatography and somatospection depend not only on trans-situational and transcultural markers of individuality, nationality, and humanity, but also on a kind of sliding scale of symbolic restrictions on other social identities within and across cultures.

In all cultures, bodies are sexed and in most contexts gendered. In the modern West, accepting Nietzsche's dictum that the soul is a name for something about the body, this is true up to an ontological threshold whose passage entails a very different conception. Ontologically essential selfhood, nationality, and human beingness are thought to escape the bonds of sex/gender into a consubstantial identity. Because male and female are equally human, Human Being must itself be ungendered, an in-dividual, that is, indivisible substance: so insists the dominant logic of ontology that constitutes the possibility of all the modern West's major social ideologies, including Olympism for those who regard it as such.[9] But where the body is the privileged carrier of gender identity, corporeal performances like the Games cannot do much to unmark it, despite gender's quasi-segregation from the official trinity.[10] From mandatory sex tests (for females not males), to separate events for men and women, to unsanctioned but customary practices such as the separation of men and women athletes within national delegations in the opening parade, to feminist agitations over leadership and authority, gender remains highly marked in Olympic practice.

Countercurrents merely reflect the ambiguity. In speech and certain behavioral practices, Olympic champions are Olympic champions, male or female. The Olympic victory ceremonies present themselves as absolutely identical for men and women and are consciously experienced as such by all but the sharpest and most mythically inhabited observers. National medals counts—East, West, North, and South—are made gender-blind to serve in the rivalry with other nations. In many cultural discourses "explaining" the human/national/individual qualities that result in athletic excellence, most of the terms (including that one) are deployed across sex/gender lines, though not so thoroughly their distributions, modifiers, and valuations. But offstage and backstage, gender is both the chief interest and the chief irritant from the standpoint of the dominant logic. The grid of differentiated body conventions laid out by the many Olympic sports enable hundreds of cultural formations to associate and ascribe a bewildering richness of gendered meanings, from physiological capacities of the sexes, to traits of character and desire, to moral statuses, to sexual preferences, to levels of civilization. It is worth reiterating that in the United States, Olympic sport is the only televised sport that women watch in proportion to their numbers in the population. Television executives, marketing agents, and communications researchers believe that the proportion tips still more toward women in the audience for the winter Games. What is so special about those bodies for these bodies? It is exemplary to wonder.

Race, for cultures where it is marked by skin color, epicanthic eyefolds, and the like, cannot be suppressed from representation on Olympic bodies either. In similar and different ways as gender, the dominant logic of Olympic somantics both struggles against racial representations and licenses offstage fascination with them. Since no discrimination on political grounds is permitted by the *Olympic Charter*, apartheid had to be redefined as a crime against Humanity in order to throw South Africa out of the Olympic movement. Today, there are initiatives to ban countries that refuse to send women athletes to the Games, notably some Islamic and one or two black African states. But opponents have so far successfully argued that these are national cultural and religious matters, protected in the dominant Olympic scheme of things, not crimes against Humanity. In such contexts it seems that race can be humanized more readily than gender, at least for these European cultural sectors.

Within domestic European contexts, however, the opposite effect can obtain. For example, major Catalan and Spanish newspapers, including "cultured" ones on the left, for a time kept separate medals counts for "blacks" and "other races" during the 1992 summer Games. When it was pointed out to local organizers and intellectuals that this practice, if noticed, would be taken as barbaric and offensive by some of the participating nations, this was not understood, much less admitted. It was a bit easier for these same local elites to grasp the offense to some foreign guests in the illustration of a newspaper story on the lack of air conditioning in the Olympic Village with a full-page sequence of telephotos of a woman athlete undressing in her bedroom. That, after all, was "naughty," the other merely "scientific." One culture's projective imaginings of other cultures' racial codings can be even more mistaken than gender meanings.

With reference to the majority of countries where ethnicity, religion, and language are not necessarily equivalent with nationality, such characteristics can still be decoded from the competitors' names, physical appearances, or gestural styles. But this is generally far more difficult and certainly so for foreigners, that is, for the majority of persons attending most of the time to any one body's movements. The restrictions of dress to the national uniform, the only second skin allowed in official contexts, and additional constraints on body decoration due to practical requirements of athletic performance make ethnicity less of a struggle for the core Olympic logic than gender and race and more of an interpretive challenge for audiences. Further along the sliding scale, family status, class position, occupation, religious conviction, political allegiance, educational attainment, and similar identities cannot usually be decoded directly from athletic bodies. Beyond small community groups, such knowledge depends almost entirely on tutoring by the mass media, which, except in the case of a few superstars, rarely extends beyond regional or national borders.

The fact of the matter is that for most who attend an Olympic Games or who pay attention to all the participants in a televised sports contest, not just those singled out for special attention by co-national commentators, the majority of athletes and other performers *are* identifiable only as (gendered, raced, perhaps ethnicized) persons, nationals, and human-beings. The rest of what's visible and salient is dramatically limited to what their bodies can or might or did or didn't do. In this hyperstructuration, Olympic body practice intensifies the focus on some identities at the expense of others, which in turn intensifies attention to body practice itself. In so identifying performers, audiences perhaps cannot help, behind their other and more detailed self-conceptions, but so identify themselves. Especially when the contests are profound, Olympic sport brings its logic to experience in the bodies of theorists too.

Inaudibility, Invisibility, and Interconnection

The difficulty presented by such performances for professional intellectuals does not lie in some special alienation from the body purportedly entailed by mind-work.[11] Furthermore, while progressive intellectuals may be embarrassed to discover that the nation-state resides, as Elaine Scarry has put it, in the intricate recesses of their body-personhoods too, this fact cannot fully account for the effect.[12] More significant is the difficulty of establishing expertise in domains of mass theorizing licensed by the interpretive democracy of the body. Persons who know little and care less about dance will rarely defer to the dance historian or philosopher in judging "for themselves" whether observed performances are good or bad, that is, attractive, interesting, pleasing, moving, worthwhile. Rather than these aesthetic judgments and propositions, popular interpretations of sport contests typically take the form of narratives accounting for the characteristics of specific players and their connection with the outcome of the game. In America, everybody feels an even more perfect right than with dance to interpret sport if they wish. In the case of the Olympics, this presumption of authority extends well beyond the physical contests to matters of political and social embodiment. Is Olympic sport socially worthwhile? Are the Olympics over-commercialized and politicized? Do they promote nationalism over internationalism? Researchers seldom elicit "don't know" or "not enough information to judge" responses to such questions, ironically undermining their own prestige as experts in the very act of getting clean "scientific" data.[13]

Conditions are rather different in several capitalist democracies of Western Europe, where the Olympics are more widely considered a social and cultural movement, their institutional complexity is better known, and the existence of expertise, certainly in the political and artistic domains, is more frequently conceded. The process of interconnected differentiation characterizes closely related cultures as much as it does historically distant ones. At the same time, it is as difficult for ordinary Germans or French to imagine a people without a federal sports minister and ignorant of even the names of their IOC members and NOC chiefs as it is for ordinary Americans to imagine the situation in Germany or France. The constitution of difference through the same forms does not necessarily or even often produce even bilateral awareness of the differences thus constituted. Instead, the apparentness of the forms themselves and of foreign bodies practicing with them reinforces the ordinary tendency toward mistaking local meanings for general ones. Extending to the whole plural world of Olympic relations, it might be said that through the connective power of their forms, the Games augment intercultural mistakenness even as they reduce gross Otherness.

There is a further clue in this to the problem intellectuals have with such globalizing objects. It is not principled opposition to ignorance and illusion so much as the social specialization of intellectuals in the insistence that the world is ultimately knowable. The Olympics demonstrate that it clearly is not. There is no center, in any absolute sense, to them and no other center can overhear, or overhearing register, or registering interpret more than a tiny dram of the vastly plural and highly segregated dialogues of which the Games consist. The lesson is hard to incorporate, even for fulltime researchers long since resigned to documenting and analyzing restricted interconnections. Over time, these relational values can be composed into a mosaic, but one that will never offer up any total pattern more substantive than the general logic of intercultural relations previously described. I conclude with an example indicating how "global performances" are in fact virtual spaces established within a network of local/national ramparts that no group oversees entirely, in either sense of the word. The whole world, or a significant cross section of it, may indeed be watching together, but the notion of a fully common object is—for officials, performers, ticketholders, telespectators, and researchers—a grand illusion in the Freudian sense, that is, a wish fulfillment.

Carnivalization and the Somantic Commons

In February 1992, I flew directly from the opening ceremonies of the Albertville winter Games to a meeting of the Dance History Scholars Association in Riverside, California. Conception and production of the Albertville ceremonies had been entrusted to Philippe Decoufflé, a brilliant young choreographer with the Paris Opéra and DCA dance companies and director of innovative music videos and commercial advertisements. Decoufflé had come to wider public attention for choreographing the "Danse Clog/Marseillaise" segment of Jean-Paul Goude's Revolutionary Bicentennial procession. The Albertville ceremonies therefore promised an innovative experimentation with mating the genres of Olympic ritual, open-air dance festival, and television spectacular, in the context, moreover, of celebrating Europe '92 and articulating France's place in it at a time of widespread domestic perception of French cultural and political malaise.

Preoccupied with preparations for the Barcelona summer Olympics, I had been unable myself to document the backstage deliberations and struggles over the Albertville ceremonies. Significantly from the standpoint of the international academic "division of labor," no group of French or other researchers had assigned themselves this task. Still, I would have the ethnographic observations of the live event from a small team of Olympic social historians and anthropologists from five countries to compare with the exegesis and reception of the performances by a professional segment of North American telespectators, the dance historians and choreographers assembled in California. I had not pre-recruited this audience in any way, and the American press had done nothing to publicize the identities and ambitions of the ceremony's creative directors. Moreover, there was no reason to believe that the dance historians differed much from compatriot intellectuals and mass publics in pre-typifying the Olympics as just a big sports and commercial television event, not a world ritual or international arts event. However, everything we have learned about American Olympic television audiences allowed me to predict that a substantial number would tune in anyway, precisely because these were the Olympics, and therefore I believed I could expect interesting and helpful analysis of the place of Decoufflé's, choreography in the aesthetic and social history of modern European dance.

The first expectation was confirmed as a significant proportion of the scholars present when my interests were announced—some two dozen, all but two of them female—came up to say they had watched the event. But the second expectation was absolutely dashed. The performances in Albertville had been as remarkable as anticipated, but the American dance experts had seen next to nothing of what I'd traveled to hear them contextualize and interpret. I had somehow forgotten they'd be watching it on television. Out of illusory desire for an interesting and rich international communication, I'd slipped myself into the mistaken logic that automatically associates interconnection with commonality, in this case television technologies and shared performative visual objects.

Despite years of documenting the cultural and occupational proclivities of American Olympic broadcasters, I failed to anticipate the transformative differentiation they would generate once again, the ramparts that would be thrown up between the spaces where the two groups of bodies were in motion. My body could over-fly the physical distance, but little of what it carried in its somatic memory of the performance *in situ* would turn out to be present, even on a simple visual plane, in the bodies of telespectators on the other side. Despite the vast outlays of effort and money and the huge buildup to an extensive prime-time special, the window opened in the walls by CBS had been comparatively tiny—indeed, scarcely bigger than a television screen tuned to network prime-time.

Another "global event" turned out to be Humpty Dumpty after the fall. Or rather, the event consisted in scatters of shards requiring laborious efforts at assemblage and with no guarantee beyond the existence of empty transcultural forms that any whole corpus was there to be constructed at all. For the ethnologist, the assembly/construction process entails collection of more and different texts, more flying around for interviews, new comparisons, reselection of analytics, the drafting of academic conference papers, accommodation of further differences and variations, trial publications, responses to official criticism—just the sort of distancing translation of performing bodies into textual representations that Olympic practitioners and authorities scorn. Many partial assemblages of this sort lie about the ethnologist's work space, none ever to be completed by the Promethean standard of Western social theory. Humpty Dumpty is, after all, a children's story.

CBS television understood little and communicated less about the specific intentions and contexts of the performances created by the French artists and producers. Verbal commentary by the anchors—a former professional baseball player and an ingenue-reporter—consisted almost entirely of names and labels, statements of gross theme and trivial fact, and stylized expressions of pleasure and approval. Right down to its self-parodying moments, the commentary replicated a common form of American discourse about dance. Approaching the finale of Decouflé's *grand spectacle*, the announcers bumbled so badly that their directors cut away from them to a studio show.

Choreographers and dance scholars are hardly dependent on the verbal commentary of amateurs when they can observe the bodies in motion for themselves. But key segments of the Albertville performances were not "covered" at all, only indexed in the briefest visual and aural snippets. As several said in California, "It looked like something really interesting was going on, but you couldn't really tell." The live performance was scheduled to last three hours and ten minutes, and in actuality took closer to three hours and forty-five minutes. The CBS broadcast (tape-delayed but presented as if it were live) lasted three hours, but the ceremony itself was given only one hour and thirty-one minutes of actual coverage. This, moreover, is a generous measurement, including indirectly related commentary without ceremony visuals and talking heads on other subjects, with the performance reduced to aural or visual backdrop. The remainder of the CBS program consisted of commercials, prerecorded features, and sports events previews and reports.

The Olympic opening and closing ceremonies are divided into two kinds by the charter and custom. The official ritual practices form a core controlled by the IOC and only limited customizing is possible by the local Organizing Committee of the Olympic Games (OCOG) and its team of national specialists. These practices include: the parade of nations; Olympic flame, flag and anthem performances; athletes' and judges' oaths; speeches by the IOC and OCOG chiefs; and rigid protocol surrounding the chief-of-state and his or her declaration of opening of the Games. In terms of the global logic of cultural economy, this domain represents the explicit dominance of transnational forms in the constitution of international performances, with local/national cultures as inflecting servants and dependencies. The second domain consists of cultural performances—music, dance, costume, scenario icons and narratives, social categories, cultural styles—surrounding the ritual core. These are almost fully matters of local and national creativity. The OCOG answers to the IOC and international opinion only for their tastefulness, inventiveness, symbolic connection to some aspect of Olympic ideology, and their joyful, celebratory character. In terms of the world logic and in complementary opposition to the ritual core, they represent the dominance of local and national cultural expressions—including cosmopolitan claims and aspects—over and through transnational artistic and social forms.

The CBS program began with an auspicious genre framing: "Tonight we open with a combination of ceremony and celebration. You'll see both carefully prescribed rituals, as well as some of the wildest and most inventive choreography you could ever imagine." Reproduction of official Olympic performance categories and, in particular, use of the term *ritual* have been extremely rare in the history of American network coverage. However, "ritual" succeeds "ceremony" as the categorical term, and the modifier "carefully prescribed" can be understood to shift the connotations toward "required formalities" and away from religious references. The latter seem to be the main irritation about using the term *ritual* in U.S. public culture. The assertions "*We* open with" and "you'll *see*" reinforce this shift: the former by refusing to identify the Olympic movement or the IOC as the authorities and by appropriating ownership to the American media itself, the latter through a verb more appropriate to spectacle than to ritual engagement.[14]

Indeed, spectacle quickly became the dominant genre marker in the commentary, replacing even ceremony by the middle of the broadcast. When the initial group of performances gave over to the core Olympic ritual (with the formal entry of IOC President Juan Antonio Samaranch and then of François Mitterrand into the stadium) no explicit verbal notice of the genre shift was made. The announcer merely stated, "We'll be back for the parade of nations," then cut away to commercials. Completion of the ritual phase (with the oaths) and transition to the main set of artistic/French performances (effected by an extraordinary Marseillaise) were marked by the commentators. "Protocol is over, now the fun begins." Ritual had declined into protocol and celebration into generic fun. "Next up the entertainment part of tonight's celebration. Believe us, you won't want to miss it." But miss it you did on CBS. Of the forty-four minutes of first-phase cultural performances, CBS presented (in the loosest definition of the term) some nineteen. Of the official ritual segment's fifty-six minutes of actual performance, the network showed some forty-three, mostly the parade of nations and Olympic flame-lighting. Of the third phase of cultural performances, CBS showed some twenty-nine minutes out of a scheduled thirty-five and actual fifty. Though the number of shots increased, the coverage was actually more superficial than that afforded the initial sequence of dance and music. The commentators could make no connection with any substantive historical, cultural, or geopolitical theme. The only intention or function by which to measure "choreography" was its entertainment value.

This interpretation was implicit from the very beginning of the telecast. An opening feature mentioned key geopolitical contexts of Albertville: the fall of the Berlin Wall, the breakup of the Soviet Union, the unification of Europe, the end of the Cold War in sport. But it was segregated from the framing of the cultural performances themselves with the statement cited above. The empty categories Choreography and Celebration were made to reproduce an American cultural disjunction between politics on the one side, and art, sport, and ritual on the other. Choreography as a category was filled in a variety of ways by Americans for American audiences. The genre marker indexed the professional identity of the principal creator and most visible performers. Rather than "the dances," which would imply some thematics to the performances themselves, there was "dancing and music" with the focus on an individual author. Decoufflé's name was pronounced four times in the course of the program (or rather, mispronounced, despite showy efforts at French). The fact that most of the performers were "professional dancers from Paris" was pointed out and the one reproduction of authorial intention CBS did manage was recognition that dance, sport, and circus were being reflexively related as body arts. However, the circus component was reduced to a matter of Decoufflé's biography, and the relational dance-sport choreography, while evocative and generative in several shots, was summarily interpreted as "just a case of athletes [dancers] honoring athletes." The commentators referred to differences between the dance version of a sport movement being portrayed and the version in the sport contest itself. They seemed unable to grasp that relations of similarity and difference in the three body disciplines were exactly what the collaborators had set out to embody and explore. Certainly no indication was verbally given that there might be a conflict of interpretations. For example, the performances could be read as privileging dance as the art required to make sport bodily practice visible and fit for contemplation, whereas sport could do nothing for dance movement except perhaps bring it to mass attention through finding a place for it among athletic contests. In the culturally and professionally constituted vocabulary of CBS, Celebration meant freedom from conflict, hence also from any intellectual interest. Entertainment— or more precisely, the media instruction "you are being entertained"—was the only value.

That the sport-dance-circus triad of tropes and many of the specific choreographic mediations in Albertville are almost indexical of the Paris avant-garde of the 1890s and 1920s, was brought out by neither the American media nor the Albertville designers, at least in any texts I have seen. Yet even with the limited visual information provided them, this was what all the dance historians pointed out or agreed with. In harmony with the logic and form of the spectacle, but also with the theme of France out of the doldrums and again a wonder to the world, everything in Albertville had to be new, daring, bizarre, innovative. CBS aped this language to its own purposes. Neither the avant-garde nor the media of the 1990s had much use for the avant-gardes and journalisms of the 1890s or 1920s. That these were the decades in which Coubertin and his colleagues founded the modern Olympics in Paris and then reconsolidated them after the First World War was explicitly alluded to only in the speeches, not in any of the artistic performances, in Albertville. This suppressed historical relation signaled a suppressed sociopolitical reading of contemporary Europe and France peeking out everywhere from what French papers the next day adored as the *magie découflante*. "*Superbe, époustouflante de créativité . . . un rêve diaphane, aérien, jeune, poétique et joyeux*": the sophisticated Paris newspapers differed little in their prose from *Le Journal du Dimanche* or *Le Dauphiné*.

The differences between this language and CBS's adjectival exclamations (wild, unusual, inventive) lay in more than hyperbole and subtler vocabulary. They indicated a radical difference in conception between the designers and the American reporters and large segments of their respective cultures. With astonishing consistency of intention, Decoufflé, Joseph Racaille, Rebecca Adam, Philippe Guillotel, Guy-Claude François, Véronique Defranoux, Martin Messonnier, and the rest of the collaborators had attempted not only to festivalize but to carnivalize the entire Olympic opening ceremony. The full authority of the OCOG, embodied in its leader, Jean-Claude Killy, bent itself to the festival theme of joyful play. Killy ended his dedicatory speech by quoting Coubertin that "the formula for Olympizing oneself" is to be joyful: "*Et maintenant, à vous de jouer.*" The end of the Cold War; the unification of Europe; the economic and political dramas of France, the Savoie, and their relation; the sports contests to come: all these were proclaimed as joys to be enjoyed. Their dark sides and crippled politics were suppressed as the collective wish for happiness found itself claimed by the logic of the performative illusion, just as the fearful sociopolitical homologies between the last fin-de-siècle and the present one sought to hide themselves in the substitution of putative postmodernism for the high modernism it really was.

Carnivalization added quite another dimension, an intensifying logic, to this joyful concealment. The performances sought to upend solemn joy in a riotous, or at least surprising, surplus of signifiers. Through their costumes, movements, and fantastic engines and apparatuses, the performances cited Bosch, da Vinci, and the Surrealists, as well as Nice, the Cirque, the Ballet Russe, and the Paris music hall. What relevant Olympic order the choreography offered in dancing the movements of winter sport, it simultaneously disordered through the appearance of completely unrelated fantasies. It could be said that the high-tech mediations of every performer and performance—electronics, mylar, rollerblades, elastic cordage, spandex, computer-driven risers, cranes, cables, gigantic windsocks—made implicit connection with the high-tech, telecentric winter sport of today's Olympic body practice. But that reading would prove to be as much a stretch for French commentators as for American.

Of course, it is a matter here of carnival motifs and representational logics, not of carnival experience, for four thousand athletes and officials, six thousand journalists, thirty-five thousand spectators, and a mass television audience confined to their places. But for this much alone, American broadcasters had no cultural reference and no real interest. Fun is fun, entertainment is entertainment: *We're* the experts bringing it to you. Habitués might well conclude from what came over the air that the network had never seen the scenario, attended the rehearsals, or interviewed any of the principals. Ordinary American viewers could be forgiven for thinking that the entertainment values of a big happy show were all anyone in Albertville or the Olympic movement ever sought to attain. When Mitterrand, Samaranch, and the other dignitaries were forced by the stadium crowd to do the wave (or rather the *ola*, as it is named and assigned cultural provenience in French), CBS saw only more happy fun, not the spontaneous working out of carnival logic in which the people refused to let the bodies of power hold their poses while citizens danced. With implicit cultural recognition of carnival politics and with the Socialists falling from power, the French media emphasized the moment. Few newspapers the next day failed to highlight the news and the photo of an unsmiling Mitterrand with his arms stiffly over his head. *"Le Président, six fois, fit la 'ola.'"*

But French state power, invested in Mitterrand's body, also escaped the carnivalizations that the designers boldly extended into the ritual core itself. The boundary between the opening performances and the Olympic ritual was made to consist in the formal arrival of the chief-of-state into the stadium. Usually he or she enters from a tunnel directly into the dignitaries' stand, walking to the place of honor which the Olympic authorities already occupy as their own. For those present it is typically not a highly dramatized moment. But in Albertville, Samaranch and Killy walked to meet Mitterrand, who entered the stadium through the main athletes' gate, then proceeded on a leisurely stroll of power across the length of the main performance space. No head-of-state had entered an Olympic stadium this way since Hitler in 1936. The image of power was domesticated by attaching hand to Mitterrand's hand the body of an eleven-year-old girl who greeted, then walked with him. Séverine du Peloux was a local schoolgirl whose dress contained the colors of Savoie and combined folk dress motifs with the avant-garde costume elements shared by other performers. In this extraordinary image, male was joined to female, state to nation, and patriarchal representation to community reproduction. This was not a woman, but a little girl, an embodiment of the powerful state-virgin symbolic relation that Sherry Ortner has analyzed.[15] Séverine would return at the close of the official ritual phase to sing an a cappella Marseillaise, the national anthem of the host country having been given a position of honor much more marked than usual. Transformed into an ambiguous Marianne, Séverine rose on an elevator toward the heavens in a spotlighted darkness. Coming from her mouth, the famous verses of the Marseillaise had an eerie effect. Two Frenchwomen seated near me refused literally and figuratively to stand for it. "That song," said one to her companion, "is too damn bloody." My Québequois colleague elsewhere in the stadium reported the same experience, and three days later Mme. Mitterrand herself was quoted in the papers as wondering whether it wasn't time for France to get a new anthem. The dramatic embodiment of the virginity-blood-war-community-state-nation-ness complex of signifiers, set apart with a solemn sacrality in a context where everything else was festivalized and carnivalized, had destabilized the local whole. The CBS directors had implicitly been captured by this symbolic logic, inter-cutting shots of Séverine's and Mitterrand's faces, but the American commentators could only pronounce the episode "moving" before moving on to commercials.

Enclosed within these twin performances of French exceptionalism and power were other symbolic gender mediations of the state-nation relation, this time in the international key. As is customary, the flags and delegations in the Olympic parade of nations were preceded by beautiful young adult women from the host country bearing the name placard of each guest nation. In a mythic motif familiar to anthropologists as part of the stranger-king complex and a leg-endary practice as foundational in European history as the first chapters of Herodotus, ethnic and political boundaries are constituted by bearing women across them. Here, native girls are sent out to invite, honor, and domesticate the foreign invaders.[16] But the designers had created a remarkable image for this pur-pose. The signboards were attached to the heads of their bearers, while their torsos were encased in and formed the axis of a transparent plastic globe filled with white feather snow. Their bodies evoked the world of Paris fashion models, as did their mincing gaits imposed by little scalloped skirts confining their lower legs and suggesting the Red Queen from *Alice in Wonderland* to some observers. By keeping their arms moving front to back, these women teasingly revealed and concealed their bodies in the little snowstorms they created within their bubbles. Wearing only sheer and translucent body stockings, the effect was one of semi-nudity. Embroidered around the pelvic area of each model's second skin were, to cite the press kit scenario, "symbolic pictures of each represented country," that is, emblems associated with the various foreign cultures in France. These were difficult to make out from the grandstands, and the American television neither mentioned nor, for obvious reasons, focused the cameras on them. But the ob-vious ones, like the green shamrock over the buttocks crack of the standard-bearer for the Republic of Ireland, revealed the general code, as did the alternately bemused and guiltily distracted expression on the face of the male Irish flagbearer as he passed our section, his eyes and the tip of his flagpole re-peatedly drooping toward the derrière just in front of him.

The bubble-girl image was astonishing and from a semiotic point of view absolutely brilliant in its ordered multivocality. In their advance explication, the designers noted that their basic inspiration was a transnational tourist object, the "snowy souvenir ball" which conventionally bears a place-name and localizing motif within or upon it. Evocations of both Paris couture and the "French post-card" added meanings from this domain of intercultural communication through tourist commodities. With what degree of authorial awareness I don't know, the image simultaneously reproduced a carnival motif from late medieval and early modern France, known to folklorists and art historians from wood block prints and manuscript illustrations. *La Folie des Hommes ou L'Homme Renversé (ou Le Monde à Rebours)* generally features the same figure, torso englobed by the world sphere, but typically male and carried upside down, legs in the air, by fools, grotesques, or savages, including Negroid women.[17] The Alice echo in the skirt belongs to this domain of signifieds. A host of other sexual, fertility, and pregnancy meanings may attach for various cultural audiences to the figure. Its deep structural gendering of the host nation-foreign state relation in European tradition has already been pointed out. A further transformation of this marriage of male/female and French/foreign codes was literally pronounced in the public address welcome for every national delegation, themselves incorporating male and female champions or not, depending on the society. An enthusiastic male voice greeted each in French and a female voice in English, not with a simple calling of the official name of the country as is customary, but with what the published scenario described as "two classical Alexandrian stanzas" and what to many ears in the stadium was ridiculous doggerel. ("Here they are, they've all come to see ya'. Let's welcome the athletes from South Korea!")

Consistent with the aesthetic and moral intention of the whole, an attempt was here being made to render nationality and the nation-state into festival and even carnival joy. The problem was that having made marked exception for their own sacred national emblems, French people were doing this without permission or consultation to the national symbols of other peoples, and culturally distant and antagonistic ones among them. In breaching the ritual frame—a fundamental and still current French meaning of *protocole* is proper handling of the national emblems of others—the designers created pleasure for some but queasy feelings, diplomatic gaffes, and complete outrages for others. The uneasiness of the American broadcasters was made explicit when the first bubble-girl came up on the television screen. "I guess we should say something about the women leading the [delegations]," said the male commentator. "What an outfit!" replied his female partner. Instead of any mention of the snowball souvenir motif, the male commentator attempted an obviously prepared joke. "I guess we could say that the Savoie is trying to take the world by storm." "Yes," replied his partner, "The more you wave your arms, the bigger the blizzard." Despite its striking presence in subsequent pictures, they returned to the figure only once thereafter. "Quite a storm brewing there," she remarked over one bubble-girl close-up. "Yea, that blizzard you were talking about." It was left to other Americans we talked to later, including female athletes and officials, to name the offense as sexism, one suggesting that it was demeaning for women Olympians to march in following "naked girls."

For others the storm brewed up over the "poetic" introductions. "South Korea" is "The Republic of Korea" to its officials, and the difference is highly valent. Mild diplomatic protests were lodged. But the worst problems were created for Islamic countries, and in particular for Algeria, the second delegation and France's former colony and most recent enemy in war. For some years the Algerian authorities have tried to make the same compromise with religious "fundamentalists" that King Hassan pioneered for Morocco. Young Algerian women would be permitted to compete as athletes internationally, to study and work abroad, and to represent the country in similar foreign contexts. But upon marriage, traditional proprieties would reobtain. Having recently voided elections and arrested Islamic party leaders who had gained in them, the country's "secular nationalists" wished aggressively to restate their vision of Algerian social order. They selected a woman athlete as Algeria's flagbearer in the Albertville opening ceremony. Then their old colonial and present labor immigration oppressors, the French, arranged things so the national flag would be juxtaposed with and even touch another, outrageously undressed woman whose indigenous European meanings made absolutely no sense in Algerian culture. The next day a photograph of the horrifying sight of the national flag sandwiched between these two now-associated types of woman, the "modern" Algerian and the decadent French, appeared in major opposition newspapers and was widely reproduced in the pamphlets and broadsheets of fundamentalist groups. No festival this, in the Algerian filling-in of the empty forms of Olympic ceremony and its abstract social categories of Individual, National, and Human.

I am unable to report the reactions of the Albertville authorities, when and if they became aware of the scandal, intercultural antagonism, and countering of current French foreign policy created by their carnivalesque innovations so brilliant from a European point of view. (Decoufflé was surprised to learn of it all in a June 1993 conversation with me.) I have heard other French and European Olympic elites react to the news with a dismissive contempt rooted in familiar Orientalist stereotypes. Who are "the Arabs" to protest over the demeaning use of women? Moreover, this hypocrisy merely registers a lack of cosmopolitan sophistication in the arts and culture. (A postcard currently popular in Paris depicts a European woman clad only in black lingerie shadowing a stereotypical sheik in the streets.) Perfectly well aware of these attitudes, Algerians have been loath to reinforce them by protesting too loudly. At Olympic meetings the following summer, Algerians present were eager to discuss the imbroglio in private but to let it go in public, in the name of Olympism and International Goodwill. For the same reason at the same meetings, Americans and Canadians declined to press their skepticism over the choice of a black woman immigrant to France to take the athletes' oath or the dubious images of music hall negritude incorporated into the Albertville choreography. Samaranch had long since dismissed out of hand North American, Asian, and Latin American protests over the European Community's payment of millions of dollars to be specially represented in the ceremonies despite the fact that the EC is not an Olympic-competent body and the charter forbids political advertising at the Games. That the bubble-girls' skirts were differently colored for EC nations than for all others surely was a minor point that could concern only wayward anthropologists.

The day after the opening ceremony, CBS television broadcast an interview with Jean-Claude Killy in which he responded to compliments on the performance with grateful humility. "We did not imagine that the opening ceremony would be so well perceived." This slip in English registers the deep irony in these global body performances. Killy and his colleagues had not and probably still have not seen the full American broadcast of what they created, nor could they readily imagine that Americans, including sympathetic dance historians in California, had been able to perceive so little. Multiplied a thousandfold, this is what the phrase "the whole world is watching" really means. The interconnective powers of the body not only entail but depend on what cannot be perceived, on the mistaking of common empty forms for shared substantive meanings, on powerful and dramatic intervalations that conceal all the segregated spaces that cannot and perhaps should not be filled in together.

NOTES

1. In classical Greece, the θεωροι were state ambassadors to the public games (or to the oracles). Related lexical forms connote the spectacle itself, identifying it with "seeing the world."

2. Roland Barthes, "Myth Today," pp. 109–59; "Change in the Object Itself," pp. 165–69.

3. Rothenbuhler, "The Living Room Celebration," pp. 61–81; "Values and Symbols," pp. 138–57.

4. On the emptying out and refilling of transnational forms, see my *Brides of Victory*. On the cultural logic of the contemporary "world system," see Sahlins, "China Modernizing, or Vice-Versa," pp. 78–96. On postnational identities, see Appadurai, "Disjuncture and Difference," pp. 1–24.

5. I capitalize concepts that have the status of empty transcultural forms, mythic figures in Barthes's sense. Readers will recognize other candidates to the roster. Indeed, this strategy is meant to raise the question of which terms, if any, in the text are not already subject to this process.

6. This locution is inspired by Artaud's remark, but still more so by the scenarists and choreographers of the astonishing opening ceremonies of the 1988 Seoul Olympic Games. In keeping with the universal humanism of Olympic ideology, the official theme and slogan for these ceremonies was "Toward One World: Beyond All Barriers." At the same time, in their five years of heated deliberations over these performances, the hundred-odd Korean academics, cultural specialists, and artists who created them sought a single metaphor to encapsulate the challenge. They chose "The Wall." (I am drawing here on the field work of Dilling. See her "The Familiar and the Foreign," pp. 357–77.) The producers were highly self-conscious that their task required embodying Korean culture in a way that made it internationally communicable yet not reinforcing of Western Orientalism, domestically plausible yet presentable on a most untraditional, spectacular, high-tech, and mass-mediated stage. Their interculturally heroic efforts resulted in a universally appreciative public commentary in the West but could not prevent causal attribution to "colorful folklore" and "Eastern mysticism."

This more benign form of Orientalist parochialism extended to Western intellectuals and academics as well. When informed that Baudrillard and Lyotard were cited at least as frequently in the Seoul committee's discussions as King Sejong, Shin Chae-hyo, or any other Korean cultural figure, the reaction of such persons, in my experience, has been disorientation, disbelief, even a sense of being threatened.

7. See MacAloon, "Olympic Games and the Theory of Spectacle," pp. 241–80.

8. Equally a scandal to classical liberal and Marxian theory, nationalism has come in for a special anathema in the Western social sciences. Even writers as different in theo-

retical and methodological orientation as the historian Eric Hobsbawn and the anthropologist Bruce Kapferer concur in associating the phenomenon with primordial evil. See
Hobsbawn, *Nations and Nationalism Since 1780*, and Kapferer, *Legends of People*. Kapferer
came to his comparative nationalisms approach in part through fieldwork at the Los Angeles Olympic Games. Readers of his work might not be prepared to have found him
conducting interviews outside the Olympic Village day after day with an Australian flag
tied around his neck. Neither were the reporters from the elite MacNeil-Lehrer public
television program who spent hours interviewing him. Though Kapferer gave them
plenty of "good interview" pithy quotes with high gesture, he was completely excised
from their final program on "Anthropologists Study the Olympics." Real professors may
be patriots and perhaps even nationalists, but they certainly can't show it in such an
open way and expect to be taken seriously. That sort of thing is for rubes and common
people.

9. The conception here of the relation between ontology and ideology generally
follows Kapferer. See Kapferer, *Legends of People*. I likewise believe that mystification lies
in the exclusion, not the inclusion, of ontological dimensions in social scientific analysis.
At the same time, ontologies are products of cultural history like any others, only perhaps
of longer gestation. On the European transformation into modern individualism of medieval scholastic and patristic Christian debates on indivisible substances, see Weintraub,
"Autobiography and Historical Consciousness," pp. 821–48.

10. I use the term *trinity* quite purposely. The gendered term here, the category
Gender itself, bears the same ambiguous relation to the National-Individual-Human
identity that Mary does to the trinitarian deity of Christianity. The implications of this are
not cultural-historical only. On the one side, they validate Barthes's account of the modern
mythic as consisting in naturalized concepts. But on the other side, in this case for masses
of Christians, mythic figures in the more familiar sense of personified divinities have hardly
been replaced in toto by *mythe d'aujourd'hui*.

A dialectic between these two conceptions is probably essential to understanding
what I have called the semantic filling-in of empty forms of Olympic practice among such
groups, indeed for understanding the general and naturalized acceptance of embodiment
itself as the preferred mode of instantiation and realization. The domination of the concept, in particular traditions under the press of requirements for transcultural interaction,
may have augmented rather than weakened the power of the body in modern systems. If
so, this somantic corporeality would be only another instance of "the primitive" turning
out to be a projective artifact of specifically modern conditions.

11. This is a guild myth of distinction in Pierre Bourdieu's sense (*Homo Academicus*)
and a general rhetorical strategy by which a martial and virile democracy tries to level one
of its elites. The strategy has featured the turning of one group of body intellectuals against
another in the common battle for institutional recognition and prestige. One thinks of the
long and sad rivalries among theater people, physical educators, plastic artists, sportsper-
sons, dancers, and musicians for intellectual legitimacy in the American university. Perhaps
it is only poetic justice that, having allowed themselves to be divided and conquered, they
are as an ensemble defenseless today, when "the body" is all the critical rage and the subject has been thoroughly shanghaied by unscholarly and unpracticed amateurs of "cultural
studies" in higher-status departments. The latter's rhetoric of heroic canon-busting within
their own disciplines has effectively masked their colonialist operations against the marginalized fields.

12. Scarry, *The Body in Pain*, pp. 108.

13. Rothenbuhler, "Values and Symbols," pp. 138–57. Conventional sociology of
sport has understandably preoccupied itself with perceived and actual social stratification
and segregation and gender, race, and class mobility in sport. But it has overlooked the
phenomenon of the general cultural right to interpret which gives clear and consistent
meaning to the conception of sport as "the democratic art form." It is the latter which
conditions and helps explain many peculiarities of the former.

14. See MacAloon, "Theory of Spectacle," for detailed analysis of these genre categories and framings.

15. Ortner, "The Virgin and the State," pp. 19–35.

16. These structures and practices are analyzed in detail in MacAloon, *Brides of Victory*.

17. I'm grateful to Barbara Babcock for pointing out this connection.

P. STERLING STUCKEY

Christian Conversion and the Challenge of Dance

> No thanks to the slaveholder nor to slavery that the viva-
> cious captive sometimes dances in his chains; his very
> mirth in such circumstances stands before God as an accus-
> ing angel.
>
> —FREDERICK DOUGLASS

Highly prized for the labor extorted from it, the African body was also the object of exploitation for sexual reasons related to its labor value. Sexual abuse of Africans began during the Atlantic voyage, the passage of slave ships from Africa to the Americas, so from the start of the trade and slavery whites engaged in forced miscegenation with blacks. A repulsive yet desirable object to many whites, the black body posed problems of a psychological nature for them. This was unavoidable for those who associated blackness with dirt and lasciviousness and evil as did many white Americans. In this regard, their observations on slave dance reveal enough of their own anxieties and longings to form a chapter of their psychic history. Reference to their psyche points up how fraught with irony the theme of the body and dance is when the black body is the object of inquiry.

The gun and whip, prominent features of the apparatus of control in round-ing up Africans, were used during the Atlantic voyage. At times during this voyage, there was the insistence that Africans dance to assure whites that they would remain lively enough to be delivered to the auction block in North America. In fact, the total being of African men, women, and children was the object of enslavement, and it was not uncommon for the branding iron to be used to identify them. But this was not the only brand they wore, for uncounted thousands wore that of the whip. In either case, to dance with such scars on one's body meant that, no matter how true to traditional dance forms a particu-lar African dance was, a new history of dance had begun.

Like the sky above and the beat of anguished hearts, the moves of dancers were no mere social construct; their melancholy rhythms were as elemental as the flow of ocean currents, as real as the agony of those in the fetid holds of the death vessels. All who survived that passage would dance with such memories in mind. It is the greatest irony, therefore, that from the start in America dance by blacks was considered a measure of their frivolity.

The failure of whites to understand African spiritual and artistic values made it easier for slaves to use dance to exploit crevices in the system of slavery. Attempts to wipe out African culture did not succeed largely because the master's ignorance lasted throughout slavery. Slaveholders never understood that a form of spirituality almost indistinguishable from art was central to the cultures from which blacks came.[1] Distinguishing between the two for the African was like distinguishing between the sacred and the secular, and that distinction was not often made. African religion, therefore, could satisfy a whole range of human needs that for Europeans were splintered into secular compartments. This quality of culture helps explain why, for the descendants of Africa in America, the sacred so easily satisfied the deepest "secular" needs, and the two long remained the same when that which was sacred was labeled secular by outsiders. The sacred for slaves, as for Africans, was not demarcated by time: Threads of spirituality—of art itself—were woven into the fabric of everyday life. In fact, dance was the principal means by which slaves, using its symbolism to evoke their spiritual view of the world, extended sacred observance through the week. In an environment hostile to African religion, that denied that the African had a real religion, slaves could rise in dance and, in a flash, give symbolic expression to their religious vision.

Dance was the most difficult of all art forms to erase from the slave's memory, in part because it could be practiced in the silence of aloneness where motor habits could be initiated with enough speed to seem autonomous. In that lightning-fast process, the body very nearly was memory and helped the mind recall the form of dance to come. For in dance, such is the speed with which the mind can work, and the body respond to it, that the time between thought and action all but disappears. In a sense, then, the body is mind, and is capable of inscribing in space the language of the human spirit. When the tempo slows, of course, the body configures what the mind more easily recalls.

Yet at times, dance can begin so spontaneously that the thought somehow seems to follow the deed, and self-doubt, especially under those circumstances, can be made to yield ground. When that occurs, the mind is taken for a ride even before it is aware of wings beneath it. That reality, as much as any other, raises questions about the alleged mind-body dichotomy. In any case, threats and ridicule, even when backed by brute force, were not always a match for dance, which at times swept along participants even happily.

In a culture in which dance is highly valued, its basic ingredients are not likely to be forgotten, at least as long as one maintains lucidity. In this regard, age is vastly more important when one is younger than later, for the dancer who begins early remains a dancer, and people generally dance more readily than they sing. When that culture is also a highly musical one, then dance and music propel each other, and seldom is there one without the other, or joy without both in some form. Such values have their own momentum and can travel across borders with the victims of the most horrid forms of oppression.

In discussions of the movement of theory across borders, not enough attention is given to art. A certain elitism prevails, with the masses the object at which theory, fashioned by intellectuals, is sometimes targeted. In other words, the values of the masses are not founding stones of the house of theory, as in the work of an intellectual like Paul Robeson, who was interested in the movement of theory, especially as affected by sensibility, across borders.[2] It is therefore essential to distinguish between forms of ideology and the limitations of those forms, between theory based mainly on abstract reflection and theory derived from the concrete experiences and aspirations of humanity.

The Ring Shout entered as an ideology embedded in artistic experience, a form of dance ceremony in which a religious vision of profound significance was projected even as it underwent transformation in the face of the pressing challenge of slavery.[3] The more subtle and disguised the ideology of a greatly outnumbered and enslaved people, the better their chances of realizing crucial cultural and political goals. In this regard, the ideology of Africans in North America could hardly have been more effectively disguised, since dance to most Europeans was empty of sacred content and to Africans sacred like prayer. A radically different aesthetic masked a multitude of cultural differences between whites and blacks.

Since dance is the artistic means by which rhythm takes observable form, rhythm was as often seen as expressed by the slave, its imprint thereby the more indelible. And since the rhythm of sacred dance was, for the African slave, often the rhythm of "secular" dance, slave dance was rich enough in emotional content and complexity to have substantial cognitive value. Small wonder that Robeson believed that rhythm can lead to its own form of consciousness. But it was hardly necessary for Africans to think of dance during the middle passage to bring its forms of expression with them. The forms most valued were best remembered and most tenaciously clung to because they also enjoyed pride of place in the subconscious.[4]

If dance in all its complexity could survive the psychic pain of the middle passage, new work places and arrangements in North America would prove no real barrier to the perpetuation of rhythm-consciousness. Though rooted in the African village, it was a consciousness consonant with the Age of Technology, in fact that gave it, with mounting complexity of sound, its artistic beat. Yet dialectically, sacred rhythm was the strongest conceivable force, in African terms, against the mechanical movements of an emergent capitalist world. Even before slaves and their descendants heard the machines, the forced labor extracted from them that made slavery a profitable part of the economy led them, after work, to draw on dance as a main form of recreation and relief.

There is no indication that any other group of workers in modern history brought such reliance on dance, to say nothing of the purposes to which they put it, to their daily lives. Relying on dance as much as they did assured reliance on music, and the rhythms of both reached the cities in the late nineteenth century to provide the complex underpinnings of jazz. Moreover, African-style dance was done to the blues, often to the playing of musical instruments that were remarkably similar to those in Africa. In that development, dance was a means by which the past itself paid homage to a new creative form.[5]

But a deeply perplexing problem had to be solved before the blues—and jazz—could be created. There was the initial absence of a common spiritual vision to guide Africans in their new lives as slaves. African dance, in their desperate situation, was their greatest spiritual and political resource, enabling them to recall the traditional African community and to include all Africans in their conception of being African in America. They discovered, despite the presence of different ethnic groups—Ibos, Akans, Bakongo, and Ashantees, among them— that they shared an ancestral dance that was common to them in Africa. Just as they crossed actual boundaries in being brought to America, enough were able to make an imaginative retreat to the ancestral home to discover, in the Ring Shout, the ground of cultural oneness. This dance was known to most slaves, whose people had mainly come from sections of Africa in which, as the Circle Dance, it was associated with ancestral ceremonies. Since respect for elders, who were nearest to being ancestors, was native to black Africans, such ancestral concern was a precondition for their formation into a single people, a process in which Africans irrespective of age and gender participated.[6]

They needed, in other words, to fashion a form of dance in slavery that was consonant with the religious values of the majority of Africans, an especially daunting problem. Yet to begin with circular dance was to suggest a certain wholeness that encouraged the spirit of community. With the rhythms directed at ancestral concerns, a powerful means of reinforcement was introduced as the dancers moved counterclockwise in the ring. In that way, symbol and substance were fused and essential oneness of spiritual outlook achieved. The complexity of the process, its grounding in profound human need, is demonstrated by the degree to which, in the Shout, requirements of the sacred were fulfilled in the most profane of settings, that of slavery.

It is difficult to conceive of more ironic circumstances than when the African danced the Shout and slaveholders, with overwhelming power at their command, looked on with contempt and loathing. Ironic above all because, through the Shout at its highest point of resonance, the ancestors and the gods exerted supreme power over the dancer. At such moments, dance was at war with the values of the master class. But the slave master could hardly have sensed such depth of protest. In any event, when slaves danced the Shout and sang spirituals they were chastised by whites for doing so. Their determination to dance, despite possible punishment, in some measure restored the body's place in spiritual terms, and in that sense was an act of physical renewal as well.

Where there was exposure to Christianity, Christian elements in time became integral to the ceremony as it revolved in a counterclockwise direction with slaves singing spirituals, to rhythmic clapping of hands and stamping of feet. Moreover, as Thomas Wentworth Higginson and others have reported, slaves improvised while shouting and sometimes shouted alone, as some hummed or sang when alone.[7] A description of the more prevalent group shout, witnessed late in slavery, suggests something of its power, why it was a source of concern to Christians.

The true "Shout" takes place on Sundays or on "Praise"-nights through the week, and either in the praise-house or some cabin in which a regular religious meeting has been held. Very likely more than half the plantation is gathered together. Let it be the evening and a light-wood fire burns before the door to the house and on the hearth. . . . The benches are pushed back to the wall when the formal meeting is over, and old and young, men and women, sprucely-dressed young men, grotesquely half-clad field-hands—the women generally with gay handkerchief twisted about their heads and with short skirts—boys with tattered shirts and men's trousers, young girls barefooted, all stand up in the middle of the floor, and when the "sperichil" is struck up, begin first walking and by-and-by shuffling, one after the other, in a ring. The foot is hardly taken from the floor, and the progression is mainly due to a jerking, hitching motion, which agitates the entire shouter, and soon brings out streams of perspiration. Sometimes they dance silently, sometimes as they shuffle they sing the chorus of the spiritual and sometimes the song itself is also sung by the dancers. . . . Song and dance are alike extremely energetic, and often, when the shout lasts into the middle of the night, the monotonous thud, thud of the feet prevents sleep within a half mile of the praise house.[8]

I.

Harold Courlander has written in *Negro Folk Music, U.S.A.* that an ecstatic breaking point often occurs when the dancer is seized by possession, and that state was no doubt a main factor in some Christians opposing the Ring Shout, especially in the context of a scene such as the one just described. But in that case slaveholders, having fled before the advance of Union troops, were not present to oppose the dance. Efforts at opposition, however, surely occurred, and that opposition carried with it the assumption of African mental, cultural, and physical inferiority. Since racism allowed such assumptions among those who knew that Africans entered America already knowing how to cultivate crops such as rice, cotton, and tobacco, major sources of income for the country, it should not surprise us that slaveholders had no respect for the dance most revered by slaves.[9]

As they stood by, or hid in the shadows, and watched slave dance, all manner of guilt and longing in some whites caused them to associate the Shout with sex. Such a misconception was applied to slave dance generally and to black life as a whole as whites projected their desires onto blacks. And it is possible that the recoil of whites from sacred dance stemmed from having considered it, in some measure, profane, especially when pelvic movement was involved. Such an attitude was opposed to that of the African, who had little conception of sexual activity, in and of itself, as dirty. This needs to be taken into account to understand the African conception of art as it relates to the sacred, a subject about which no one has written more perceptively than Roland Hayes. "To native Africans," he writes, "sexual intercourse is creative and holy, allusions to it in their songs are respectful, not obscene." In a passage that takes in dance, he adds that the "bodily movement which accompanies the performance of the songs of love is not vulgar to African eyes. On the contrary, it is an artistic symbol of exalted experience."[10]

The bodily movement of the Ring Shout was considered anything but exalted by white Christians, who associated it with sexual activity and barbarism at a time when sacred dance was no longer a force in Western religious ceremonies. Yet the Shout had so strong a hold on slaves that slave conversions to Christianity were overwhelmingly in that context. In fact, opposition to the Shout was perhaps the principal means by which slaveholders attempted to break the mold of African culture in America.

Courlander argues that a compromise was struck between master and slave. In *Negro Folk Music, U.S.A.*, he writes that the "Shout is a fusion of two seemingly irreconcilable attitudes toward religious behavior." According to Courlander:

> In most of Africa, dance, like singing and drumming, is an integral part of supplication. . . . In the Euro-Christian tradition, however, dancing in church is generally regarded as a profane act. The Ring Shout in the United States provides a scheme which reconciles both principles. The circular movement, shuffling steps, and stamping conform to African traditions of supplication, while by definition this activity is not recognized as "Dance."[11]

Definition holds, we are told, that by no longer crossing their legs during the Shout, slaves were no longer dancing. But there are problems with Courlander's notion of reconciliation, one of which is that he never raises the question of whether the crossing of legs was ever a part of the Shout. For obvious reasons, this is a crucial consideration. If the crossing of legs was never a part of the Shout, then of what significance was the slave's refusal to cross his or her legs? Except perhaps as a means of perpetuating the illusion of compromise, of what significance was the expulsion of those who violated the alleged decree? Equally troubling is Courlander's failure to tell us when and where slaves first ceased crossing their legs during the Shout. Moreover, he fails even to refer to the logistics involved in the movement of the prohibition from one plantation to another in the rural South. Related to this matter is the degree to which the Shout was revered by slaves and on what occasions and where it was performed. To alter one's performance at a slave funeral or in a cemetery when slaves were alone, unless of one's own volition, would be preposterous in a people as subtle as we know them to have been.

A certain confusion is at the heart of Courlander's argument, for he admits that the Ring Shout "is dance (contrary to the premise of the participants). . . . "[12] Is it being suggested that slaves did not know they were still dancing? If so, it is an argument that cannot be taken seriously. Given Courlander's conviction that some compromise was reached, he would have been more credible had he argued that some slaves tricked the master into believing that they were not dancing while knowing they were. But given the characteristics of the Shout, even had slaves initially crossed their legs when Shouting and later ceased doing so, the performance would conform to African traditions of dance supplication. This leaves the master in a position similar to that of Covey, the overseer who, beaten by Frederick Douglass, proclaimed victory after being released from the grip of the young slave.[13]

Not only was the Ring Shout not static following its crossing of borders—for one thing, the mood of the dancers changed dramatically in the slave environment—there was no single Shout on which Christians could focus hatred. Now that meant the problem of opposing the Shout was compounded in ways whites could hardly understand. The more powerful yet more subtle Shout in which the dancer leaps into the air, turning in a counterclockwise direction, merits mention as a means by which *individual* Ring Shouts were similar to, yet different from, the more standard Ring Shout. Fredrika Bremer provides a fine description of this subtle form of inscribing in space, through dance, one's religious values. She describes solo performances of groups of Africans leaping and spinning in the air in New Orleans in the 1850s and calls the effect of the whole an "African Tornado,"[14] which is richly suggestive since tornadoes, in this hemisphere, move in a counterclockwise direction. Variants of this type of Shout were found elsewhere in the South and even in the North and should be kept in mind when considering Courlander's argument regarding reconciliation.

Slave resistance to efforts to oppose the Shout help one appreciate the resilience and determination of those who entered the ring to dance. One instance of such resistance in the 1830s involved a man who would later be eminent among his people, the Reverend Daniel Payne of the African Methodist Episcopal Church. A fervent opponent of the Shout, Payne observed it on many occasions without once raising the issue of the crossing of legs, revealing instead enormous hostility to the ritual as a whole. His hatred of the Shout, in fact, was such that he even opposed the singing of spirituals in his church in Baltimore. There was no doubt in his mind that the Shout was an expression of heathenism as remote from Christianity as could be imagined. Indeed, he opposed it with such vigor that one Sunday two black women rose from their seats and, reaching the pulpit, clubbed him and his assistant pastor. Payne's attempt to end the singing of spirituals and sacred dance failed, for he fled the church.[15]

In the 1850s, the Shout was practiced in Georgia under the very noses of slaveholders at massive camp meetings. Fredrika Bremer reports that at a meeting near Macon one night, three to four thousand blacks and whites were present as white and black preachers addressed the throng, the blacks preaching to blacks, the whites to whites, as flames rose behind them, illuminating the scene. For the slaves, the religious service under the night sky was more formal than those held later in tents in which they were housed. Entering one, Bremer found a group of black women "Dancing the Holy Dance," or Ring Shout, and states: "This dancing, however, having been forbidden by the preachers, ceased immediately on our entering the tent. *I saw merely a rocking movement* of women who held each other by the hand in a circle, singing the while."[16]

Since Bremer writes that such tents could be seen "all over" the grounds—they housed perhaps as many as two thousand slaves—it is reasonable to assume that such holy dancing went unnoticed in most of the tents. Thus, slaves active in Christian worship remained at home with African religion on entering the tents for more private worship ceremonies. Often appearances, one can conclude, concealed the deep complexities and ironies of slave worship experience at such camp meetings.[17]

The presence of the Ring Shout in the North during the antebellum period greatly complicates matters for Courlander's thesis, for one must ask if Southern slaves somehow got word to free blacks and slaves that they were not to cross their legs when Shouting. It is not likely that slave runaways entered the North to reveal the prohibition when the master was not there to give it substance. What is more likely is that the Shout developed there largely on its own with no prohibition about leg crossing. Let us take the classic case of Philadelphia's fifth ward. W. E. B. Du Bois, in *The Philadelphia Negro*, writes of a church in that ward that was established in 1837, that, in Du Bois's words, represented "the older and more demonstrative worship." He then quotes from an article by the Reverend Charles Daniels that describes another variant of the Ring Shout, one that involves worshipers leaping into the air, as in the New Orleans church, but from a rotating ring. This Shout, with its leaping twist, was vastly more difficult for white Christians to understand. According to the Reverend Daniels:

> It took an hour to work up the congregation to a fervor aimed at. When this was reached a remarkable scene presented itself. The whole congregation pressed forward to an open space before the pulpit, and formed a ring. The most excitable of their number entered the Ring, and with clapping of hands and contortions led the devotions. Those forming the ring joined in the clapping of hands with wild and loud singing, frequently springing into the air and shouting loudly. As the devotion proceeded, most of the worshipers took off their coats and vests and hung them on pegs on the wall. This continued for hours, until all were completely exhausted, and some had fainted and been stowed away on benches or the pulpit platform. This was the order of things at the close of sixty years history.[18]

Du Bois adds, probably also recalling his earlier experiences in the backwoods of Tennessee, "The writer scarcely does justice to the weird witchery of those hymns sung thus rudely." And he notes (the year was 1899) that "there are dozens of such little missions in various parts of Philadelphia. They are the survivals of the methods of worship in Africa and the West Indies."[19]

Again with no reference to foot crossing, Daniel Payne describes a so-called bush meeting that occurred in 1878 in Philadelphia, more than a decade following the end of slavery, but during the time the Ring Shout was being done in that city's fifth ward:

> After the sermon they formed a Ring, and with coats off sung, clapped their hands and stamped their feet in a most ridiculous and heathenish way. I requested the pastor to go and stop their dancing. At his request they stopped their dancing and clapping of hands, but remained singing and *rocking their bodies to and fro*. This they did for about fifteen minutes. I then went and taking their leader by the arm requested him to desist and to sit down and sing in a rational manner. I told him also that it was a heathenish way to worship and disgraceful to themselves, the race, and the christian name.[20]

As weak as the case is for crossing legs when Shouting, there appears to have been a slight foundation in reality for it. It is likely that there was some discussion of this matter with some slaves acting on the "prohibition," for there are references in some sources to slaves *seeming* not to dance in a ring in the presence of whites, as in the example from Bremer, which could have been related to the crossing of legs. Moreover, there is the suggestion in one spiritual, in Alan

Lomax's view, of strictures against the crossing of legs when Shouting, though walking is referred to in the song:

> Sister, better mind how you walk on the cross,
> Yo foot might slip and yo soul be lost.

Lomax provides an interesting possible context for understanding why some slaves might have *gone along* with white warnings against leg crossing in the Shout. "Whereas a wide stance was usual in black African dance," he writes, "a narrow stance with foot crossing is typical of clogging or stepping or other forms of West European dancing. The newly converted slaves came to view foot crossing as a lure of Satan."[21]

That the crossing of legs thesis could have been accepted for so long is a measure, above all, of the failure to appreciate the power and complexity of African culture in slavery. Had the work of Marshall Stearns received the attention it has long deserved, generations of scholars could have avoided wasting time by believing the indefensible. "The Protestant religion discourages dancing and the playing of instruments," asserts Stearns. For those with that view, "dancing is defined as crossing the feet, and in this religious ceremony of West Africa [the Ring Shout] the dancers never cross feet anyway."[22]

II.

With the Ring Shout as pivot, black dance radiated outward in America to become a formidable presence. It was a dance that seemed to generate change, possibly because, as with African art generally, the great constant *is* change, improvisation being its motor. In the Shout, the Negro spiritual and essentials of jazz dance evolved. The Ring Shout was the immediate context in which these forms developed during and after slavery, probably because it was more directly tied to the ancestral past, a source of creative inspiration for the African. The presence of the motions of jazz dance in the Shout—the movements are frozen in time in the photographs found in Lydia Parrish's *Slave Songs of the Georgia Sea Islands*—is startling not only because that dance is sacred but because it is so modern despite its emergence centuries ago.[23] The complexity of the rhythms to which it is danced, their function as a kind of metronome for our age, is the surest evidence of the Shout being attuned to modern needs.

A variant of the Shout with even closer ties to jazz dance is done on John's Island off the coast of South Carolina at Moving Star Hall, a place of worship that is attended by a mainly elderly congregation, though it is led by a relatively young preacher. So close is this sacred dance to hip jazz dance of the fifties, sixties, and the present that it is indistinguishable from it. Did it precede, and if so by how long, that precise style of dancing in dance halls? Or was this full-blown expression of jazz dance developed in the ring? In this latter regard, it should be noted that the Moving Star Hall worshipers reluctantly admit to Ring Shouting "when the spirit moves" them. In any case, the dancers could easily be dancing to jazz music as they move their elbows somewhat like pistons, coordinating them to the beat of the music, shuffling first one and then the other foot as the opposite arm, left or right, reaches a high point.[24]

The fact that elements basic to jazz dance were in the Ring Shout, awaiting the sounds of jazz music, is astonishing. And since those elements, especially the positioning, at times, of the elbows, respond to the music of the spirituals, the influence of that music on jazz reminds us of the roots of jazz and jazz dance in the sacred. It is small wonder that generations of jazz artists have borrowed—and continue to borrow—from the music of the church. Yet one of the best-kept secrets is the role of certain segments of the black church in rooting out sacred dance and opposing any connection with jazz and the blues. With Methodists in the lead, these segments took an extremely retrogressive, harmful line.

But they did not triumph, for black religion at its best is rooted in ground that recognizes little distinction between sacred art and "secular" forms flowering from it. The Shout was the initial source of such flowering. Its spiritual transport and frequent association with sorrow—with funerals and memories of the ancestors, to say nothing of the pain of slavery—reflect extraordinary depth of human experience. Small wonder, therefore, that the blues quality of jazz, a sadness miraculously mingled with joy, also finds resonance in the Shout. Only Frederick Douglass and James Baldwin have adequately treated the problem of the oneness of joy and sadness in black music, and I have discussed this elsewhere.[25] But I want to suggest here that those seemingly opposite qualities— qualities of sacred blues—characterized the feelings and thoughts of those who danced the Shout.

This comes through powerfully in *The Fire Next Time*, whose charging rhythms, over a handful of pages, carry black music criticism to heights not achieved since Douglass. Though Douglass remains the master theorist of black music, having formulated basic principles for his time and ours, he did not link dance to music, a curious development indeed for him. But Baldwin does. In *The Fire Next Time*, the collapsing of categories, the movement from one determination to another, is the secret to his genius as dance takes its rightful place with music:

> There is no music like that music, no drama like the drama of the saints rejoicing, the sinners moaning, the tambourines racing, and all those voices coming together and crying holy unto the Lord. There is still, for me, no pathos quite like the pathos of those multicolored, worn, somehow triumphant and transfigured faces, speaking from the depths of a visible, tangible, continuing despair of the goodness of the Lord. I have never seen anything to equal the fire and excitement that sometimes, without warning, fill a church, causing the church, as Leadbelly and so many others have testified, to "rock." Nothing that has happened to me since equals the power and the glory that I sometimes felt when, in the middle of a sermon, I knew that I somehow, by some miracle, was carrying, as they said, the "word"—when the church and I were one. Their pain and their joy were mine, and mine were theirs—they surrendered their pain and joy to me, I surrendered mine to them—and their cries of "amen!" And "Hallelujah!" and "Yes Lord!" and "Praise His name!" and "Preach it, brother!"

> sustained and whipped on my solos until we all became equal, wringing wet, singing and dancing, in anguish and rejoicing, at the foot of the altar.[26]

Go Tell It on the Mountain contains some fine writing on dance. In this work, another solo Shout is revealed, as was increasingly the case when slaves and their descendants moved into churches. The Shout in the novel is done to the music of the piano and tambourine as the whole congregation rises to support the shouter as the dance begins. The rhythms are complex, and the high point of possession occurs. But there is something about the movement of the arms as the dance begins, about dance to percussive sound, and dance leading to possession that link the performance style to that of the Ring Shout. Indeed, Baldwin provides the best description on record of the solo Shout, of its power and place in communal consciousness and collective performance. The call and response that marked the spiritual and artistic interplay of the preacher and his congregation is paralleled, in subtle but powerful ways, by that of sacred dancers. His early years as a preacher in Harlem storefront churches enabled Baldwin to view religion at its center, and that together with his extraordinary command of both music and dance enabled him to fashion this stunning tableau:

> On Sunday mornings the women all seemed patient, all the men seemed mighty. . . . [Elisha] sat at the piano, singing and playing; and then, like a great black cat in trouble . . . he stiffened and trembled, and cried out. *Jesus, Jesus, oh Lord, Jesus!* He struck on the piano one last, wild note, and threw up his hands, palms upward, stretched wide apart. The tambourines raced to fill the vacuum left by his silent piano. Then he was on his feet . . . the muscles leaping and swelling in his long, dark neck. It seemed that he could not breathe, that his body could not contain this passion, that he would be dispersed into the waiting air. His hands, rigid to the very fingertips, moved outward and back against his hips, his sightless eyes looked upward, and he began to dance.

Elisha's dance, in the center of a circle of dancers, soon took on a driving, juba-like quality as he kept time, much like a black Baptist preacher, for himself and for those responding to him:

> Then his hands closed into fists, and his head snapped downward, his sweat loosening the grease that slicked down his hair; and the rhythm of all the others quickened to match Elisha's rhythm; his thighs moved terribly against the cloth of his suit, his heels beat on the floor, and his fists moved beside his body as if he were beating his own drum. And so, for a while, in the center of the dancers, head down, fists beating, on, on, unbearably until it seemed the walls of the church would fall for very sound; and then, in a moment, with a cry, head up, arms high in the air, sweat pouring from his forehead, and all his body dancing as though it would never stop.[27]

Such was the environment that nourished generations of jazz and blues musicians and dancers. On the other hand, there is little doubt that the music and dance of the church have been influenced by black "secular" forms of music and dance, that there was ongoing reciprocity between the two from an early period following slavery. Such reciprocity, for all the opposition to it by some church-goers, has been no less enriching spiritually than artistically. Paule Marshall treats this theme, and does so brilliantly:

> And suddenly there it was: that strangled scream, stolen from some blues singer, that he was noted for. Each Sunday he carefully husbanded it, unleashing it only when he felt it was time to move the sermon to higher ground. From all over the church the amens rushed forward to embrace it. The dust motes in the spring sunlight slanting into the pews from the windows broke into a holy dance.[28]

NOTES

1. See Stuckey, *Slave Culture*, chapter 1.

2. See Robeson, "I Want to Be African," pp. 55–59. Also see Stuckey, *Slave Culture*, chapter 6.

3. This process of change is discussed at some length in Stuckey, *Slave Culture*, pp. 25–43.

4. Robeson, "To Be African," p. 58.

5. Lomax, *The Land Where the Blues Began*.

6. The role of the ancestors, long neglected by students of black culture, has been treated throughout Stuckey's *Slave Culture*. Ancestral concerns of blacks in the Americas, expressed through dance, are treated in groundbreaking ways by Marshall in *Praise Song for the Widow*, pp. 231–51.

7. Stuckey, *Slave Culture*, p. 25.

8. *New York Nation*, May 30, 1867.

9. Stuckey, "Ironic Tenacity," pp. 23–32.

10. Hayes, *Angel Mo' and Her Son*, p. 29.

11. Courlander, *Negro Folk Music, U.S.A.*, p. 195.

12. Courlander, p. 196.

13. Douglass, *My Bondage and My Freedom*.

14. Bremer, *America of the Fifties*, pp. 276–78.

15. Payne, *Recollections of Seventy Years*, pp. 92–94.

16. Bremer, *America of the Fifties*, p. 119.

17. Bremer, *America of the Fifties*, pp. 18–20.

18. Du Bois, *The Philadelphia Negro*, pp. 221–22.

19. Du Bois, *The Philadelphia Negro*, pp. 221–22.

20. Payne, *Recollections*, pp. 253–54.

21. Lomax, *Where the Blues Began*, p. 494. Levine quotes ex-slaves on the Shout and the crossing of legs: "Hit ain't railly dancing 'less de feets is crossed"; "dancin' ain't sinful iffen de foots ain't crossed." Levine, *Black Culture and Black Consciousness*, p. 38.

22. Stearns, p. 13.

23. Parrish, between pages 144 and 145. Parrish remarks in the caption: "Margaret, on the Left, Demonstrates the Correct Position of the Arms and Feet in Shouting." If that is in fact their correct position, then there is remarkable correspondence of hands and arms in Shouting and in jazz dance.

24. Thanks to Bernice Johnson Reagon, I had the opportunity to attend services at Moving Star Hall in the spring of 1986.

25. Stuckey, "Ironic Tenacity," pp. 33–35.

26. Baldwin, *The Fire Next Time*, pp. 47–48.

27. Baldwin, *Go Tell It on the Mountain*, pp. 15–16.

28. Marshall, *Praise Song*, p. 199.

Bodily Interventions
into Academic Disciplines

MARIO BIAGIOLI

Tacit Knowledge, Courtliness, and the Scientist's Body

Traditionally, history and philosophy of science represented themselves as disciplines dealing with the products of minds rather than bodies. Slowly, this picture began to change as a result of the work of Kuhn and Feyerabend. Kuhn hinged his then-radical view of scientific change on "tacit knowledge"—a notion he borrowed and articulated from Polanyi and Wittgenstein.[1] Philosophers of science of the logical empiricist tradition had presented the link between the scientists' linguistic categories and the physical world as established by operationally explicit "correspondence rules." Kuhn, however, began to argue that the understanding of how scientists connect observations to linguistic categories cannot be reduced to explicit rules, but rather needs to be seen as the tacit result of their training and the "gestalt" they developed through that process.

Following a different path, Feyerabend linked radical scientific change to the development of new "natural interpretations." For instance, looking at Galileo's eventually successful attempt to legitimize the telescope as a producer of evidence contradicting the traditional Aristotelian cosmology, Feyerabend argued that the acceptance of these observations was not rooted in Galileo's ability to put forward a detailed description of the telescope's image formation through the refraction of light rays. Rather, Galileo presented an alternative "philosophical package" (and a new notion of evidence) and found a new audience for it.[2] In short, one had to be willing to accept a specific tacit knowledge (Galileo's "way of seeing") in order to trust his instrument and observations.[3] The acceptance of telescopic evidence as unproblematic was what Feyerabend called a "natural interpretation."

I would argue that it has been through Kuhn's emphasis on tacit knowledge or Feyerabend's introduction of the notion of natural interpretations that recent science studies have slowly made room for the role of the body in the production of scientific knowledge. In their initial formulation, Kuhn's and Feyerabend's categories were still more about minds than bodies. Yet, by showing that the connection between things and words was not a transparent matter of correspondence rules but relied on the training of one's perception, they began to "embody" the mind of the scientist—though this embodiment was initially limited to the perceptual apparatus. As we will see in a moment, from Kuhn's and Feyerabend's initial emphasis on mental embodiments in terms of perceptual apparatuses and their training, historians and sociologists of science have moved toward the consideration of the experimenters' bodies and their role in the replication of experiments. By doing so, science studies have eventually encountered the problem of mapping the disciplining of the body through which tacit knowledge is acquired—a problem they share with several of this volume's contributors who focus on other forms of bodily performances.

Let us sketch this trajectory. According to Kuhn, a science student learns how to apply theories by being exposed to specific paradigmatic exemplars, that is, by being taught how to reduce different events to a specific class of phenomena—one for which the student has been given a paradigmatic solution. Through these exemplars, the students gains competence in the paradigm's linguistic categories. In short, a scientist's ability to see a specific event as belonging to a certain category of processes results from she or he having been *shown* examples, *directed* to equivalent cases, etc. It is not "natural" to assume that the laws that account for the orbits of planets work also for the trajectory of a stone thrown by a slingshot on earth. Aristotelian philosophers did not think so. That different phenomena are perceived as belonging to the same category does not derive from them being "naturally identical" but from a specific training that makes the scientist ignore what is different about them and focus, instead, on some similarities—similarities that are emblematic of that specific paradigm.[4] The perception of the identity of different phenomena is not the result of nature per se but of how nature is taxonomized by that paradigm.

To summarize, not rules but *ostensions* (something that escapes complete formalization) teach a graduate student how to become a scientist. To put it differently, it is through *practices* that students are taught how to model specific natural processes by perceiving Wittgensteinian "family resemblances" between them and the paradigmatic case study they have been exposed to during their training.[5] Finally, following Wittgenstein's argument against the existence of "private languages," Kuhn has argued that scientists cannot make explicit or fully verbalize the rules according to which they operate. In short, tacit knowledge is presented as necessarily escaping full mapping while, at the same time, being crucially important to the production of scientific knowledge. As one may expect, Kuhn, Feyerabend, and their followers have been often charged with relativism (or even irrationalism) because of this feature of their views of scientific change.

More recently, the scope of tacit knowledge has been expanded by the shift of focus in science studies from theories to *practices* and *experiments*—a shift associated also with the adoption of ethnographic methodologies within science studies.[6] In fact, the learning of paradigmatic examples (the training into perceiving family resemblances) does not occur simply through problems and exercises to be solved *on paper* but is often rooted in *laboratory practices* involving the student's ability to manipulate experimental apparatus—to "tune" it so that the "correct" outcome of an experiment will result.[7] In a sense, the connection between a theory and the "out there" is learned by the student as she or he learns how to *move around* and operate in a laboratory (or in the field) and to tinker with instruments. Tacit knowledge is of the body as much as of the mind.

As shown by Collins's work on the role of instruments and laboratory practices in the construction of scientific knowledge, the replication of experiments often depends on people moving from the original laboratory to the one where the experiment is going to be replicated.[8] The accurate verbal description of the original experimental protocol and experimental apparatus is generally insufficient to allow others to replicate it—especially when that experiment has not yet been accepted and canonized by the community.[9] For instance, Collins has shown that the construction of the TEA laser (initially developed in Canada in the late 1960s) was not achieved in other laboratories by scientists who just read published descriptions of the device. Rather, the successful replicators were those who visited the originating laboratory and had repeated contacts with the original developers.

Also, he noticed that "scientists did not know whether they had the relevant expertise to build a laser until they tried it."[10] The replicators' skills were opaque to their own holders. It was not by putting in writing what they knew about it that they could realize whether they were "ready" to replicate it. Instead, that could be done only by actualizing their skills by constructing the device and see if it worked. Collins's thesis does not hold only for recent science. It has been corroborated with evidence from earlier periods by Shapin and Schaffer, who have argued that, in the 1660s, the successful replication of Boyle's experiments with the air pump was rooted in the replicants' direct witnessing of Boyle's pump and not just in their access to Boyle's published descriptions of his apparatus and experimental protocols.[11] All these case studies show that the knowledge necessary for the successful replication traveled with bodies and not only with texts.[12]

These different case studies indicate that it is not simply that an experiment is "right" because it can be replicated, but it also becomes replicated by being accepted as "right." More precisely, a disputed experiment becomes undisputed (that is, replicated, canonized, blackboxed) when people begin to accept the experiment itself, the apparatus with which it has been performed, and the bodily skills of the original experimenters *as the term of calibration for their own replications*. In a sense, one has to accept an experiment before one can reproduce it. Of course, the power and credibility of the person or team that proposes an experiment has much to do with its acceptance and replication by others. Similar power dynamics are to be found in the case of the physics graduate students described by Kuhn who accept the ostensions provided by their teachers or textbooks (and the tacit knowledge that goes with them), also as a result of the authority they attribute to those sources.

In short, these studies of the closure of scientific disputes through the replication of blackboxing of an experiment and its apparatus hinges on the notion of skill, a body-related version of tacit knowledge. In a sense, one party's ability to have one's experiment blackboxed depends on that party's ability (or power) to have its skill accepted as the term of reference for the experiment's replication rather than by having it fully spelled out in terms of explicit rules of behavior. If one expected experiments to be replicated by having their proponents spell out fully the experimental protocols, one would get in a deadlock; skill (like tacit knowledge) is something that cannot be made fully explicit. This is what Collins has called the "experimenter's regress."[13] To avoid it, one has to trust the experimenter's body and its skill, its bodily tacit knowledge. Once one's skill is accepted, it becomes part of the "bodily canon" of the branch of science to which that experiment belongs, very much like a certain form of tacit knowledge (in the Kuhnian or Feyerabendian sense) becomes the unspoken foundation of a given paradigm or "natural interpretation."

More recently, Collins has explicitly articulated the cognitive dimensions of skill and tacit knowledge by tracing their implications into the debate over the cognitive limits of artificial intelligence. One of the most powerful arguments about the limits of artificial intelligence was developed by Hubert Dreyfuss, who drew on the work of Wittgenstein.[14] Wittgenstein had argued that a member of a given language game could not fully verbalize the rules underlying that game. As we have seen, this argument was also at the base of the notion of tacit knowledge and skill as used by Kuhn, Feyerabend, and Collins. Dreyfuss moved from Wittgenstein's argument and claimed that one of the structural limits of artificial intelligence (and in particular of so-called expert systems) was that it relied on the codification of human cognitive skills into a computer program. Because the human expert could not produce a complete codification of the rules according to which he or she operated, the computer was bound to run an "incomplete" program. Wittgenstein's thesis provided Dreyfuss with an a priori argument about the computer's inability to simulate a human expert's "tacit knowledge" by showing that the transfer of expert knowledge from humans to computers was bound to be incomplete. One could say that the computer could not be as "smart" as a human not only because of its limits in simulating the behavior of the human "mind," but also because it could not replicate the expert's "bodily knowledge."

Moving from this scenario, Collins has argued that the roots of the limits of artificial intelligence are sociological as much as philosophical. Basically, what the computer can reproduce are those forms of human cognition that have been *socially* blackboxed.[15] Once a human cognitive activity has become "solidified" or "canonized" because of social pressure and reinforcement, then the skills required for its performance become increasingly standardized and transferable both to a wider sector of social actors and to a machine. We have seen that after the closure of a scientific dispute, the experimental apparatus involved in that dispute becomes increasingly reproducible. Eventually, it becomes blackboxed to the point of incorporating much of the skill necessary for its "proper" operation. It becomes "user friendly". Collins's argument about artificial intelligence hinges on his treating a computer as a scientific instrument being operated after the closure of a dispute. Therefore, when it works in simulating human cognition, the computer does so not so much because it has a "smart" architecture or a powerful processor but because it incorporates social practices and bodily skills that, by that time, have become "unproblematic". Paradoxically, it is a fully socialized nature that can be "replicated" by a computer.

To summarize, as beliefs in simple correspondence rules have left the stage, the considerations about the body and its training have entered debates in science studies and philosophy of the cognitive sciences. However, this is true more in principle than in practice. In fact, by looking at recent science studies literature (which tends to concentrate on recent or contemporary science) one is struck by how little "body talk" is to be found there. True, we have much interesting work on the scientific construction and representation of the body (Foucault, Laqueur, Schiebinger, Jordanova, etc.), but we find very little on the disciplining of the *scientist's body* and on the cognitive implications of this process.[16] While the spotlight is no longer on the metaphysical foundations or formal aspects of scientific theories but on body-centered or body-dependent categories like practices, instruments, experiments and laboratories, the research still tends to emphasize the mentalistic rather than bodily dimensions of tacit knowledge. The inherent elusiveness and opacity of skill is creating formidable problems to its study.

This neglect is probably related both to the ephemeral nature of the traces left by the body's skill and to text-oriented or quantitative interpretive tools typical of historians, sociologists, and philosophers of science. While it is impossible to trace changes in the scientists' mental categories and infer shifts in their tacit knowledge by taking a diachronic look at scientific literature, it is much more difficult to write a history of the changing skills that went into replications of experiments and in the production and calibration of experimental apparatus. While scientific articles (and sometimes manuscript papers) are often accessible, a history of instrument-building, replications of experiments, and the shifting tacit knowledge that went with them tends to become an often impossible archeological feat because it is usually impossible to go back and find or operate the original instruments in their original setting and setup.

These empirical problems may be somewhat less severe when we study a period in which the scientists' protocols of argumentation and behaviors had not yet conspicuously differentiated themselves from surrounding cultural practices. After the scientists' professional culture became specialized (and therefore local), a historian faces a situation in which the evidence about and traces of the scientists' skills are limited to the artifacts and texts of that community. Instead, if we study early modern scientists active within the culture of the princely court or of gentlemanly circles, we can utilize a much wider range of evidence about the bodily skills—skills that were integral to their self-fashioning as natural philosophers and that framed their argumentative and experimental performances.

Together with other historians of science, I have begun to argue that the legitimation of the new natural philosophy in the seventeenth century was rooted in its practitioners' adoption of forms of argumentation and presentation of the self consonant with courtly etiquette and gentlemanly codes of behavior.[17] Because of this homology between the bodily and discursive culture of the court and that of natural philosophy, and because of the distinctively performative character of science in this period (experiments were often seen as spectacles and philosophical disputes tended to be perceived as courtly theatrical events), we can draw from the many etiquette handbooks and court treatises to reconstruct some aspects of the scientists' "performances" and the tacit knowledge in which they were rooted.

There is a point that needs to be stressed to understand how this literature can be brought to bear on the reconstruction of the scientists' skills: the homology between courtly discourse and presentation of the self. Court literature shows that one's "gracious conversation" was the oral analog of one's elegant presentation of the self.[18] Both expressions were instances of one's "courtliness" and were evaluated according to similar codes. For instance, being badly dressed or behaving awkwardly was read as a sign of uncourtliness, and one who was badly dressed or displayed an unelegant demeanor was expected to be a pedant, a bore, and a coarse speaker. An elegant demeanor and an elegant conversation were signs of one's "virtue" (the essence of courtliness). This "virtue" (also referred to as *sprezzatura,* that is, nonchalance) was, like tacit knowledge, something that was not fully reducible to a set of explicit rules of behavior. While etiquette books provided useful guidelines, one needed to have some natural gift, some *je ne sais quoi* to allow him or her to become a "natural" courtier.

As shown by Castiglione's *Book of the Courtier,* one could not fully describe what *sprezzatura* or virtue was about. For instance, Castiglione could not (or chose not to) offer a *definition* of courtliness but could only present a fictional conversation at court in which the participants agreed to play the game of "forming in words a perfect Courtier."[19] His was not a treatise that spelled out the courtier's tacit knowledge but rather a fictional description of a parlor game about the ideal *representation* of the courtier. However, that Castiglione did not present his work as a textbook of etiquette was not just the result of the elusive nature of the courtier's tacit knowledge. That court *sprezzatura* could not be spelled out was crucial to its social effectiveness. Its elusiveness allowed it to be presented as a mysterious quality not unlike nobility: Either you had "it" or you did not. As with Collins's argument about how the elusiveness of tacit knowledge created a space in which power could play and eventually bring a scientific dispute to closure, the opacity of *sprezzatura* was central to the prince's self-representation as somebody who could "certify" true courtliness. But being a perfect courtier meant to be a perfect, "natural" subject—somebody who happened to have the right subject-ivity. In fact, to have the right type of subjectivity meant to have the "right attitude" about being a subject of the prince.

Therefore, the opacity of *sprezzatura* allowed the prince to set the standard for the perfect behavior of the subject (one that would confirm his identity as prince) by giving "ostensions," not rules. The prince alone could "calibrate" his courtiers. To spell "out" those rules would have been equivalent to giving "away" the definition of sovereignty—something the prince could not and did not want to do. Thanks to the opacity of *sprezzatura,* the prince could represent himself as powerful without really saying why he was so. In a strong sense, the opacity of *sprezzatura* allowed for the representation of sovereignty as a "mystery of state."[20]

In short, behaving and speaking in a courtly fashion was not just a "professional skill" but rather the demonstration that one was a person worthy of that title—a legitimate subject of power. Non-courtiers were, in fact, not seen as "persons" but rather as members of the "masses." They too were subjects, but did not participate in the construction of the power-image of the prince. Courtly nonchalance was not a matter of rhetorical style, but it was a way of constructing oneself or, more precisely, of representing oneself as having the only acceptable type of subjectivity. This was a prerequisite to having one's claims taken seriously. While, in later science, credibility became connected to professional training, institutional affiliation, and peers' recognition, the natural philosopher operating within the court or aristocratic culture constructed her or his credibility by displaying "virtue." Therefore, to look at these non-verbalizable modes of presentation of the self is not just to study the scientists' "literary style" but the discursive "I do not know what" that provided the *conditions of possibility* (in the Foucauldian sense) of their claims about the natural world.

The pervasive and constitutive role of *sprezzatura* and gentlemanly politeness in seventeenth-century natural philosophy emerges from a variety of sources. For instance, Shapin and Schaffer have argued that Boyle's experimental philosophy was predicated on gentlemanly etiquette. The experimental philosophers' ban on the pursuit of final cause and their commitment to a scientific discourse that interpreted empirical evidence without invoking comprehensive philosophical systems (like Aristotle's) aimed at avoiding dogmatism that could lead to bitter, honor-tainting disputes. This concern for the maintenance of proper gentlemanly interaction among the certifiers of scientific claims was codified in their notion of "matter of fact."

A matter of fact was not just a fact. It was a specific claim constructed through an appropriate "etiquette of inquiry." By being a local claim unconnected to dogmatic philosophical systems it did not threaten the honor and status of the gentlemen involved in its construction and therefore allowed them to certify it. It was "true" precisely because it fit gentlemanly etiquette. I would say that the new notion of evidence introduced by experimental philosophy was a form of "solidified politeness" in the sense that the "solidification" of a matter of fact resulted from its unthreatening features, which allowed the gentlemen to argue politely and, by doing so, eventually "close" it.[21] In a sense, the turning of a claim into a "matter of fact" rested on the blackboxing of the gentlemen's tacit knowledge as gentlemen. A claim would become a matter of fact only through the gentlemen acting like gentlemen around it. A matter of fact was a "gentlemanly disciplined" form of evidence.

Galileo provides further examples of how courtly *sprezzatura* was central to the acceptance of his scientific claims and practices. As we have seen, courtiers differentiated themselves from the masses by possessing virtue or *sprezzatura*. Such a virtue was routinely opposed to "pedantry," which was seen as the sign of one's technical and therefore low-class background. To be a pedant meant to have dogmatic opinions, to be unable to argue as a "free-thinker," to be slave to a philosophical system, to be unable to "play." In short, somebody who sought final causes or was prisoner to a philosophical system did not display the "intellectual nonchalance" required of a courtly cultural performer. While some of these issues informed Boyle's development of a noncontentious and polite experimental philosophy, they were used by Galileo in a more aggressive fashion. His recurrent attacks on the Aristotelian philosophers and the Jesuits rested on the social trope of the pedant—a trope that gained its power from its role within court culture.[22] He was not just a "modern" fighting the "ancients." His attack on ancient authorities was not just in the name of the "modern" science but also in the name of court culture.

The new natural philosophy he was elaborating was one predicated on courtly *sprezzatura*. The ancients (and those who saw them as authorities) were not just wrong, they were "uncool." Galileo's adoption of a nonchalance-based style was crucial because, as in the case of his attempted legitimation of Copernican astronomy, he often could not offer conclusive proofs for his specific claims nor could he justify philosophically the superiority of his method over that of the "ancients." Consequently, to some extent, Galileo's success rested on his supporters' buying into his "language game," that is, into *believing* in his agenda (if not in all his specific claims) rather than in asking for metaphysical arguments about the soundness of his method. In a strong sense, the "tacit knowledge" of the courtiers became the "tacit knowledge" in which Galileo's "form of scientific life" was rooted.

The reception of his astronomical discoveries provides an example of this process. As we have seen, Feyerabend has argued that the acceptance of Galileo's telescopic evidence signified the adoption of a different tacit knowledge. I would add to this that courtly *sprezzatura* played a crucial role in the process. Courtiers and gentlemen were likely to accept Galileo's instrument and the evidence it provided also because their culture may have prevented them from asking the questions that were likely to problematize the credibility of the telescope. As mentioned, Galileo could not provide a satisfactory explanation of the process of image-formation through the telescope. But the exhaustive description of the optical processes underlying the behavior of the instrument that philosophers and mathematicians would have expected from Galileo was not something that courtiers were likely to appreciate. That type of discourse was of mathematicians and philosophers, not of courtiers. They tended to perceive that discourse as technical and therefore "pedantic." That Galileo could not provide such an exhaustive set of "correspondence rules" did not seem to be a serious handicap for courtiers. Actually, they were not culturally disposed to even ask for that. What Galileo was offering them through the telescope was not just a "marvel" (something that fit the courtiers' taste) but also a notion of evidence that was not pedantic. Galileo's was "cool evidence." If the closure of Boyle's "matters of fact" rested on gentlemanly (unspeakable) politeness, what allowed for the closure of the dispute over Galileo's telescope was also the tacit knowledge of the courtiers—their "virtue" and *sprezzatura*.[23]

It may seem that what I am discussing in the case of the courtiers is something different from the tacit knowledge and skill encountered in Wittgenstein, Kuhn, Feyerabend, and Collins. The answer is both yes and no. Of course, in the case studies presented by Collins and his followers, we find a very circumscribed form of skill connected to the replication of an experiment or to the reproduction of a piece of apparatus while, in the case of the court, the skills entailed by the new natural philosophy appear "softer" and usually connected to forms of argumentation rather than to "hard" practices like tinkering with experimental apparatus. However, underneath these important differences we find that courtly demeanor and gentlemanly mannerism framed the conditions of possibility of Galileo's and Boyle's "forms of life" in ways that are quite similar to the way in which modern paradigms, natural interpretations, or the replication of experiments rest on tacit knowledge.

The differences among these forms of tacit knowledge result not only from the increasing specialization of scientific culture, but also from the different regimes of power in which seventeenth-century natural philosophers and modern scientists operated. For instance, Collins has argued that power plays an important role in the closure of scientific disputes and in the consequent blackboxing of specific claims. The tacit knowledge that gets blackboxed is the one that fits (and reshapes) the power field of that scientific community. Collins's work (like that of Kuhn) rests on the assumption of the scientific community having some degree of separatedness (though not necessarily of isolation) from society at large.[24] The language game they consider is that of a quite specialized "tribe"— one that has developed peculiar forms of tacit knowledge. Instead, in the case of Boyle and especially Galileo, the field of power in which their discourses developed was still quite undifferentiated from (or at least porous to) the broader regime of power that framed "high" culture in general. For instance, Boyle's "form of life" was directly framed by the political discourse of seventeenth-century England, while Galileo's courtly scientific discourse was largely framed by the discourse and power regime of political absolutism as expressed by court culture.[25] Therefore, the different forms of tacit knowledge and subjectivity we encounter in the seventeenth and twentieth centuries are genealogically connected by a long process of professional differentiation and disciplining.

In recent years, the disciplining of subjectivity has been seen as emblematic of the development of modernity. Although the main elements of this view can be traced back at least to Weber, it is in the work of Elias and Foucault that we find a fuller development of this perspective. However, Foucault has claimed that such a disciplining of subjectivity did not apply to the mathematical sciences. In a sense, his concern with the development of the life, medical, and "human" sciences focused on their role in the disciplining of the subjectivity of those who are *subjected* to power rather than on the way in which the holders of this knowledge were disciplined themselves by the same process. Not the scientist but the insane, the criminal, and the medical patient are the center of Foucault's attention. I would argue that it is because of his lack of emphasis on the scientist's body that Foucault has found himself unable to see how disciplining was crucial to the development of the modern physical sciences.

Although the work of Elias does not deal directly with the production of scientific knowledge, some of his reflections may help correct this blind spot in Foucault's model. Elias offered a comprehensive view of the development of modernity by relating it to the disciplining of feelings and behaviors that resulted from what he saw as the increasing interconnectedness among the members of society. This pattern was exemplified by the long transition from the feudal system, characterized by loosely connected local lords and kings, to the highly centralized court of an absolutist prince like Louis XIV (an institution he saw as the forerunner of the modern state). From this evidence, Elias argued that the development of increasingly polite manners and intricate court etiquette resulted from the need to have many powerful people (the king and the court aristocrats) interact at increasingly close quarters.

However, it is not that undisciplined behaviors would have been simply "unpleasant": They would have disrupted the collective process through which court society held together and framed the construction of identity of its members.[26] This, I think, is homologous to how impolite manners would have disrupted the certification of "matters of fact" by disrupting the gentlemanly identity of those involved in that process. Elias argued that the sense of individual identity experienced by courtiers was a social construction: To be an individual meant to be a highly socialized being—something that could be achieved only in a closely interconnected society. In a sense, Elias provides an important complement to Collins. While Collins has argued that the "hardness" of claims about nature results from their being very social, Elias indicated that the "hardening" (or blackboxing) of one's identity was rooted in its being tightly constructed through intense and continuous interaction with other people on whose confirmation that sense of identity rested.[27] Moreover, what was being produced through these interactions was not just individual identities but the prince's power as well. Power was not just the external cause of the courtiers' self-fashioning but also its result.

Elias's work suggests how the processes of the "blackboxing" of subjectivity and of claims about nature are produced through homologous processes through which power and status (and therefore credibility) were constructed. Self-fashioning, world-fashioning, and the construction of authoritative discourse were all components of an interconnected process. Consequently, I would suggest that the emergence of modern science may also reflect a disciplining process that has led to a very specific form of bodily and mental "etiquette" within the context of an increasingly interconnected and authoritative scientific community. It is the specificity of this "etiquette" and of the related regime of power and credibility that may account for the specific characteristics of scientific knowledge.[28]

In a sense, a scientist's manipulation of an instrument to have it yield meaningful results may not be unlike the bodily skills expected of a courtier to achieve the appropriate presentation of the self. Similarly, a scientist's reading of a given experimental report as confirming or refuting a given theory (one in which her or his professional identity and career may be at stake) may be commensurable to the processes by which a courtier reads the signs of favor, interest, or coldness as they are conveyed by the demeanor of her or his fellow courtiers. Both perceptions result from specific forms of disciplined subjectivity and bodies rooted in specific regimes of power. Both cases exemplify a culturally constructed behavioral response (one that cannot be reduced to unambiguous algorithms) that relates one's subjectivity to the signs encountered in his or her power-laden socio-professional environment. While the regimes of power and the related social structures changed remarkably from the seventeenth century to today, the processes that linked self-fashioning to world-fashioning are comparable. In short, courtly *sprezzatura* (the result of court disciplining) and modern scientists' tacit knowledge (the result of professional disciplining) result from, I believe, analogous processes.

I would like to conclude by going back to the problem of mapping the tacit knowledge in which claims about nature and the replication of experiments are rooted. Previously, I argued that this task may be easier in the seventeenth century than in the twentieth because of the relative lack of differentiation between the tacit knowledge of the natural philosophers and that of gentlemen and courtiers, and because of the wealth of texts on courtly and gentlemanly behavior. While I would still maintain that point, there is a caveat that needs to be addressed. In particular, the differences between these two historical periods rest on the quantity rather than the quality of evidence available about them.

As we have seen, the verbal description of experimental apparatus and protocols has been shown to be insufficient for the replication of a claim before closure is achieved. Similarly, we find frequent remarks in court literature that how-to books of court etiquette were poor vulgarizations of "real" courtliness and that one who relied on them exclusively could not achieve real *sprezzatura*.[29] However, this is the point of view of those who needed to defend the uniqueness of their social identity by declaring it irreproducible by the masses. Quite probably, etiquette textbooks were useful (at least to some extent) to those who wanted to fashion themselves as courtiers in the same way that, after closure, a textbook becomes a powerful resource for the professional initiation of a "novice." In short, in both cases the problem is not with the essential limit of texts in conveying bodily knowledge, but rather in how blackboxed that bodily knowledge was by the time it was inscribed in a text. Etiquette textbooks were probably reliable guides about "mainstream" courtliness, though they may have been insufficient to convey the "cutting edge" in courtly behavior. As we have seen, similar considerations apply to the ability of scientific textbooks to provide the proper "ostensions."

Consequently, while etiquette textbooks allow us to get a more detailed picture of the tacit knowledge of, say, Boyle or Galileo, the basic interpretive problem is left unsolved. Historians of tacit knowledge (whatever the period they may be investigating) can study tacit knowledge after it has been reified either in a text or in a device. This is not simply to say that the observers' knowledge is always a posteriori. If that knowledge has not been blackboxed, a posteriority cannot guarantee access to it. Also, as we have seen, being a participant does not allow one to spell out his or her tacit knowledge either: One can perform it, but full verbalization is bound to remain another matter.

NOTES

1. Polanyi, *Personal Knowledge*; Wittgenstein, *Philosophical Investigations*.
2. The law of refraction had not yet been formulated and, moreover, Galileo did not seem to be familiar with the leading text on optics, Kepler's 1604 *Ad Vitellionem paralipomena*.

3. Feyerabend, *Against Method*.

4. Actually, the notion of tacit knowledge problematizes the very concept of similarity. In fact, once one argues that the perception of similarities is the result of training, the very notion of similarity rooted in inherent features of nature becomes problematic.

5. Kuhn, "Second Thoughts on Paradigms," pp. 293–319.

6. See, for instance, Latour and Woolgar, *Laboratory Life*; Knorr-Cetina, *The Manufacture of Knowledge*; Latour, *Science in Action*; Lynch, *Art and Artifact*; Traweek, *Beamtimes and Lifetimes*; Shapin and Schaffer, *Leviathan and the Air-Pump*; Galison, *How Experiments End*.

7. Kuhn, "The Function of Measurement," pp. 178–224. See also, Atkinson and Delamont, "Mock-Ups and Cock-Ups," pp. 87–108.

8. Collins, "The TEA Set," pp. 165–86; "The Seven Sexes," pp. 205–224; *Knowledge and Controversy*, pp. 3–158; Gooding, *The Uses of Experiment*.

9. Collins, "The Seven Sexes," pp. 207–208; Shapin and Schaffer, *Leviathan and the Air-Pump*, chaps. 5–6.

10. Collins, *Changing Order*, p. 56.

11. Shapin and Schaffer, *Leviathan and the Air-Pump*, chap. 6, "Replication and Its Troubles," pp. 225–82.

12. As a counterexample, Schaffer has looked at a case in which the original experimenter was not forthcoming in sharing information about his experimental protocols and apparatus but offered "generic" descriptions and did not allow for a public witnessing of his experiments. This was the case of Newton's prism-based work on the decomposition of white light into its constitutive colors. Because of Newton's reluctance to transfer his "skills," the debate did not reach quick closure but eventually forced Newton to withdraw from it to avoid accusations of having produced experimental artifacts. Closure was achieved only sometime later when Newton managed to "canonize" his experiment through a different path, that is, by deploying his newly acquired power as president of the Royal Society. See Schaffer, "Glass Works"; Gooding, *The Uses of Experiment*, pp. 67–104.

13. Collins, *Changing Order*, pp. 129–57.

14. Dreyfuss, *What Computers Can't Do*.

15. Collins, *Artificial Experts*.

16. A partial exception to this is Simon Schaffer's intriguing "Self Evidence," pp. 327–62. However, after addressing very clearly the connection between the problem of the disciplining of the scientists' bodies and that of other subjects of power (along the lines provided by Elias), Schaffer's narrative does not analyze this connection in the seventeenth and eighteenth centuries but focuses on what he takes to be a crucial turning point in the early nineteenth century: the systematic transfer of tacit knowledge from scientists to instruments. In short, he does not focus on the disciplining itself but on its problems and their eventual "solution." On the disciplining of the practitioners' bodies, see also Graham Gooday's piece, forthcoming in *Technology and Culture,* on the laboratory-based training practices of late-nineteenth-century English physicists, and the special issue of *Social Epistemology* on "The Historical Ethnography of Scientific Rituals."

17. Shapin, "The House of Experiment"; "A Scholar and a Gentleman," pp. 279–327; Biagioli, "Scientific Revolution," pp. 11–54; "Absolutism, the Modern State, and the Development of Scientific Manners"; Daston, "Baconian Facts," pp. 337–63.

18. Arico, "Retorica barocca come comportamento," pp. 338–56.

19. Castiglione, *The Book of the Courtier*, p. 25.

20. On this issue, see Marin, *Portrait of the King*; Kantorowicz, *The King's Two Bodies*; and Biagioli, *Galileo Courtier*, chap. 1.

21. Biagioli, "Scientific Revolution," pp. 32–39.

22. Biagioli, *Galileo Courtier*, chaps. 2, 5.

23. Biagioli, *Galileo Courtier*, pp. 90–101.

24. Collins's notion of "core set" is crucial here. See his *Changing Order*, pp. 142–67.

25. On this aspect of Boyle's work, see Shapin and Schaffer, *Leviathan and the Air-Pump*. On Galileo's science and the discourse of absolutism, see Biagioli, *Galileo Courtier*.

26. For a concise description of Elias's thesis, see Roger Chartier, "Social Figuration and Habitus," pp. 71–94.

27. What I am saying about Collins applies to Latour's model as well.

28. Because someone may think of this as a Latourian statement, let me point to a crucial difference. Bruno Latour, in *Science in Action*, has tried to describe the difference between modern Western science and traditional or non-Western forms of knowledge as something along the lines of Jack Goody's argument in *The Domestication of the Savage Mind*. That is, he has stressed the different devices (writing, printing, imaging systems, experimental apparatus, and laboratories) that broadly demarcate these two sets of cultures. The differences in these two types of knowledge are largely the result of the different ways people operate and think in environments populated by very different sets of knowledge-making devices. However, because neither the self nor the body play a relevant role in Latour's picture, he has not considered the "disciplining" of the scientist's body as playing any role in the workings of science. Technological developments *per se,* not the disciplining of the body (and mind) in a framework characterized by those developments, is Latour's key to understanding the workings of science.

29. See, for instance, Whigham, *Ambition and Privilege.*

SUSAN McCLARY

Music, the Pythagoreans, and the Body

Stanley Cavell has observed that "the absence of humane music criticism . . . seems particularly striking against the fact that music has, among the arts, the most, perhaps the only, systematic and precise vocabulary for the description and analysis of its objects. Somehow that possession itself must be a liability."[1]

The situation Cavell describes has dominated discussions about music throughout most of Western history—at least as far back as Pythagoras (sixth century B.C.), who grounded his metaphysics on correspondences between harmonic intervals and mathematical proportions. Plato transmitted this under-standing of music in his description of the "music of the spheres" in the *Timaeus*; Gioseffo Zarlino used it to justify the compositional preferences of Renaissance Venice (although he had to expand the mystically potent numbers from Pythagoras's four to six in order to accommodate the thirds and sixths to which sixteenth-century ears were addicted);[2] and Jean-Philippe Rameau updated it in eighteenth-century France to legitimate the newly domesticated procedures of tonality:

> It is to music that nature seems to have assigned the physical principle of those purely mathematical principles about which all the sciences revolve. I mean the harmonic, arithmetic and geometrical proportions from which re-lated proportions derive and which manifest themselves the moment a resounding body is made to vibrate.[3]

Today's music theorists operate under similar premises, but with a mathematical palette that now includes set theory.[4]

If we were to judge from the writings of theorists alone, music would seem to be an airtight medium—the manifestation, as Rameau claimed, of "purely mathematical principles." The body apparently has no place in this schema: Rameau's "resounding body" might be a string or a trumpet, but it certainly is not a sentient being with arms and legs.

However, another strand of documentation concerning music can likewise be traced back to Greek antiquity: namely, music as a social practice. This tradition lacks music theory's beautiful systems; more often than not, it surfaces in the form of diatribes against what are perceived as abuses of music's sensual dimension. And it is here that a wide variety of relationships between the body and music may be glimpsed—usually as infractions that ought not to occur, but that do, in fact, happen, regardless of how stringently the Pythagoreans try to restrict music to mathematical meanings.

Thus Plato sought to exclude from the republic those practices that appealed to the body—the music of women, slaves, youths, the "effeminate" Lydians—and to privilege Dorian practices—the music that enhanced the regimented order of Spartan troops.[5] So great was Saint Augustine's vulnerability to the sensual pleasures of music—pleasures that incited his unruly body—that he contemplated banishing it from worship.[6] John of Salisbury attacked the new polyphonic techniques of the twelfth century by claiming they were calculated to produce a "titillation between the legs."[7] And Adorno argued that the rhythmic impulses of jazz induce a desire for self-castration—a desire to surrender the rational faculties that had guaranteed Western domination over the body (and everything else associated with the "nature" side of the usual stack of binarisms).[8]

In other words, however airtight the speculative systems of music theory might be, in real life the body constantly intrudes into this domain—and it always has. More and more it seems to me that what truly organizes music in the West is the tension between the inescapable body and the West's deep-seated need to control or transcend that body through intellectual idealism. In this, music resembles many other Western cultural enterprises, except that—as Cavell points out—it has seemed more successful than most, owing largely to our ability to generate perfect fifths from 3/2 proportions and ill-tuned triads from the overtone series.

Yet as soon as musicians begin assembling those "mathematically pure" elements into music, they enter into a discursive field, much of which (rhythmic patterning, qualities of motion, representations of affect or desire) is grounded in experiences of the body. And the impact of music on the listener's body can be profound. As Raymond Williams has written:

> We are only beginning to investigate this on any scientific basis, but it seems clear from what we already know that rhythm is a way of transmitting a description of experience, in such a way that the experience is re-created in the person receiving it, not merely as an "abstraction" or an emotion but as a physical effect on the organism—on the blood, on the breathing, on the physical patterns of the brain. . . . It is more than a metaphor; it is a physical experience as real as any other.[9]

Given the interdisciplinary activity now focused on the body, the time would seem ripe for examining music from this perspective. And it would be convenient if our task were simply to follow a single, stable entity—the body—as it has been represented through various musical styles. But historians have come to realize that the body itself has always been a contested category, that its experiences differ radically according to time, place, social class, gender, ethnicity, age, and much else. In other words, we cannot appeal to the idea of a trans-historical body. Moreover, music does not just reflect: It also shapes. It serves as one of the principal media by means of which we come to know our bodies (available kinetic vocabularies, cultural modes of erotic pleasure, and so on). Consequently, there is no immutable bedrock—either the body or music—upon which to base a clear linear history. Yet the very interactive relationship between music and the body only raises the stakes, making it all the more pressing that we start addressing this medium and its influence on social identity.

Let us begin with an example that is relatively easy to document. On May 12, 1965, producer Jerry Wexler approached some studio musicians during a recording session and said, "Why don't you pick up on this thing here?" He then executed a brief physical gesture for the musicians. Guitarist Steve Cropper later explained:

> [Wexler] said this was the way the kids were dancing; they were putting the accent on two. Basically, we'd been one-beat-accenters with an afterbeat, it was like "boom dah," but here this was a thing that went "un-chaw," just the reverse as far as the accent goes. The backbeat was somewhat delayed, and it just put it in that rhythm, and [drummer] Al [Jackson] and I have been using that as a natural thing now, ever since we did it. We play a downbeat and then two is almost on but a little bit behind, only with a complete impact. It turned us on to a heck of a thing.[10]

The resulting tune, Wilson Pickett's "In the Midnight Hour," is significant for several reasons. As Cropper's testimony indicates, it gave rise to a new style of soul music and provided Stax Records with the boost it needed to make it a viable presence within the industry. Thus, whatever it was that was invented during that session quickly became a hot commodity that was exploited for all it was worth. But "Midnight Hour" also introduced into the broader public sphere a new way of experiencing the body, and it quickly became part of a widely shared vocabulary of physical gestures and expressions. If you know this recording, its rhythms are indelibly engraved in your kinetic memory. At the mere mention of its title, your muscles coil up in Pavlovian anticipation of its groove.

As Cropper says, it soon turned into "a natural thing" for him and other musicians; it became virtually transparent. Yet Cropper's own account of how it came into being indicates how very constructed this "natural thing" was. He reveals with stunning clarity the historicity of musical grooves and, consequently, the historicity of the body. Moreover, he bears witness to the circularity between physical gestures and musical imagery, as the band seized a motion already practiced by one set of kids, figured out how to simulate that motion in their rhythms, and sent it out through the mass media to millions of others who responded enthusiastically in their turn. Music depends on our experiences as embodied beings for its constructions and its impact, but our experiences of our own bodies—our repository of proper or even possible motions and their meanings—are themselves often constituted (to a much greater extent than we usually realize) through musical imagery.

The classic response of fans to a tune like this is: "It's got a good beat. You can dance to it." Critics often dismiss such statements as evidence of the mindlessness, the lamentable absence of discrimination in pop music reception. However, if you watch fans dance to "Midnight Hour," you will find that they have (in Wexler's words) "picked up on this thing here": Those microsecond delays translate—as though without mediation or consultation with the higher faculties—into a very specific set of gestures highlighting the butt. For the duration of the song at least, the body and even subjectivity itself are organized by its rhythmic impulses.

The fact that music can so influence the body accounts for much of music's power. But its power is not restricted to the activity of dance: The ability of music to mold physical motion often has ramifications that extend much further. As Plato wrote, "For the modes of music are never disturbed without unsettling of the most fundamental political and social conventions."[11]

Of course, "Midnight Hour" does not address social issues at all. Yet its success on the U.S. pop charts counts as a triumph of African-American countermemory. For what got unleashed with "Midnight Hour" is a form of physicality that is indispensable to African-American dance and music, but that mainstream America in 1965 still regarded as shameful. Under the influence of its groove, many white listeners started experiencing their own bodies in terms of an African-American sensibility. The impact of this and similar tunes on white Americans contributed to the political climate of cultural crossover in the sixties, the Civil Rights Movement, as well as what came to be called "sexual liberation."[12]

This is not to deny the commodity dimension of "Midnight Hour": The lure of commercial success obviously motivated Wexler, as it no doubt inspired Cropper, Jackson, and Pickett. Yet the fact that a tune is constructed to maximize its ability to make money (as this one clearly was) does not mean that its social effects are negligible. Indeed, if we started eliminating from consideration all music designed for profit we would be left with precious little to hear; the debates concerning music and commercial mediation go back to the twelfth century, when the problem was how to regulate urban minstrels who peddled their wares.[13]

More often than not, it is those in positions of authority, those who want to maintain the status quo, who have waged war on music that is bought and sold. Some of the most profound changes in musical style have come from those who do not have access to official means of support (such as patronage or grants), those who necessarily rely on the market and popular acclaim. And their music frequently appeals unapologetically to the body (to the "baser instincts," as detractors say), making the intersection between sensuality and money always a hotly contested terrain.

Yet it is that scandalous open market, where consumers pay to have professional musicians push their buttons, that has produced the music we care about, whether the myriad genres of African-American music that have influenced bodies all over the globe since the advent of recording (Adorno's dreaded mechanical reproduction) or, as we shall see, the sixteenth-century madrigal, opera, and even tonality itself.[14] Without question, we need to attend closely to how those who profit manipulate our reactions. But students of popular culture who hasten to trash all commercial music betray how little they know about Western music history.

The small revolution initiated by "Midnight Hour" is one that I can recall myself, for mine was one of the many bodies transformed to some degree by that song. Pickett's recording—complete with precisely those grooves laid down that day in 1965, as well as the inimitable grain of his voice—remains available for us to experience firsthand, although the moment of its initial impact has left only traces in reviews, accounts such as Cropper's, and memories such as mine. To bodies accustomed to this groove and its spin-offs, "Midnight Hour" no longer sounds novel; it is part of a now-natural set of gestures, and it may even invoke nostalgia for what seems today a more innocent time. The fact that we have a recording of "Midnight Hour," in other words, does not guarantee that we know how to write its history or gauge its impact.

The task facing a historian attempting to reconstruct the influence of such songs on bodies during the 1960s is rendered immeasurably more daunting as we proceed back in time and into musics that have been canonized precisely because they appear to have transcended the body. We possess few theoretical documents that deal affirmatively with relationships between the body and music, especially in comparison with the heaps of Pythagorean-based accounts available. Given the lack of prestige (not to say the hysteria) usually attached to the body, musicians rarely explain what they do in those terms. The effects of the body thus slip through under the guise of proper idealist syntax and are difficult to ferret out again—especially if the music is deliberately performed, as it often is today, in such a way as to eliminate gesture.[15]

In place of sound recordings, scholars studying earlier music must rely on notated scores—scores that provide only a schematic impression of the pitches and metric relationships within a composition. Moreover, we are inevitably influenced in our readings of that notation by our twentieth-century sensibilities.[16] And even if we realize in the abstract that our experiences are historically constituted, we can never fully grasp how and in what respects they differ from those of other moments.

Yet it is possible to recover some of the bodily basis of music, as well as its influence on and by means of the body, in earlier periods. As we have already seen, historical documents of various sorts (policy statements, polemics, etc.) often suggest how the body was understood with respect to particular musical repertories.[17] Furthermore, some of the research done in other disciplines sheds light on music. For instance, the notion of erotic "friction to heat" in the late Renaissance, as developed by Thomas Laqueur and Stephen Greenblatt, can help us account for some of the most basic procedures of early seventeenth-century music.[18] Most important, the music itself presents a wealth of evidence. To be sure, we must learn how to read the historically specific codes of each style in order to make use of this information. But much of it is quite obvious, if we permit ourselves to hear it.

Let us remain for a while with pieces designed specifically to engage the body in dance. The early 1600s actually yielded a close parallel with Wilson

Pickett's later transformation of the Western body through non-Western practices. For among the trophies acquired through the plunder of the New World was a style of dance music called the *ciaccona*.

Historical sources differ a bit with respect to the origin of the *ciaccona*; some attribute it to Peruvian Indians, while others suggest the input of African slaves.[19] Both possibilities seem musically plausible: The tunes played by Peruvian street musicians today still resemble the *ciaccona*, and the genre's characteristic cross-rhythms survive in African-based dance music throughout the Americas. (Of course, a cultural fusion of this sort could not have taken place without the violent displacement and forced commingling of these two populations by the same colonial taskmasters who also exported the *ciaccona* back to Spain. Thus, while admiring the power of this music and its impact on Western culture, we should not forget the vast human suffering and injustice it represents by virtue of its very existence.)

We are able to reconstruct something about this music by means of the many seventeenth-century attempts to capture it in Western notation, which functioned both to preserve it and to domesticate it for purposes of European appropriation. The process of the *ciaccona* is a relatively simple one. It involves a very short pattern, sometimes as brief as four seconds, that is merely repeated as long as the dance goes on. What compels the repetitions is a groove of jazzy cross-rhythms that engages the entire body—especially the lower torso, which jerks in response to the strong off-beat accent right after the beginning of each bar.

Once the *ciaccona*'s infectious rhythms hit Europe, it sparked a dance craze that inspired a familiar set of reactions. On the one hand, it was celebrated as liberating bodies that had been stifled by the constraints of Western civilization; on the other, it was condemned as obscene, as a threat to Christian mores. But most sources concurred that its rhythms—once experienced—were irresistible; it was banned temporarily in 1615 on grounds of its "irredeemably infectious lasciviousness."[20] Nor was social pedigree a sure defense against contamination; even noble ladies were said to succumb to its call. Like soul music at a later historical moment, the *ciaccona* crossed over cautiously guarded class and racial boundaries. Whatever the *ciaccona* signified in its original contexts, it quickly came to be associated in Europe (by friends and foes alike) with forbidden bodily pleasures and potential social havoc.

Many literary sources bear witness to the effects of the new dance. For instance, the lyrics for one extended *ciaccona* describe a funeral at which the priest slips and sings out "vida bona"—the signal for the *ciaccona* to begin. The officiating clergy, the nuns, and even the corpse respond by wiggling and leaping with uninhibited glee. When they go afterwards to beg forgiveness, the bishop asks (strictly as a point of legal information) to hear one refrain and spends the next hour gyrating with his skirts raised; his congregation shakes the house for another six. At the conclusion of this carnivalesque fantasy, the bishop forgives his flock.[21]

Not surprisingly, settings of the *ciaccona* quickly flooded the market, helping to expand the emerging industry of commercial music publication.[22] Even high art composers scrambled to get in on the action (a sure way of defusing the trickle-up effect of lower-class fads), and *ciaccona* patterns and rhythms resounded

Ex. 1a **CLAUDIO MONTEVERDI (1567-1643)**
Zefiro torna (1632)

through both secular and sacred repertories during the first half of the seventeenth century. Its energies, in fact, contributed to the on-rushing quality of motion that characterizes early tonality. One could argue, in other words, that the procedures later described by Rameau in terms of "purely mathematical principles"—the procedures we like to regard as proof of Western musical supremacy—bear witness to the West's encounter with the Native American/African body and its rhythms.

The most famous *ciaccona* setting to come down to us is Claudio Monteverdi's *Zefiro torna* (1632), an accompanied duet for two tenors. The poetic text hails the return of spring and spins out verse after verse enumerating the season's delights, but toward the end the anguish and alienation of the poet's inner self suddenly erupt into the text, setting up a stark Petrarchan contrast with the splendor of the natural world. For most of the duet, the *ciaccona* proliferates its dance pattern with reckless abandon, each temporary conclusion breeding only the

Ex. 1b

desire for yet another repetition (see figure 1a). As the lines concerning the poet's emotional state appear, however, the music swerves into a concentrated passage featuring some of the most chromatic, dissonant writing available to the manner-ist avant-garde (see figure 1b). The duet ends pivoting between the overwrought agony that guarantees the "authenticity" of the subject's interiority and the care-free, seductive *ciaccona* rhythms of "nature," of the body. Note that this "body" is no longer the body of color from which the *ciaccona* was taken; it now stands for the "universal" (that is, white) body—albeit a body yoked explicitly in binary op-position with the tortured, deeply feeling mind.[23]

Performance decisions matter enormously for compositions like this one. One of the earliest available recordings was a lugubrious rendition conducted in 1937 by Nadia Boulanger. Boulanger appears to have taken as her cue the "true" (that is, anguished) feelings of the poet as they are revealed near the end, and she

Ex. 2 **JEAN-BAPTISTE LULLY (1632-1687)**
Alceste (1674), Prologue
La Nymphe de la Seine—Récit

read the entire duet accordingly. One listens in vain for any trace of African or Native American influence—or, indeed, of dance and the body—in this performance. But more recent musicians have understood the semiotic implications of the *ciaccona* and have produced versions closer to the above description. The performance by Nigel Rogers and Ian Partridge, for instance, infuses the opening sections with a physicality that makes it quite obvious what the fuss over the *ciaccona* was about: One truly does not want that groove to stop, even if civilization itself is at risk.[24]

Dance is not always associated with carnival or subversion, however. As part of his absolutist agenda, for instance, Louis XIV employed dance and its supporting music to regulate—indeed, literally to *synchronize*—the bodies and behaviors of his courtiers.[25] In accordance with Louis's priorities (motivated at least as much by political as aesthetic considerations), French musicians maintained dance at the center of their activities. Even vocal pieces usually conformed to the rhythmic impulses of dance-types. Thus, the first task in composition or performance was to provide the kinetic base for the dances that were so central to court life.[26]

Let us take as an example a brief *récit* from the prologue to Jean-Baptiste Lully's opera *Alceste* (1674) (figure 2). As with most of the spectacles designed for

Louis's court, this prologue presents an allegory in praise of the Sun King, commemorating an earlier triumph over Franche-Comté. A figure identified as a "Nymph of the Seine" bemoans the absence of her "hero" and languishes while awaiting his return. Eventually, the hero's victory is announced with suitable fanfare, and Louis himself is fêted—honored both as the principal spectator of the drama about to unfold and also as the principal spectacle around whose glory all else revolved.

The nymph's utterance adopts the rhythmic impulses of the sarabande, which (like the *ciaccona*) was rumored to have descended from a New World ritual noted for its wild sensuality, but which had long since been tamed into the most stately of the courtly dances. Its principal identifying mark was a slow triple meter in which the second beat received unexpected emphasis, associated in dance practice with a lift onto the toes that was sustained for the remainder of the measure (not an easy feat, given the tendency of ankles to wobble). It is the resulting contrast between motion and suspended animation that characterizes the sarabande and that informs the nymph's discourse, even if she only sings it. A set of conventions designed for regulating the body pervades the *récit* from its note-to-note sequences to its periodic phrases that correspond to groupings of dance steps. And although Lully sprinkles his tune with graces (indicated by the marks above the staff), these ornaments serve as much to reinforce the crucial gestures of the dance as to adorn the melody.[27]

The nymph's *récit* follows the formal plan of a *rondeau*, in which a refrain returns between slightly contrasting sections (ABACA). In this particular *rondeau*, the refrain itself operates recursively as an ABA structure. The first line, "Le Héros que j'attens ne reviendra-t'il pas?" divides symmetrically, each half contained within two measures, thus setting the pace, the norms against which the rest of the *récit* unfolds. With the second phrase, "Serai-je toujours languissante / Dans une si cruelle attente," the nymph begins to resist the established rhythm. As she works toward continuous motion and delays accents to the third beat, she threatens (as much as was allowed within this style) to overflow the bounds of the expected phrasing. But reason saves the day: Her increased animation leads back safely to the opening line, which recontains and seals the refrain with a gesture of closure.

Lully's strategy recalls one of the instances of *bon goût* recorded so admiringly by Madame de Sévigné. A young woman of the court had been jilted by the Chevalier de Lorraine. When she encountered him one day, she launched into a tirade against him. He—ever mindful of her best interests—deflected attention to the pet she had with her: "That's a pretty little dog you've got there. Where did you get it?" As Madame explained it, the Chevalier thereby preserved the lady's dignity, restraining her from a display of passion that would have proved distasteful to the community.[28] This extraordinary disciplining of both body and feelings was accomplished through the internalization of rules of rational order. That Louis succeeded in seducing the French nobility into this ideology is nothing short of astounding, and it is in part the product of the strict regimen of dance and its music to which his courtiers were subjected.

To be sure, the nymph's *récit* does contain conventional signs of sorrow: the minor key, the halting motion, the drooping melodic lines, the yearning appoggiaturas (ornaments that delay expected arrivals but that also enhance by "leaning" into them), or the depressed altered pitch on "cruelle" and in the harmony of m. 3. But these are subordinated to the exigencies of the dance rhythms and groupings. And this turns out to be typical also of French performance treatises; whether the issue is violin bowing, text declamation, or ornament placement, the metrical impulses always constitute the deciding factors.[29] Emotional expression is rarely addressed; formal precision presides.

Modern scholars and performers have tended to ignore French seventeenth-century music, for these pieces only work if a bodily sense of weight-shifts or lifts-onto-the-toes can be perceived in the music, and such gestures depend on details of timing as minute as those described above by Cropper. But our problem is not only the difficulty of reconstituting nuances in the absence of any heard experience of the music. Far more daunting is a conceptual barrier, grounded in the mind/body metaphysics that have dominated thought about music since the nineteenth century: Most modern performers actively resist having to factor in the body when studying "purely musical" phenomena. If French music relies on the body, then it would seem to be trivial as *music*; if it works as *music*, then the body ought to be irrelevant.

Fortunately, the emergence of historical dance has done a great deal to ameliorate this situation.[30] The better early-music performers now learn the steps of the courante or sarabande; like Cropper in the "Midnight Hour" session, they try to make their music "pick up on this thing here." Needless to say, these processes are circular: Musicians reconstruct their performances by watching reconstructed dance, and dancers modify their gestures in accordance with the rhythms they hear the musicians play. But at least these two fields have begun to reestablish the crucial interdependence of music and the body at this moment in French history.

To return to Lully: If the criteria of expression or formal innovation were brought to the nymph's *récit*, the piece would scarcely even count as competent. As we have seen, the affective devices Lully employed are quite minimal; this clearly is not his principal concern, nor would we expect it to be, given French taste. Moreover, the *récit* remains within the most restricted of harmonic and structural conventions. What it *does* offer, however, is a subtle series of nuances made up of varying degrees of motion, hesitation, and stability. If we are sensitive to the kinetic impulses of the sarabande, then the constant pulses that emerge with the words "dans une si cruelle attente" is exquisitely tense: a detail that breaks momentarily with the regularity of the surrounding context and makes the return to the refrain and its lifts all the more gratifying.

The listener's body can vicariously experience those tentative hoverings, the unanticipated sequence of continuous steps, the reestablishment of equilibrium, but only if the performers articulate with the physical precision of French dance the delicate nuances indicated by Lully's ornaments and placement of harmonies. Performed well, the *récit* gives the illusion of presenting the aural equivalent of a geometrical pattern or a theorem in the physics of motion; human expression seems almost trivial in comparison with this embodiment of Pythagorean order.

Like any repertory that influences the body, French seventeenth-century music went far beyond simply facilitating social dance. The fact that French courtiers were encouraged—indeed, required—to participate in dance does not indicate any particular liberality in the *ancien régime*, since Louis used dance self-consciously as a means of social control. Proper attitudes were inscribed on each body, which was expected to behave in perfect unison with all the others. Through dance and its music, the Sun King could watch the social world moving with one accord to the tunes he called. Dance music at the French court thus filled functions similar to those Plato had designated for Dorian music in his republic. If French music exhibited extraordinary grace, this grace was to signify the joy of submitting to authority; ornaments made these moments seem like the voluntary surrender to *bon goût*.

These ideological relationships among dance, music, the body, and the state apparently had to be carefully protected from alternatives. At least this seems to be the issue in the many polemical wars that sought to ward off the influence of foreign musics. For instance, in his account of the hysteria over music generated during the *guerre des bouffons*, d'Alembert presented the following satirical version of the argument he opposed:

> All liberties are interrelated and are equally dangerous. Freedom in music entails freedom to feel, freedom to feel means freedom to act, and freedom to act means the ruin of states. So let us keep French opera as it is if we wish to preserve the kingdom and let us put a brake on singing if we do not want to have liberty in speaking to follow soon afterwards.[31]

D'Alembert here parodies a kind of slippery-slope logic, whereby we slide rapidly from music to feeling to action to collapse of the state, exactly as in Plato, whom this passage deliberately echoes in its apparent horror of liberty. The assumed culprit here is neither the luxury-loving Lydians so despised by Plato nor the purveyors of soul music condemned by evangelists in the 1960s, but rather the usual demonized Other of the French establishment: Namely, the Italian music that had swept through and conquered the rest of Europe precisely because it offered "freedom to feel."

At first glance, Italian genres seem far less grounded in the body. Although dances occasionally appear, they certainly do not constitute the core of the repertories' premises, as they do in France. Indeed, the regimented patterns required by the dance are quite antithetical to the impulses of the Italian imagination.

The Italians sought primarily to invent a musical vocabulary for simulating—and stimulating—the passions. Although they seemed more concerned with the experiences of the interior self, their images were understood fundamentally in terms of the body and its movements. Thus, sadness was represented by musical analogues to the body as it suffers grief, with slow, drooping motions; anger was recognized by its angular, aggressive gestures; anguish (as in *Zefiro torna*) by its painful dissonances; happiness by its rising, ebullient qualities; and so forth.[32] It is within the context of the sixteenth-century madrigal that composers first began to develop this musical vocabulary for denoting human feelings. Along with its other constructs, the madrigal produced the earliest explicit musical representations in the West of desire and pleasure, all spelled out in lavish detail.

One of the first international hits of this repertory was Jacques Arcadelt's *Il bianco e dolce cigno* (1539), in which the lyrics compare the swan who sings while dying to the lover who likewise "dies," but does so happy (if "weeping"), in keeping with the cliché of orgasm as a little death. Throughout most of his setting, Arcadelt maintains an extraordinary degree of decorum—the four polyphonic voices (which represent, by convention, a single subjectivity) usually sing the text simultaneously, almost as in a hymn. Occasionally, a word with special affective weight, such as *"piangendo"* (weeping), leads the composer to indulge in a harmony that slips away temporarily from the rationality-defining mode, but then he quickly pulls the process back to orderly behavior (figure 3a). The effect is one of barely managed restraint, for those few "slips" imply the presence of an immense tide of subjective excess just beneath the surface. In other words, the music creates the illusion of public speech and, at the same time, the subject's private *frissons*, his interiority (which are, of course, publicly constructed through the codes Arcadelt is here helping to invent).

At last, with the lines, "If in dying I feel no other pain / I would be content to die a thousand times a day," the dam breaks. The voices that had been held together so tensely up until this point suddenly split apart; each in turn peaks, then cascades downward (figure 3b). Parts enter at spaced time intervals, such that the centered subject now dissolves into multiple, overlapping attempts at climax and closure. Each line seeks desperately the sweetness of the cadence, yet their phased superimposition causes them to cancel each other out. Every moment of would-be conclusion is swept along in the delicious flood of release, until gradually they all subside—rocking to a point of repose under what sounds like a sustained and pious "amen."

Not surprisingly, *Il bianco e dolce cigno* was copied, arranged, and republished all over the continent, for it featured an extraordinarily graphic simulation of the phenomenological state of orgasm. It also gave rise to a large number of imitations, many of which tried to surpass the power of Arcadelt's original.[33] (One of the reasons composers were so reluctant to abandon the artificial convention of representing a single subjectivity with multiple voices is that such imagery can only be constructed with a polyphonic ensemble. The extensive duet repertory in the 1600s was designed to accommodate both the speech-like declamation deemed necessary for dramatic realism *and* the simulations of interiority in which the Italians remained invested.)

Without question Arcadelt's imagery is highly stylized—it does not, in other words, represent an unmediated experience of sixteenth-century sexuality. Moreover, Arcadelt did not invent this image *ex nihilo*: Such patterns abound in, say, the masses of Josquin, in which the swirling imitative counterpoint at the climax of a Kyrie invites the surrender to religious ecstasy. But Arcadelt evidently perceived a similarity between the effect of such moments in Josquin and the experience of sexual release, and his madrigal permitted the imagery to cross over into the secular realm of bodily representation.

By around 1660, Italian music had produced not only the means for delineating affect and specific subjective images, but also the glue that held everything

Ex. 3a   **JACQUES ARCADELT (c. 1505–1568)**
Il bianco e dolce cigno (1539)

Ex. 3b

together: a set of procedures later known as tonality. From the moment tonality was "naturalized" in eighteenth-century France as the product of mathematics and physical acoustics, it has been accepted as having nothing to do with social construction or passionate expression. It is simply "the way music goes." Yet an examination of the emergence of these procedures reveals that this too, the most powerful of the devices produced by the seventeenth century, was largely grounded in the body.

Tonality involves instilling in the listener the expectation that closure is at hand and then manipulating the resultant expectation by delaying its gratification. Sometimes this process is tied to verbal rhetorical skill (closure awaits the conclusion of the argument), and in such cases it may seem to have escaped the body. But because it developed primarily in the context of lyrics concerning desire, it also operates effectively and self-consciously as an erotic trope.[34]

Let us take as an example Cleopatra's aria "V'adoro pupille" from Handel's *Giulio Cesare* (1724), for although Handel was a German working in England, he was one of the foremost composers of Italian opera at its peak. Cleopatra sings this aria at the beginning of Act II as a way of seducing Julius Caesar, whom she needs for political purposes. She has Caesar brought to a mysterious place where she choreographs their encounter with utmost calculation. First, she has a harp-infested orchestra play the sensuous ritornello to her aria. Caesar (good creature of *opera seria* that he is) knows that someone is *supposed* to sing following a ritornello—but nobody does. He is intrigued by this proferring and frustrating of standard conventional behavior, inquires urgently about what is happening, and is virtually beside himself before she even appears. After two trick starts, Cleopatra makes her entrance.

The words she sings are standard stuff: "I adore you, eyes, arrows of love; your sparks are welcome to my breast." Thus it is largely up to Handel to work whatever magic can be generated for this critical scene. Interestingly, he has Cleopatra sing a sarabande, as did Lully's nymph. The prescribed dance impulses shape her rhythmic flow too, especially at the beginning, establishing immediately that the unknown woman is a lady of cultivated courtly habits. But Handel's sense of the body extends far beyond the metric patterns required by the dance; in fact, once the sarabande is established as the foundation for the aria, it is overladen with several other levels that compel the listener's attention.

Just as Cleopatra aroused and manipulated Caesar's expectations before her entrance, so her melodic line provokes and enacts trajectories of desire (figure 4). She begins brazenly, decisively announcing "V'adoro" in the high part of her range. But having thrown down that gauntlet, she retreats to middle range where she modestly, even haltingly (in keeping with her sarabande rhythms) presents the remainder of her invocation. Nothing remains of that exhibitionistic opening except its ornament, which gets duplicated in each successive unit as her line advances toward tonal closure. Handel has her offer herself right off the bat—then act as though it never happened. We don't need a music theorist to tell us that the high note cannot just be abandoned; as she draws her line ever further away from the opening gambit, our desire to hear that note again—to have it fulfill its promise—becomes more and more pressing.

We get part of our wish with the second line, "le vostre. . . . " As Cleopatra continues her process toward securing closure, she twice arches up suggestively to caress that isolated high note. She hasn't forgotten it and certainly

Ex. 4   **George Frideric Handel (1685-1759)**
        Giulio Cesare (1724), Act I, Scene 2

doesn't want us to, even though she hasn't let us know quite yet what it means. With the next phrase (beginning again with "V'adoro") she makes her metaphors explicit. Her melodic motion begins to surge past the silences that had parsed

Ex. 4

out the first phrase, and she rises—through a sequence that spells growing
desire—from one end of the scale to the other, thus consolidating union between the two vocal registers she had opened up. The high note no longer
stands as a distant object of desire; her melodic line advances step by rational
step until it bends to embrace the high note from on top, thus absorbing it into
her orbit. A more dazzling example of suturing would be difficult to come by, as
Caesar's imperial body (along with the listener) is hooked into her fantasy of
erotic intermingling.

Ah, but perhaps Cleopatra has given away too much too quickly. After a
roulade that crowns the moment of imagined consummation (and incidentally,
the conquest of the secondary key area), she reverses her strategy and separates
the two lines again. It would almost seem as though the union never had taken
place, except that she seems ever more reluctant to leave that again-distant high
note alone. Each time she approaches closure, she reaches out to re-embrace the
higher register, thus converting what ought to have been a regular four-bar
grouping into an eight-bar series of desire-motivated transgressions that postpone
the anticipated arrival and stretch willfully out of proportion the phrasing implied by the well-behaved dance.

Her cadence, when it finally arrives, is back in the lower part of the range.
The startlingly abject quality of this conclusion opens up a kind of vacuum into
which the orchestral ritornello spills. Her taunts leave an energized gap that invites Caesar to act out physically what she has implied through notes alone. Nor

is this the end, for "V'adoro pupille" (as Caesar well knows) is a da Capo aria, in which the opening A section is succeeded by a contrasting B section, followed by a reprise of A ["da Capo" = from the head]. In keeping with performance practices of the day, the repeat of A was the opportunity for the singer to demonstrate the extent of his or her virtuosity through improvised ornamentation. In other words, the performer was called upon to enhance the affect and imagery of the aria, bringing it to a suitable climax and conclusion. By the end of "V'adoro pupille," we have to be convinced that the emperor of the known world has been brought to his knees and enslaved by artificially produced desires. Handel's audacious display is made possible by his body-based tropes of carnal passion and the blurring of identity that occurs with sexual contact.[35]

As Foucault has taught us, "sexuality" was not just waiting there in 1600 for a musical analogue.[36] Again, the power of music resides in its ability to construct subjective experiences that we then embrace as our own most private feelings. In an important sense, Italian composers of the Baroque took the erotic body as its playground and devised a vast array of ways of experiencing desire and pleasure, as well as gender. That their images were not universal is clear from the fulminations of French polemicists, who often found them repugnant and perverse.[37] If many of the inventions of Italian music of this time sound "natural" to us, it is because we have been so profoundly, so intimately shaped by their discursive practices.

At least it was usually apparent when these practices emerged that the erotic was at issue. But the eighteenth century witnessed a crackdown on the excesses of the *seicento*, and the devices that had been invented during the reign of Italian opera increasingly came to be subjected to rules.[38] When *Giulio Cesare* was revived in 1787, the printed libretto reported that it had been altered "to suit it to the refinement of a modern audience."[39] And the tonal dynamic of delayed gratification, which continued to fuel most Italian and German music, became so standardized that Rameau could theorize it as the latest manifestation of Pythagorean number.

The early German Romantics—while they still held music to be the abstract manifestation of desire itself—tried to erase all traces of the social realm from their medium.[40] Thus, the defenders of "Absolute" music denied the relevance of affective conventions to this repertory, even though the music (including the symphonies of Brahms, the darling of the Absolutists) continued to depend for its effectiveness upon those analogues with the body that had been established over two hundred years before.[41] And occasionally the submerged body was acknowledged, providing evidence that it still formed the basis for musical communication.

Wagner's *Tristan und Isolde*, for instance, relies on our understanding cadence as sexual consummation (as in both the Arcadelt and Handel examples above) and derives its overwhelming power by delaying for hours its long-awaited closure. Nineteenth-century French exoticism highlighted the body, albeit the colonized body of the Orientalist femme fatale (Carmen, Delilah), who infused exhausted conventions with motion and sensuality before being purged for the sake of order.[42] And the emergence of modern music at the turn of the century depended on the questioning of then-conventional images of the body or sexuality: Debussy's faun opts for sustained pleasure rather than climax, and Stravinsky's *Sacre du Printemps* threatens to overthrow civilization and its discontents by enacting what we are invited to hear as the primitive body and its yet-unrepressed violent impulses.

Serialism recaptured the twentieth century for Pythagoras—or at least it did in the academy. But the invention of sound recording opened the door to the worldwide dissemination of musics overtly and unapologetically grounded in the body, and the battle between idealist and body-based conceptions of music has been fierce ever since. At certain moments in the battle, advocates of popular music have tried to demonstrate that their music, too, fulfills the criteria of disinterestedness and aphysicality so central to mainstream aesthetics: Schenker graphs of Beatles songs, pitch-class analyses of Coltrane, or anti-disco campaigns by rock critics all bear witness to attempts at liberating popular music from the body in order to redeem it.

I would prefer to settle the dispute in the direction of the body, to hear music—whether Lully, Brahms, or Wilson Pickett—always as grounded in the body, albeit in radically different ways of experiencing that body. Of course, those who value music because it transcends the body are not likely to concede easily to this position. Many continue to regard the body with loathing, and for them, acknowledging an erotic component in a composition means degrading it.

Yet I would like to see the history of music reconstructed from the point of view of the body, in part because it is such an important issue among today's musicians. A number of women artists, including Pauline Oliveros, Laurie Anderson, Diamanda Galas, Meredith Monk, and Madonna, foreground the body in their work, producing images that reconfigure ideas of both music and the body.[43] Our current concerns with the body in music—by the women just mentioned, as well as Prince or John Zorn—make better sense if we understand them not as aberrant, but as part of a struggle that has been going on at least since Plato.

But I also want to relocate music in the body because it is the best way I know for understanding music history in general. The histories transmitted in leading textbooks and journals tend to offer a succession of perfect, orderly artifacts that cannot be permitted to signify lest they signify the body. Controversies of the past disappear, along with any notion of why styles change, for music can only maintain its Pythagorean purity if we erase the bodies it shapes and that shape it. To be sure, studies based on contingencies such as the highly mutable body are bound to seem messy in comparison with the mathematical charts we like to flaunt. But they also promise to make visible and audible the power music has exercised in the social world. And because of the extraordinary specificity of musical artifacts, such work also can contribute heavily to projects seeking to reconstruct the history of the body.

NOTES

1. Cavell, "Music Discomposed," p. 186.
2. Zarlino, *Istitutioni harmoniche* I, chap. 14.
3. Rameau, *Démonstration du principe de l'harmonie*, p. 103. The domestication of tonality is discussed later in this chapter.
4. For example, see Forte, *The Structure of Atonal Music*.
5. Plato, *Republic*, 424b–c and 398d–99c. References to women occur in *Protagoras*, 347c–d; to youth and the challenging of authority for the sake of pleasure in *Laws*, 700–701.
6. St. Augustine, *Confessions*, pp. 238–39.
7. John of Salisbury, *Policratus*, p. 7.
8. Adorno, "Perennial Fashion—Jazz," p. 129: "The aim of jazz is the mechanical reproduction of a regressive moment, a castration symbolism. 'Give up your masculinity, let yourself be castrated,' the eunuchlike sound of the jazz band both mocks and proclaims, 'and you will be rewarded, accepted into a fraternity which shares the mystery of impotence with you, a mystery revealed at the moment of the initiation rite.'"
9. Williams, *The Long Revolution*, pp. 66–69. For a sustained account of the bodily basis of epistemology in general, see Johnson, *The Body in the Mind*. The discipline of music therapy has long focused on the effects of music on both mind and body, but its findings have largely been dismissed as "applied" research. While therapists tend not to address historical issues, their findings could contribute invaluable empirical information to all studies concerned with music and the body.
10. Cropper, quoted in Stokes, Tucker, and Ward, *Rock of Ages*, pp. 293–94.
11. Plato, *Republic*, 424c.
12. For more on how popular music contributes to social formation, see Lipsitz, *Time Passages* and "Ain't Nobody Here but Us Chickens" in his *Class and Culture in Cold War America*, pp. 195–225. See also McClary and Walser, "Start Making Sense," pp. 277–92; and Walser, *Running with the Devil*.
13. For a fascinating study of the early history of commercial music in the West, see Page, *The Owl and the Nightingale*. In the Middle Ages the genre most often condemned as both lascivious and commercial was, of all things, the carol.
14. For an excellent account of early Italian opera as an openly commercial enterprise, see Rosand, *Opera in Seventeenth-Century Venice*. Rosand demonstrates how standard formal and tonal procedures developed as ways of accommodating the rapid rate of production demanded by entrepreneurs and audiences.
15. Professional music training drills students in how to minimize the body in their performing activities: All "extraneous" motions, such as foot-tapping or dramatic gestures, are discouraged—often through physical punishment. Such suppression of bodily activity and its attendant tensions often results in severe, permanent injuries. But the phenomenon of "playing hurt" is only now being studied seriously; ideological denial of the body's participation in music has long made such injuries literally unspeakable and, consequently, invisible—even (or particularly) in conservatories where cases occur with alarming frequency.
16. Richard Taruskin has been particularly insightful in his linking of present-day practices for early-music performance and the priorities of mid-century modernist aesthetics. See, for instance, his "The Pastness of the Present," pp. 137–207.
17. See, for instance, Leppert, *The Sight of Sound*.
18. See the discussion in "Constructions . . . Dramatic Music," in my *Feminine Endings*, p. 37. I draw in this account on Laqueur, "Politics of Reproductive Biology," pp. 1–41, and on the application of Laqueur's idea to literature in Greenblatt, *Shakespearean Negotiations*, pp. 66–93.

19. See Hudson, *Passacaglio and Ciaccona*, p. 4.

20. Bianconi, *Music in the Seventeenth Century*, p. 101.

21. These anonymous lyrics appear in Hudson, *Passacaglia*, pp. 7–8. Marino wrote an extensive account as well. See also the excerpts in Cervantes's *La ilustre fregona*, in Biaconi, pp. 101–102.

22. For more on the subsequent history of the *ciaccona*, see Hudson, *Passacaglia*, p. 11, and Bianconi, *Music in the Seventeenth Century*, 103–104.

23. Eventually the *ciaccona* lost its rowdy qualities altogether. Its French spin-off, the *chaconne*, was used for static (that is, "timeless") formal rituals at ends of ballets. Even in Italy and Germany, it came to serve merely as a technique whose repetitive qualities made it ideal for depicting obsessive states of mind, as in Bach's anguished *chaconne* for solo violin.

24. *Virtuoso Madrigals*, Archiv 2533 087, under the direction of Jürgen Jürgens.

25. See Little, "Dance under Louis XIV and XV," pp. 331–40. For more on the political dimensions of dance and music at Louis's court, see Isherwood, *Music in the Service of the King*. For more on the links between culture and politics at Versailles, see Marin, *Portrait of the King*, and Burke, *The Fabrication of Louis XIV*.

26. See, for instance, Cooper and Zsako, "Georg Muffat's Observations," pp. 220–45.

27. Lully began his career as a fourteen-year-old dancer in an Italian opera troupe visiting Paris. When the troupe returned home, Lulli/Lully remained, insinuated himself into Louis's favor through his abilities in dance, and eventually was granted a monopoly over most musical production at court. It is, therefore, not surprising that he bent official style so as to spotlight his own talents.

28. As recounted in Mellors, *François Couperin*, p. 32.

29. Cooper and Zsako, "George Muffat"; Bacilly, *Art of Proper Singing*; Couperin, *L'Art de toucher le clavecin*; Mather, *Interpretation of French Music*.

30. For a summary, see Little, "Recent Research in European Dance, pp. 4–14. For examples of dance applied directly to musical performance, see Little, "The Contribution of Dance Steps," pp. 112–24, and Hilton, "A Dance for Kings," pp. 161–72.

31. d'Alembert, *La Liberté de la Musique*, p. 48.

32. See, for instance, Zarlino, *Istitutioni harmoniche*, IV, chap. 32, pp. 177–78. Subsequent theorists were influenced by Descartes's *The Passions of the Soul*. For an eighteenth-century account of musical affect, see Mattheson, *Der vollkommene Capellmeister*. For a philosophical discussion of these issues, see Kivy, *The Corded Shell*.

33. For instance, Giaches de Wert's madrigal "Tirsi morir volea" ("Tirsi wanted to die")—which involves a shepherd who must delay orgasm until his partner is ready to "die" with him—pushes the tension of yoked declamation almost to the breaking point, as Tirsi seems to be virtually grinding his teeth in anticipation and frustration, before the explosive simultaneous orgasm finally occurs. These are among the first compositions self-consciously modeled on the experience of sustained sexual tension, climax, and release. Needless to say, this remains an extremely popular pattern in later music, even when it is not acknowledged. See my *Feminine Endings*, especially chapter 5.

34. See my "Constructions of Gender." I am at present writing a book, *Power and Desire in Seventeenth-Century Music*, which will deal with this issue in greater detail.

35. Handel was unusual for his time in creating sympathetic depictions of powerful, desiring women in his operas and oratorios. Gary Thomas has made an excellent case for understanding Handel as having been affiliated with a same-sex subculture. See Thomas, "Was George Frideric Handel Gay?" While it has not yet been generally accepted, Thomas's thesis might help explain Handel's subversions of accepted gender roles in his music: his displacement onto female characters of qualities usually reserved for men and his critiques of patriarchal privilege in, for instance, *Jephtha*.

36. Foucault, *The History of Sexuality*. See also Abelove, "History of Sexual Intercourse," pp. 125–30, on how social configurations of desire may have altered material conditions such as population growth.

37. See, for instance, Le Cerf de La Viéville, *Comparison de la musique italienne et de la musique française*, in *Music History*, pp. 489–507.

Among the bodily effects of *opera seria* most disturbing to the French was the featured display of castrati (Caesar had been sung originally by Senesino, a famous male alto). Nowhere in Western culture has musical taste imposed its priorities so directly on the body as with this custom, in which mutilation produced males who could dominate in the high registers "naturally" reserved for women. Perhaps the most compelling (certainly the most entertaining) source concerning the castrati is in Rice, *Cry to Heaven*.

38. See again Rosand, *Opera in Seventeenth-Century Venice*.

39. Lang, *George Frideric Handel*, p. 148.

40. For instance, Ludwig Tieck heard in the symphony "insatiate desire forever hieing forth and turning back into itself," and E. T. A. Hoffmann wrote of the "infinite longing" in Beethoven. See Dahlhaus, *The Idea of Absolute Music*.

41. See my "Narrative Agendas in 'Absolute' Music."

42. See my *Georges Bizet: Carmen*, and the chapters on Carmen and Salome in my *Feminine Endings*. See also Clément, *Opera, or the Undoing of Women*, and Kramer, "Culture and Musical Hermeneutics," pp. 269–94.

43. See my chapters on Anderson and Madonna and the section on Galas in *Feminine Endings*.

RANDY MARTIN

Agency and History:
The Demands of Dance
Ethnography

There are no wings in Judson Church. Stained glass. A marble altar. A gilded organ. These and not the conventional tokens of theater architecture are the markers of a space transformed. In an evening of works shared by two choreographers, dancers in the last piece of the concert await their moment of display in a gallery immediately above the audience. In anticipation of their own performance, they witness now in others what others will soon see of them. They join in the audience response to this just-completed spectacle that they are now called upon to provide. Dancers descend from this elevated perspective down a narrow staircase and walk along the audience's flank, brushing against the perimeter of that congregated body as if to measure its density. They enter the darkened space that holds a diffuse focus. The markings of "church" at Judson—quite eccentric no doubt to the experience of a good part of the crowd—is enough of a departure from the familiar to grant the performers the distance that will privilege their activity as spectacle, despite their entrance on the scene through means of such casual contact.

What has accumulated over three months of rehearsals at sites with little resemblance to this one will now dissolve in fourteen minutes of performance. The transcription from spaces of rehearsal to that of performance has occurred only once in a run-through of the piece an hour before the concert. This concert is one of a series of single evening showcases. Without presumption of repetition, four of us assume places in the darkness that we take as the illusory origins of something that culminates but did not actually start here.

I sit furthest downstage watching, along with the audience behind me, the minimal beginnings of a recurrent gestural phrase, suggestive of but without specific signification. Kim, who sits perched on the edge of the marble altar, appears silently absorbed in these gestures. I share in the audience's gaze upon these initially tiny movements, but with a decidedly more instrumental interest. One of those movements brings me to join in their general articulation, and by so doing, to depart from that gaze which had effectively formatted the performance space and as such enabled the performance.

There is now music to provide an aural frame of reference for the four of us and allow the visual dependencies among us to abate. The escalating movement, punctuated like so many questions still listening for response, brings me from the floor to my feet. Randa intervenes on my behalf. She takes over the weight that had been me free-standing. She flips it, shifts it again, and departs. Corporal interdependency continues in a duet with Greta composed of a series of embraces that slip away as we grasp for them. Well inside of the piece by now, the movement that has brought me here is all linked through permutations and disruptions of that initial gestural phrase. The physical contact of two yields to the unison of four in the first frontal encounter of performers to audience. There are no lights angled at the stage at Judson Church that normally would blind performers to those who gaze upon them, generating the visual asymmetry upon which spectacle depends. On the contrary, the general illumination does little to discriminate between the two parties and in the moments of movement that open outward, it is possible, albeit only fleetingly, to regard them as they do us.

Soon this mutuality of regard will become more explicit. The unspeakable state of my body as an object of the gaze is broken when I address the audience. "I suppose you were hoping to get some sort of meaning out of that? Well did you?" These words carried my gaze back to the gazers and inquired as to what their sight had seen. But my momentary fixity could only bring me to gaze without being able to sustain such a visual stance. In movement, the boundary between the volume of the performance space and that of the audience could be effaced. Motion, collected in me as a medium of exchange between the history of rehearsals and the aggregated body of the public, operated across that divide. In sight, I could not match the mass of audience with its detail. There was the brown beard against blue plaid sitting in front and, several rows back, the glasses' curve matched in a facial furrow. Such sightings had to be quickly relinquished to preserve my own visuality as something available to the audience and to lend my corporeality to those three to whom I owed an immanent allegiance.

Racing through the space in a collision course with audience and lofting myself into verticality, I am caught by three standing in for many more beyond them. In the seamless circulation of weight that is dancing, what was caught is now deposited for the transit of others. These exchanges continue, enlisting others to effect the equivalent of localized polar shifts. Whole bodies are remapped along altered axes of arrival and departure. Soft folds for sudden landings are created where there were flat surfaces associated with the boundaries of self–containment. The boundaries have been redrawn so persistently as to inflict a partial meltdown of that familiar da Vincian figure in its orb. For inside that sphere is no longer a renaissance of singularity exposing its genius. The canvas has been torn, and, like figures momentarily released from the stillness of representation, we pour through the openings. There is now little movement that proceeds unmediated through the body of others. Space has become dense and bodies permeable to the point of narrowing the differences between them. It is possible to extend in a direction where no one yet stands and find support by the time of arrival.

Such explicit collectivity, dependent as it is on proximity, yields to an expanding distance among the four of us. The suggestion is made through movements echoed peripherally among us of that prior community of proximity, now continuing without touch, implicating not only ourselves in a shared project but also those others upon whose gaze we have come to depend upon for our continued activity. But the piece ends. All of the motion in the space collects the place we each occupy as we regard those who gaze upon us. Only their applause will break that tenuous obligation and with it, our mutual unities disperse.

The genealogy of that other unity is much more difficult to trace than that of the performers. Like the latter, it is occasioned by and enables the performance but unlike the dancers, whose specific unity has a prior history, audience is only constituted by that particular instance of the dance. Despite its indications of specialized activity, Judson Church is not as directive as some performance spaces are in that process of self-constitution. Without a functioning proscenium, the audience itself serves as a physical boundary of the performing space. The illumination of that space, which signals the opening of the dance piece for the audience, finds them scanning what lies before them, looking for the dance. Given the absence of focused pools of light that can be created by the panoply of instruments that Judson lacks, or other visual aids, and the minimal beginnings of this particular piece, it is not unlikely for an active participant of the audience to locate the initial movements of the figure upstage after the dance has already begun. For audience then, it is the work of their gaze that sets the piece in motion. Given too that the space is as wide as it is deep, the distance between dancers with which the piece begins imposes a certain sense of loss, introduced as a suspicion that there may be more activity on the periphery of one's gaze than at its focal point. Watching the piece entails looking for something to look at. The carved details and inscriptions of the church may provide as likely a momentary resting place for the gaze as others in the audience, which is arrayed in a U–shape around the performing space.

The shifting character of the gaze is activated by the specific inscription of the choreography in this space. Yet the promise of the choreography—to deliver the space whole to an intended viewer—is violated in the very act of viewing. This occurs not simply because each participant in this activity sees it from a different perspective, but because the different perspectives are generated by an indeterminate but distinct process of audition, a tryout, so to speak, for the senses. What audience shares, then, is not what it has seen, as if the dance produced a common set of images exposed to a population with diverse propensities toward their reception (the model of mass media), but rather a common predicament of looking for the dance as they view it. This predicament is not inconsistent with the idea of this piece of choreography, as evidenced in the constant shifting of who moves through space and who moves in place in the opening sections of the work, or who moves and who observes or speaks in the latter part of the dance.

There are, no doubt, moments of common focus for the audience that the choreographer has designed into the piece, and these make the reflexivity of viewing more immediate. When the muteness of the dancers is broken by the initial address to the audience, their common attendance to what they have heard breaks their own silence. The creakings of chairs and clearings of throats, the prior noises of the listeners, that usually go unrecognized as solitary acts of self-acknowledgment, are now expressed as laughter. The laughter in this case was not a common roar that might have come from the spongy mass of a homogeneous body in attendance. It was instead punctuated through the house, accumulating its aural presence after the performer who had uttered that first statement had gone on to other activities. Part of what the audience was trying-out for was the assertion of its capacity for evaluation. The audience was listening to itself.

Its other opportunity for audition comes when it brings the piece to a close. Applause emerges at the moment of the audience's fullest self-recognition. It is occasioned certainly by the dancer's activity, but it is a response to a question that the audience must by this point have posed to itself. Was that the dance? By initiating this common activity, the audience renders its most instrumental imposition on the dancers—it gets them to bow—and then quite literally applauds the dancers out of the performing space. What the choreography began, getting dancers to move with something in mind, the audience here continues. But as soon as they have succeeded in their choreography, they disband themselves, leaving behind the authority their work had assigned to them.

One of them was a critic for the *New York Times* who did invoke that lost authority. Several paragraphs appeared in the "Home" section of the paper a few days later. That a review appeared at all could not be expected, especially for a concert of experimental dance that ran only for a single evening. But that it did appear meant that the dance could have an efficacy beyond the concert hall, at least in the minds of those who had not been at the event. Conventionally speaking, the review entered the dance into history by translating it into a representation that could be interpreted by others. Yet both as a document of the event in which the artistic object was presented, and as an instrument for understanding what made the event possible, the review in this rather truncated form is a weak device for historical representation. The review, the most common form of dance writing, is weak as much for how it attempts to describe the object of that performed event as for what it leaves out.

Clearly this problem of the artistic object is present for any writing about art, or, for that matter, other historical events. There is always something left out of the attempt to represent in words work executed in a nonverbal medium. But dance presents special problems of how to move between representation and object. For example, better documentation might have been provided by either of two video cameras that recorded the performance that evening. But the motional dynamics, the incessant change of bodies moving in space that dancing features as its artistic object, can only be simulated in video through an editing process that results in something distinct from the original dance. While audio recording might replicate at least the signifiers of a musical performance, video relies on a displacement of an activity that occurs within a three-dimensional space into some virtual equivalent. Videography reinscribes dancing in another medium that can introduce an awareness of how, in the production of a document, a history is written.

Yet even this more self-conscious form of documentation (when dance videography is that) focuses on recreating an event rather than on recapturing something of the social processes, namely the very participation of performers and audience, that made that event possible. Dance highlights this participation precisely because of its resistance to representation. While various systems of dance notation exist, they do not enjoy the generalized application of the musical score or dramatic script. The graphy, or writing, in choreography is an inscription of moving bodies in space and not on paper or video screen where movement activity is a precondition for inscription, rather than the other way around. The claim here is not that signals for movement patterns can never be transmitted to dancers in any media but movement, but rather that the choreographic idea is dependent on its ultimate expressive activity (dancing) for its inscription in a manner qualitatively different from any other performance idiom. For example, even where video is used in the rehearsal process it records rather than generates movement. From the perspective of the audience, given that a video imagines the perspective of a generalized viewer, as an artifact of the performance, video may readily conceal the asynchrony and heterogeneity of audience activity.

Classical ballet, hip hop, Balinese or Ghanaian dance certainly have a vocabulary established prior to a given work. Especially for the latter three forms the question of how to situate the choreographic function is particularly complex in terms of the way it is instantiated in other cultural processes. In contrast, the lexicon for modern and experimental dance is more diffuse while the choreographic role tends to be attributed indexically. This privileges the specificity of each rehearsal process to create a work of dance.

If dance lends itself only weakly to modes of representation for performers, who after all could continue to dance a given work even without its being documented, it is even more challenging to conceive of its possibility of representation for an audience. Dance is unlike language, where at least a relation of signifier and signified is identifiable if not immutable. At the "zero-degree" of dance movement, meaning is indeterminate because in practice movement lacks the discrete equivalents of sound-images that words provide. Further, the association between particular movements and concepts has not been culturally established by any equivalent of a "community of speakers" that would equate dance movement with a more generalized circulation of gestures.[1]

While dancing relies on any number of structural devices as part of the choreographic craft, even experienced dance-goers, like professional critics, do not evidence anything as efficacious as demonstrable codes of interpretation. Nor has a secondary literature emerged that has articulated a grammar of dance criticism specific to its object or a more general meditation on this predicament for the representation of dance in writing. The other side, therefore, of the resistance of the dance object to representation has been the inability to generate a theoretical language of its own or a sustained dialogue with theory from other sources.[2]

The distance between representation and object has engaged the intellectual energies of those writing on dance as a kind of bricolage where the dance event appears to occasion writerly structure. These energies have been occupied in writing on other objects by a theory that simulates the complexity of the object through the writing itself. The traces of participation, the work an audience does to create a sense of the object as it is presented to them, are nowhere to be found in the standard means of representation and documentation and as such, absent from the ways in which history is conventionally conceived.

Reception of dance, quite evident in the kinds of dancing referred to above but also characteristic of Western concert dance, is realized only in the particular performance event. The dancers constitute themselves in anticipation of perform-ance. This anticipation bears the anxiety of uncertainty, of something that can be completed only through its communication. The performance is the execution of an idea by dancers whose work proceeds in expectation of an audience that is itself only constituted through performance. The audience has no identity as audience prior to and apart from the performative agency that has occasioned it. As such, the audience is intrinsically "unstable," both in terms of its own presence and in its ability to occasion and then disrupt the very anxiety of performance.[3] At the same time, it is the work that the audience does, the participation that it lends to performance to make the latter possible, that is irrecuperable to repre-sentation. It is, like the dance activity itself, an untranslatable object. But unlike dancing, representation rarely makes an effort to recognize it.

Participation springs from this disruptive potential, an indeterminacy of representation internal to the performance. If writing and documentation cannot recuperate the traces of participation found in performance minimally, they can recognize the disruptive effects of the work of participation lost to representation. This is the problem that was hinted at in the writing that opened this chapter, writing that, in effect, stood in for the activities of performance and audience and was meant to indicate this disruption of narrative forms. In this case, one of the narrative forms depended on a kinesthetic memory of my part in the dance and the other on a video of that performance with visual and aural traces of audience in it, which I viewed six months later. What a fuller elaboration of these narra-tives would want to show was that the performance event could only be grasped through an exchange consisting of the mutual interruption and displacement of narratives. A single privileged narrative perspective, be that of the dancers, the audience, the choreographer, or critic, is not adequate analytically to the com-plexity of the event.

The shift in perspective to participation rather than representation as sug-gested by the conceptual challenges posed by dance, as the particularization of the performer-audience relation, has an import beyond dance writing. This per-spective simulates a relation of performance and audience where performance pertains to the execution of an idea implicit in the notion of "agency" and audi-ence suggests a mobilized critical presence intended by radical notions of "history."[4] This distinction points to a conception of history where historical proj-ect as the formation of an identity and historical possibility as the capacity for continued mobilization are joined, one that focuses on the moment of reception in relation to the object. The full appreciation of the place of reception, of the unstable audience, has the potential to extend an understanding of the political.

Joining the politics of history and of performance rests upon a specialized application of dance analysis. Rather than suggesting dance in any form as a model for political activity or prescribing models for political dance, both of which assume a priori responses to what can only be conjuncturally based questions, the specificity of the relations of performance and audience in dance can provide methodological insights for recognizing politics where it would otherwise be invisible. In the context of this analysis, dance should be considered an analytic frame, not the framing of a particular activity that should be extended or emulated in other social arenas.

Paradoxically, fuller recognition of the moment of reception in dance performance can be applied beyond the narrow confines of a venue such as Judson to reconceptualize the place of audience in a culture of mass communication. Typically, culture is mistaken for a market transaction that proscribes the public as passive consumers of images without the capacity for critical presence suggested by the term participation. In the market view, the image on the screen is only a decision taken that requires no further effort and disappears somewhere in the demand of the audience.[5] Even in more complex conceptions of media consumption, it is often assumed that representation is the only optic through which to view the prospects for mobilized publics or the making of history. The performer-audience relation seems closer than that of text and reader to approximating the object of history. The historical object lacks the stability of a text and the conditions of its production, suggests more participation than does the activity of interpretation or reading.

The procedure I suggest that is most appropriate for exploring the relation of agency and history simulated in performance is ethnographic. Ethnography is an appropriate method for appreciating the disruptive presence that divides representation and its object. Ethnography conveys through language that the ethnographic procedure is radically different from what it looks at. Ethnography is an activity of textual appropriation of difference that rests upon a prior cultural appropriation through colonial contact. Hence, while ethnography results in representation, with sufficient methodological reflection, it points to what is lost to representation just as does the performer-audience relation in dance.

Different versions of ethnography have projected a range of power relations, and therefore possibilities for politics, in the construction of the relationship between representation and object, whether in art or history. Traditionally, the temptation for ethnographic activity has been to preserve the exotic as an other whose very estrangement and distantiation make it available for uncritical appropriation.[6] Ethnography as a professional practice emerged within the history of colonialism as both the affirmation of the other's availability to be colonized (first territorially and then epistemologically) and the doubt that civilization could survive the loss of difference that progress would inevitably bring. Methodologically this project assumed that the distinction of self and other were as stable as the distance of ethnographer and cultural object. Instead, colonization was precisely the destabilization of those relations of identity and distance which ethnographers were, in their own work, impelled to sort out. Without a sufficiently critical conception of themselves and their social context, it was tempting to present an unreliably stable picture of difference.

Since at least the seventies, the ethnographic model has been revised in a variety of ways with significant consequences for social theory and politics. One tendency of this revision seeks, in the face of what it sees as the loss of the exotic, to locate its activity wholly within representation as a rhetorical reflection of writing.[7] Scrutinizing the authority of representation, calling into question the distance of the cultural object, asserting the partiality of truth as both "committed and incomplete" all render ethnographic practice more fully reflexive. Yet this consciousness of self can come at the expense of a comprehension of what that self appropriates and what lies beyond that appropriation. My concern is that the unruly engagement with difference that currently marks Western culture must be recognized if what reconstituted colonial energies now do to the world is to be kept alive to analysis.[8] The self–awareness gained by this expression of revisionist ethnography threatens to be recuperated within the politics of writing per se.

Given that the revision is far from complete, I would want to encourage the development of self-critical ethnography toward a strategy responsive to the demands of dance analysis presented here that would reaffirm and relocate the exotic within ethnographic representation, precisely that of the unstable audience.[9] The ethnography of this strategy consists in writing that fully displays the disruptive potential of that which it represents in analysis. Here the ethnographic field is neither the undifferentiated space of the other visited by the ethnographer nor the seamless space of representation in which an ethnographer writes. It is, rather, like dance performance, a relation of forces joined in tension yet fundamentally unlike one another. By identifying such tensions, the work of field work becomes more problematic, more contingent, and more susceptible to contention and reformation because it is constituted by difference rather than merely reflecting difference.

In this regard, ethnographic writing identifies politics where there was thought to be none. This is not to say that we should expect to hear more from the audience at Judson that night, clearly that would take some other event, tied to a sustained mobilization. But if critical analysis is to understand what keeps any audience coming back for more, if it is to grasp what sustains any mobilization irrespective of its duration, it had better attend closely to the dynamics of performance.

Difference, hitherto relegated to some exotic other elsewhere, now lies within the account of the object as destabilized and destabilizing. Context here is not what lies beyond the object, but what it cannot grasp and in failing to do so appears as a momentary assertion. If traditional ethnography had asserted the (colonial) context unproblematically as beyond the cultural object, and revised ethnography has tended to lose context to its own representation, this dance-based ethnographic prospect insinuates context in the midst of the object without it being absorbed by that object. The other, grounded in practical terms as the mobilized presence of the unstable audience, provides momentary context to the agency of the object itself, now the writing of spatial inscriptions or dancing, or of ethnographic texts.

Such a conception of ethnography could be applied to any number of situations, from television watchers to soldiers in battle, from movements of capital to those against it. But to develop its terms of analysis, it should logically begin with the highly particularized relations of dance where the participation of audience refuses to be subsumed by the representation of performance.

In the case of the audience at Judson Church, its refusal comes at the expense of its continued mobilization and, as such, the powers it appropriated during the performance are expended without recognition of their politics. Such politics would be interesting to pursue in the recent conjuncture of anxieties over dance (and other artistic) output that substitute the work of audience with a negative idealization of its capacity for reception. Instability of presence has been translated as a kind of moral fragility in need of the protections of censorship in the minds of those willing to talk about contemporary art but unwilling to see it. The invisibility of the audience's participation is misrecognized as an absence, a void into which is projected a fatuous intimacy. The materialization of publicness that performance enables is rendered in terms of an idealized Victorian privacy. Hence, in the recent attacks on performance, public demands for resources are elided with a language of protective (but highly selective) private rights that seek to exclude difference as what is constitutive of the public. Reception gets conceived as matter of simple transference of the idea of the art object to its audience, rather than a transformative social activity that brings context into performance. In this regard, such terms as shock, indecency, immorality must be reconsidered as both problems and capacities of reception, rather than properties of the object.

The Judson series was sponsored by an organization called Movement Research that had National Endowment for the Arts funds revoked for its putative foul play (it had published materials on AIDS and sexuality in a journal it produced that were considered inappropriate to art by the funding agency). It is not surprising that a critically inclined arts organization would turn to Judson Church, which has long figured as an oppositional public sphere that has included involvement with labor and anti-war movements. It is no small irony, however, that experimental work—once conceived of as autonomous from the instrumentalities of the social—would be drawn into the sanctuary of a church to escape the wrath of an assault cloaked in the mantle of religion. In this context, an ethnographically driven riposte to those whose own indecency speaks for public pleasures could have a certain practical effect.

It is not difficult to imagine other theaters of politics where such analysis might have utility. The attack on the arts is but one version of a far more pervasive lexicon of hate speech that, whatever else it does, assumes the disposition of those traditional ethnographies fully but uncritically inflected with their own colonial predicament. The contemporary others, reduced in all practical terms to a single amalgamation of gendered, sexually preferred, and racialized difference in the colonizing speech of deprecation, also assume an audience of their own kin, incapable of surviving any encounter of performed difference. The twist this is given in the term "politically correct" is that any disturbance of the self-consuming silence mandated by the discourse of polite pluralism would primitivize civil society by replacing the ordered rule of a multitudinous single voice with the noisy unruliness of many.

The pluralism of intolerance assumes that producers and receivers of public discourse cohabit socialized spaces without generating exchange—what Marx understood as mutual displacement. Specifically, with respect to dance performance, it was the incessant interruption of the gaze of performer and audience, noted in the description of the Judson performance above, that served as the very medium of exchange. How strange that in this marketplace of ideas, exchange itself is proscribed. Perhaps, to extend the market analogy to performance theory, this is because generalized exchange in this globally configured profit-taking environment is oriented toward the disappearance through representation of what it appropriates: namely, the labor that generates any social value, including the sociality and critical capacity of audience.

In these terms, the analytic gains of dance ethnography reveal the bad faith of the colonizing discourse of narrow market rationalities and supposedly non-economic irrationalities (of race, gender, sexuality, and the like). To deny what audience produces in performance is to disavow its capacity to produce its own associations, in favor of an imperative to manage its desires with respect to a world of products run wild. The protection offered trades the unruly orders of difference that constitute society for a representation of harmony that serves as a nefarious performative fiction. But the wonder of fiction is the desire it sustains for another tale to be told. The magic of dance is to deposit this desire with the audience.

NOTES

1. For a similar concern about the limits of the semiotic model for dance, see Auslander, "Embodiment," fn. 5, p. 21, citing the work of Wilfried Passow.

2. Copeland and Cohen make the point in the preface to their extensive edited volume "*What Is Dance?*" that "the dance community pays a considerable price for this bias against theory. It rarely enjoys the sort of vigorous intellectual debate that enlivens discussions of the other arts" (p. viii).

3. Blau develops this concept at length in *The Audience*.

4. This radical notion of history has by now been articulated in many ways. It could be traced initially to E. P. Thompson's work on processes of political formation, but certainly was developed by the reception of such diverse figures as Gramsci, Williams, Foucault, and Bakhtin in this country. A useful discussion, to which I am greatly indebted, of how these literatures have come together can be found in Brown, *The Production of Society*. Brown discusses the antinomies of the Thompsonian project in "History and History's Problem," pp. 136–61.

5. For a critique of the consumer model of audience in mass media, see Inglis, *Media Theory*, pp. 134–55. For an elaboration that emphasizes the "work" of consumption, see Miller, *Material Culture and Mass Consumption*.

6. Much-discussed examples of this relation of ethnographer and object can be found in the opening of the classic studies of Malinowski, *Argonauts of the Western Pacific*, and Evans-Pritchard, *The Nuer*.

7. For a programmatic statement of this inflection, see Clifford's introduction to the volume he edited with Marcus, *Writing Culture*, pp. 1–26.

8. This concern is shared by other critiques of this direction within revisionist ethnography. See, for example, Abu-Lughod, "Can There Be a Feminist Ethnography?" pp. 7–27. This concern is developed with respect to representation more broadly by Spivak in *In Other Worlds*.

9. It is worth noting that within the Clifford and Marcus volume itself there are openings in this direction. Assad suggests that "indeed, it could be argued that 'translating' an alien form of life, another culture, is not always done best through the representational discourse of ethnography, that under certain conditions a dramatic performance, the execution of a dance, or the playing of a piece of music might be more apt" (p. 159). Yet by maintaining the model of translation, Assad seems to demand less of performance methodologically than it may be able to provide. Stephen A. Tyler also points to ethnography as a "text . . . of the performed" (p. 136) but his evocation of a "cooperative story" that "should emerge out of the joint work of the ethnographer and his native partners" (pp. 126–27) and would serve through "restorative harmony" and "aesthetic integration" (p. 134) "to re-integrate the self in society and to restructure the conduct of daily life" (p. 135) threatens to extract the ethnographer's work from the social and historical conditions of cultural contact. While Assad is quite alive to the politics of these conditions, his translation model suggests autonomously bounded cultures that make the shared global context he wants to foreground difficult to recognize. In Tyler's apparent desire to transcend relations of power, global situations that shape the ethnographic encounter can be lost to analysis. The notion of a disruptive, mutual interference between the narratives of representation and its object, that in Spivak's terms "bring each other into crisis" (Spivak, *In Other Worlds*, p. 241), is intended precisely to push on the dilemma that lies between Assad's and Tyler's works.

Moving Theory across Bodies of Practice

THOMAS W. LAQUEUR

Credit, Novels, Masturbation

There is in the *Spectator* for 3 March 1711 a little "Vision or Allegory" involving dance and the subject of this paper: masturbation, fiction, and the rise of credit. The narrator dreams that he is in a Great Hall at one end of which is a beautiful Virgin, named "Publick Credit," who is seated on a throne of gold. She smiles with "a Secret Pleasure" at the Acts of Parliament, emblazoned around the walls, which had made her existence possible and she shows "a very particular uneasiness" when she sees anything approach that might hurt them. She "appeared infinitely timorous in her behaviour," seemed troubled by vapours, and was subject to "momentary Consumptions, that in the twinkling of an Eye, she would fall away from the most florid Complexion, and the most healthful State of Body, and wither into a skeleton."[1]

I am tempted to make much of the fact that her plight is remarkably similar to that of the masturbator who, in an anonymous tract by a quack doctor, came into the domain of medicine for the first time the very year of Addison's reverie. (*Onania* in 1710 also managed the stunning cultural feat of not only inventing a major disease but naming it: The link between Onan and auto-eroticism had, over the millennia, been tangential at best.)[2] But first, on to the dance.

Suddenly, the doors of the hall flew open and there appeared, the narrator continues, a half dozen of the "most hideous Phantoms that I had ever seen." "They came in, two by two, though match'd in the most dissociable Manner, and mingled together in a kind of Dance." The dance of "so many jarring Natures" reminded him "of the Sun, Moon, and Earth, in the Rehersal, that danced together for no other end but to eclipse one another." The Virgin on the throne fainted. The great heaps of gold on either side of the throne were all of a sudden only heaps of paper or piles of notched sticks; the "hill of Money bags" collapsed because only one in ten of the bags actually contained any money at all. The rest were only "full of wind."

Finally there entered "a second dance of Apparitions" more agreeably matched and "made up of very amiable phantoms." Liberty had monarchy by the arm; moderation led religion; an unidentified dancer led the genius of Great Britain. And amidst these true and real virtues in harmonious movement— amidst genuine sociability—the paper turned back into guineas, the bags swelled again, and all was set right, though the syncopic Virgin is not heard from again.

Credit—government and private paper—forms one of the loci of fiction I want to consider. Legitimized by the 1695 Bank of England Act, which allowed the regular funding of the national debt, the market in paper grew exuberantly only to burst in history's first crashes: John Law's Mississippi Bubble in France and the South Sea Bubble in England, both early in 1720. ("Bubble" meant something fragile, unsubstantial, empty, a deceptive show, as in "Why should a woman dote on such a Bubble," or in Defoe: "The Nation will find South Sea at best a mighty bubble.")[3]

Montesquieu, like Addison and Steele, makes much of the moral dangers of credit, in his case Law's various schemes: "I saw the disease spreading until it affected even the healthiest parts of the organism," writes Usbek in the *Persian Letters*, "the most virtuous men committing shameful deeds." "I saw every law of the family overthrown . . . an insatiable lust for money suddenly springing up in every heart."[4] The letter that Montesquieu chose to place next, though of course it is "dated" three years earlier in 1717, tells of how all sexual order has collapsed in the harem: Zelis dropped her veil on her way to the mosque, allowing everyone to see her; Zashi went to bed with one of her slaves; and a youth was apprehended in the garden of the seraglio.[5]

Before leaving this theme, I want to make one even more explicit textual connection between sex and economics. The well-known physician and friend of Rousseau, S. A. Tissot, who in 1758 wrote what would become the most quoted medical anti-masturbatory jeremiad in history, says the following regarding the seeds of the secret, pathogenic vice:

> Men subject themselves, to false wants, and such is the case of those addicted to self-pollution. It is imagination and habit that subject them; it is not nature.[6]

I do not offer these comments on dance, masturbation, and equity or credit markets as if the mere appearance of "intertextuality" somehow relates one bodily practice to others. Nor could I offer, or even imagine, a general account of how to set a limit on our consideration of the full range of cultural phenomena that might shed light on the body as a cultural construction. I intend, as I have already begun in a rather dogged and empirical fashion, to juxtapose texts that will demonstrate that, in the annoying but true refrain of the historian, "it is no accident that" the first novels (say, Defoe's *Robinson Crusoe* in 1719 or *Moll Flanders* in 1722), the first speculative market collapses (1720), and the sudden and unheralded appearance of masturbation as the cause of serious mental and bodily harm (*Onania* was supposedly published in 1711, although the first extant edition is 1714) are within a decade of one another.

I cannot here provide sufficient evidence to support the claim for the absolute novelty of masturbatory disease except to say that so learned a doctor as Tissot could find no classical precedents despite much effort. Also, the exhaustive *Dictionnaire Encyclopédique des Sciences Medicales*, in its entry on "Onanisme," notes that antiquity regarded onanism with serene indifference and that only in the eighteenth century did it attain considerable importance.[7] If this is indeed the case, if masturbation as a medical problem is new in 1711, the question arises: Why?

I want now to offer less an answer itself than my strategy for arriving at one. I will do so by first arguing briefly that other explanations, including Michel Foucault's, are not entirely satisfactory. I will then adduce textual links between credit, novels, and the secret vice to suggest that the common villain is fictionality, the realm of the imagined. Finally, I will speculate briefly about how these texts might be inserted into a social and political history of how the body assumes its meaning.

There is, in the first place, the view that the fear of masturbatory diseases and the mushrooming—I use the word advisedly to suggest links with the eighteenth-century usages of "mushroom," to mean the moneyed interests—medical literature that described and warned against them are explicable as a response to something in the real world: a dramatic rise in the incidence of masturbation. Possibly. More privacy in the bourgeois home; more boarding schools where the solitary vice was supposedly learned; proportionately more servants who wickedly calmed children, especially boys, by stimulating their genitals; heightened sexual desire in a world in which desire more generally was socially valorized could all have resulted in more masturbation.[8]

But we have absolutely no evidence that it actually did. And even if masturbation were suddenly rife, it does not follow that it would become the object of such anxieties and the putative cause of so much grievous bodily harm. Perhaps it is true that, as François Delaporte wrote recently, "diseases do not exist but only practices."[9] Still, fear of the plague after 1348 is more easily explicable in terms of the appearance of rats carrying fleas carrying *Yersinia pestis* and resulting in massive mortality than would be the fear of even epidemic masturbation, which, in fact, caused very, very few deaths in the eighteenth century. Whatever happened to the incidence of the practice itself, the problem is genuinely one of explaining the cultural construction of disease and anxiety about the body.

A particularly influential explanation of the rise of masturbatory disease links it to a supposedly new psychological attachment to semen, a new worry about its loss, and a new emphasis on its place in health and disease. Semen, money, and energy, in this account, are all in short supply and are profligately expended at the wastrel's peril. A certain old-fashioned humorialism thus mediates between economic and sexual irrationality so that masturbation exacts the same sort of price upon the body that failure to husband resources visits upon one's commercial activities.[10]

There are several difficulties with this explanation as a general account. If spending alone were all that was at stake, supply would ultimately regulate demand. The extreme nervousness about masturbation in this period occurred precisely because it seemed to escape an economy of scarcity, because supply seemed endless and limited only by the imagination. In the masturbatory economy of excess, there really might be a free lunch. Or, put differently, masturbation became a major concern precisely at the time when the possibility of widespread surplus, of a high demand/high wage economy was recognized by theorists.

One could, admittedly, find hundreds of appreciative quotations and citations of Tissot's famous dictum that one part of semen is worth forty of blood; it was repeated endlessly for at least a century.[11] And, spermatorrhea—the leakage of sperm, which was regarded as both a consequence of and an important stage in the patho-physiology of masturbatory disease—became a little medical realm of its own.[12] But all this does not get the historian very far in explaining the eighteenth-century appearance of a new deadly disease that was the supposed result of masturbation.

In the first place, if seminal loss were the key to the relevant patho-physiological mechanism, why was seminal loss from so-called heterosexual intercourse regarded as relatively benign, while losses from autoerotic orgasm were so fraught? Worries about illness through loss of semen were certainly not new, nor were paeans of praise to the precious fluid. Many supposed victims of masturbation, moreover, were entirely outside a putative seminal economy. Contemporary literature insists that the practice was every bit as dangerous for women, who, as everyone agreed by this time, produced no semen. The first extant edition of *Onania*, for example, admittedly provided only a few supporting examples of female self-abuse, but the fifteenth edition, sensing an earlier lack of conviction, promised still more testimonial letters to prove not only that girls masturbate in droves but also that they harm themselves by it (p. 42). Tissot thought that women no less than men "often perish the victims of this detestable lewdness" and that if anything "the malignity of the disorders occasioned by it" seems to have "a superior degree of activity among" them (1766 ed., p. 46).

And of course there was a large literature on the dangers of the solitary vice among prepubescent boys and girls who did not, it was always pointed out, ejaculate anything. "We find in the annals of medicine," explains Larousse's *Grande dictionnaire* in 1875, looking back for its lay audience on a century's observations, "plenty of cases of five, six, and eight year old children dead as a result of masturbation."[13] Obsession, not loss of precious body fluids, destroyed their immature nervous systems and constitutions generally. Thus, even if new fears about the loss of semen motivated some aspects of the rise of medical and more general concern about masturbation, it is absent from many of the sources and does not explain the phenomena *tout court*.

A new eighteenth-century interest in nerves and the brain are, I think, critical in understanding the rise of masturbatory disease, but their place in the story goes well beyond their being the carriers of excess stimulation and the agents for its diffuse actions in the body. Even if orgasm was thought to be enervating and excessive enervation dangerous, the question remains why masturbatory orgasm would be regarded as so very much more threatening than any other kind. Why, as Tissot puts it, is it "more pernicious than excesses with women?" (1766, p. 86). Even "if excess of venery is a dreadful and common cause of dangerous diseases," why should self-pollution, as an early nineteenth-century American doctor thought it was, be "tenfold more destructive"?[14] Orgasm as enervating is certainly not a new idea in 1711, masturbatory orgasm as specifically harmful comes like a bolt out of the blue.

Or to put it another way, if Nicholas Venette's advice on the permissible frequency of orgasm in heterosexual intercourse was at all representative of eighteenth-century views, it is difficult to understand, if semen and spasms were all that mattered, why even daily masturbation should be thought dangerous. Depending on age and climate—to take the extremes, a twenty-five-year-old on the plains of Barbary in the summer to a forty-year-old in Sweden in January—Venette thought that five times down to once or twice a night was fine. Women "truly do not feel themselves exhausted," no matter how often they couple.[15]

None of the above evidence argues against the fact that excessive loss of semen, the nervous stimulation of sexual excitement, and the convulsions of orgasm were regarded as dangerous by eighteenth- and early nineteenth-century physicians. My claim is rather that adducing these contemporary worries does not explain the sudden appearance of a putative new disease, and, moreover, that the tensions and inconsistencies in the medical texts belies a fundamental tension inherent in trying to construe onanism within an economy of scarcity—of semen, of nervous energy—when the danger lay in an economy of surfeit, of excess, of the "supplement." The vagueness with which patho-physiological mechanisms were articulated, the blurring of theoretical boundaries, the manifest failure to assimilate the experiences of men, women, boys, and girls under one disease entity suggest that one look outside old humoral or nervous paradigms.

There is considerable evidence for the Foucauldian account.[16] Instances of the production of discourse are blindingly evident; a truth about the body is invented, the discursive production of the pervert—the masturbator—clearly figures within "the strategic field of power relations." But the eighteenth-century epidemic of new masturbatory diseases remains problematic in *The History of Sexuality* at least if we read it, as I think we must, as making a causal argument. The specific instance of children, with which Foucault deals regarding masturbation, is relatively easy because they can be regarded as more or less passive creatures whose persons and practices are made the subject of new surveillance. But this only pushes the problem back one step—why did adults suddenly start to care so much about this particular practice—and in any case, eighteenth-century medical books are filled with confessions, real or imaginary, from grown-ups. Why now do people worry that their masturbatory practices cause impotence or vaginal discharge when late-seventeenth-century readers of *Aristotle's Masterpiece* or Venette's *Art of Conjugal Love* did not make these associations?

Foucault's chronology of masturbatory phobia is also a century or so off. He explicitly does not want to make it part of the great rupture in the mechanisms of repression that occurred in the late seventeenth century and that can be traced back through Christian sexual ethics. He wants to focus instead on the end of the eighteenth century, when there emerged, in his account, "a completely new technology of sex" of which the attack on onanism is a part. This technology in turn was part of—one might say caused by—the great shift in the nature of power that also forms the narrative backbone of *Discipline and Punish*: "the old power of death that symbolized sovereign power . . . supplanted by the administration of bodies and the calculated management of life." Sexuality as "a very real historical formation" is coterminous with a new sort of power: the replacement of "the privilege of sovereignty with the analysis of a multiple and mobile field of force relations."[17]

But the invention of masturbatory disease by an English quack doctor and a Swiss Protestant during the first half of the eighteenth century seems very far from the great shift in the nature of sovereignty associated with the French Revolution and the beheading of Louis XVI. And perhaps more important, Foucault's "pedagogization of children's sex," that is, the medicalization of masturbation, is neither temporally nor logically associated with the other relatively autonomous arenas for the production of sexuality: the hysterization of women's bodies; the socialization of procreative behavior, including the efforts to direct the behavior of the Malthusian couple; and the psychiatrization of perverse pleasure, that is, the making of homosexual pathology.

It is now past time for me to propose which "discourses and practices" do, in fact, illuminate the problem, if those adduced by Foucault do not. I was led to think about the problem of fiction and the imagination through a text by the famous eighteenth-century surgeon John Hunter. Masturbation, he writes, "does less harm to the constitution" than the "natural [act]," and intercourse with a prostitute or a woman to whom a man feels indifferent is less debilitating than intercourse "where the affections for the woman are also concerned" because the mind and the passions are less engaged in the former two than in latter case. It is the most purely "constitutional act" of the three. It is "simple." Only "one action takes place." By contrast, during intercourse with a woman for whom a man really cares,

> the mind becomes interested, it is worked up to a degree of enthusiasm, increasing the sensitivity of the body. . . . When the complete action takes place it is with proportional violence; as in proportion to the violence is the degree of debility produced or injury done to the constitution.[18]

Hunter was unique in this ordering of danger. But he led me to focus on the imagination generally, as well as on imagining the imaginary. A peculiar reflexivity, a self-containedness seems to make masturbatory imagining and novelistic imagining more dangerous than other sorts.

Once one starts looking for "imagination" in the medical literature on masturbation, it is everywhere. Yielding "to filthy Imagination" is how *Onania* described the context of self-abuse (4th ed., p. iv). As the *Encyclopédie* puts it, masturbation that "is not so frequent, which is not excited by a fiery and voluptuous imagination, which is, in a word, spurred only by one's need" is not harmful at all. But this generally is not possible and in fact the imagination has "the greatest part in the crime" and is thus most severely punished for it.[19] Masturbation can begin with some chance stimulation, writes Thomas Beddoes, the political radical, philosopher, and father of the romantic poet, "voluptuous ideas will arise in girls from any accidental irritation." But then, in those of considerable sensibility, these "ideas get possession of the imagination," causing them "to seek pleasure without any bodily irritation," that is, to indulge in the act he could not call "by the offensive name."[20]

There are lots of clues in eighteenth-century literature regarding the dangerous powers of the imagination. Most powerfully, as Condillac writes, it permits "new combinations of [impressions] at pleasure." It can play all sorts of tricks that amount to disposing our ideas "contrary to truth." The imagination is a uniquely vulnerable faculty of the mind, a weak link. "Little by little we will take all our chimeras to be realities," says Condillac, and therein lies the danger of novel reading, especially for poorly educated girls who have trouble telling the real from the fictive.[21]

The problem with masturbation and with the novel is not, of course, that those who engage in erotic self-stimulation or in reading literally cannot tell, or are mistaken about, the ontological status of fantasy. No one would claim that a character or the imagined object of desire really exists. What I think Condillac means, and what was worrying moralists generally, is that it was precisely the fictional quality of the characters in a novel or masturbatory fantasy that made them more real, more compelling, more able to arouse sentiments than so-called real characters or real sexual partners. The danger lay in representational excess, in fiction or artifice coming to supplant nature with its built-in structure of constraints.

Now we have masturbation in the realm of reading. If, as Alexander Crichton put it in 1799, insanity could be due to "disproportionate activity of the representative faculties" arising from "causes that exalt imagination," that is, "the faculty of fiction too frequently exercised" or "strong passions," we are in a position to understand not only religious manias—Tissot cites the case of an insane Moravian—but also masturbatory madness and the mental illnesses of novel readers.[22] If, as eighteenth-century doctors thought, reading books could have somatic consequences, the far greater mental excitement of masturbation would not go unnoticed by the flesh. Thomas Beddoes in 1802 attacks "books which act perniciously upon the constitution . . . novels which render the sensibility more diseased." He thinks that circulating libraries account for many of the sicknesses one finds because "the power of certain ideas to irritate organs . . . requires no illustration."[23] Robert Darnton records among the comments of contemporary readers of La Nouvelle Héloïse the following reactions. The publisher Panckoucke proclaims to Rousseau the "many tears he has shed . . . how many sighs and torments" and the renewed sensibility of his body: "my heart . . . beats faster than ever." Baron de la Sarraz thought that one should read books alone so that one could weep, as one inevitably did, at one's ease. The Marquise de Polignac declared that after Julie's deathbed scene she was past weeping and was convulsed by a sharp pain, indeed by a seizure, that became so strong that she would have been ill had she not stopped reading. J. F. Bastide was driven to bed and nearly mad by Nouvelle Héloïse, while Daniel Roguin was cured of a cold by his violent tears.[24]

These were the sorts of comments that provided further evidence, if any was needed, for the evils of novels. But there are more specific discursive connections that link masturbation to other pathologies of fiction. Coleridge thought that reading novels "occasions the entire destruction of the powers of the mind." An eighteenth-century commentator thought that they intoxicate the mind with "morbid sensibilities," that is, they render it exquisitely vulnerable to moods, feelings, and stimulus; they are to the mind "what dram drinking is to the body." Novels "affect the organs of the body," "relax the tone of the nerves," and along with music have "done more to produce the sickly countenances and nervous habits of our highly educated females than anything else." We are getting closer to masturbatory disease.[25]

If we add the view that "novelism"—*Methodist Magazine's* term—produces vacant countenances, continually feeds the imagination, ruins the lives of women by, among other things, becoming alternative "companions of their pillow," "tickle the imagination," and set up irresistible discontent, it seems ever closer to its contemporary, onanism. Novelism, like onanism, is dangerous because its protagonists are not really there and are all the more stimulating for their absence.

By linking the fantastical elements of masturbation and the novel, I want to suggest a still-broader historicist account, one that links auto-eroticism, a new genre of imaginative literature, and a much more general and far-ranging eighteenth-century debate about real versus false desire, sociability and estrangement in economic life. If masturbation is indeed a pathology of the imagination, a practice whose exercise seems to have no supply constraints, a satisfaction of endless desire by endless gratification, then perhaps it became threatening because of, or perhaps in connection with—I am not sure I want to make a causal argument—the morally disturbing qualities of a commercial, credit economy that magically promised undreamed-of abundance at the same time as it brought the problem of sociability to the fore.

Masturbation is imbricated in a discourse of the fetish that includes fiction, with its willful indulgence in the imagination, at one end and money or credit at the other. It is part of Rousseau's worry that natural self-sufficiency is being destroyed by the real and imagined needs created by commerce and sustained by a currency whose value bears no relationship to anything concrete and substantial.[26] Money, in other words, is the same sort of fetish as the masturbatory object of desire. Or it is part of the same imaginative excess noted by Maria Edgeworth, who cites a French source to the effect that: "credit—that talisman which realizes everything it imagines and which imagines everything."[27]

Real exchange, like real sex, stimulates manufacturing and sociability; a false paper economy, like masturbation, does the opposite. Conversation, the Scottish Enlightenment philosophers tell us, bridges the atomizing tendencies of market self-interest and, in a larger context, keeps the imagination in check. Solitude does the opposite. (I wonder whether one might not read Hume's juxtaposition, in his autobiography, of the fact that he spent three years in solitude in France and then produced a book—the *Treatise*, which "fell *dead-born from the press*"— as a statement about the corporeal dangers of solitary activity.[28]

If worry about masturbation is a worry about wastage, it is perhaps less about the wastage of sperm as about the wastage of a false epistemology. Credit, like the novel and the solitary vice, seems to remove one from "reality." Credit allows governments to fight wars without their populations feeling the pain commensurate with its dangers; it allows private citizens to spend beyond their means, or rather, to not know what their means really are.

I am not sure how far locating one discursive formation—that of masturbation—in the midst of two others explains much of anything. It certainly does not allow one to make a specifically political argument of the sort that Foucault makes regarding the medicalization of masturbation. Nor does it give one a warrant for the sort of connection Elias makes between a particular political formation on the one hand, and particular corporeal habits and ultimately a particular structure of personality on the other. Public masturbation, unlike public blowing of one's nose in one's sleeve, was never there to be reformed. (One could, of course, point to the well-known accounts of fondling the future Louis XIII's penis before assembled dinner guests, but this sort of behavior does not seem widespread.)

My discursive broadening of the question, however, might suggest how one would approach a social history of masturbatory anxieties. Elias's and others' suggestions that in the court of Louis XIV, for example, the ballet at Versailles and in Paris, together with courtesy, fencing, and military manuals and practice, are all part of the same history of "politesse," demand that we look beyond the particular, micro-histories of each element of this constellation for some more general and overarching account. If masturbation is not only a problem of sexuality but also of the imagination, which links it to credit and the novel, we are invited to broaden our investigations beyond the sexualized body, even broadly construed, into other realms. The history of masturbation is thus part of a history of the reconceptualization of private versus public—it has always seemed to me that the emphasis in the phrase "solitary vice" is really on the solitude, not vice—of new forms of sociability, of new ways of understanding the self in the eighteenth century. Genevan doctors, Scottish Enlightenment philosophers, London journalists, novelists and their critics very much inhabit the same world.

I imagine Betty Dodson, one of the most literarily prolific modern advocates of masturbation, taking a hot bubble bath, surrounded by candles and mirrors, relaxing, allowing her imagination full rein, telling herself, "I love you," and confronting August Tissot. They talk, not about whether masturbation is dangerous, but about how freely one can allow the mind to wander, how much control the self requires as it negotiates the hazards of social and political life.

NOTES

1. The famous allegory of "Dame Credit" is from Addison and Steele, *The Spectator*, pp. 12–15.

2. The precise date of the publication of the first edition is in doubt because no copy seems to survive, but at the latest it appeared in 1711.

3. *Oxford English Dictionary*.

4. Secondat, Baron Montesquieu, *Persian Letters*, letter 146, 269.

5. Secondat, *Persian Letters*, letter 147, 270.

6. Tissot, *A Treatise on the Curse of Onan*, p. 88.

7. *Dictionnaire Encyclopédique*.

8. The great nineteenth-century medical high priest of seminal loss, Lellemand (*Des Pertes Séminales Involuntaires*, p. 477) and the historian Edward Shorter, for example, argue that the silence of ancient and early modern doctors on the subject of masturbation

is evidence that people simply did not indulge in it very much. Shorter, *The Making of the Modern Family*, p. 99.

9. Delaporte, *Disease and Civilization*, p. 6.

10. A particularly influential version of this thesis is in Barker-Benfield, *The Horrors of the Half-Known Life*, p. 175, and chap. 15 more generally.

11. Tissot, *A Treatise on the Crime of Onan*, p. xiii.

12. Muller, *Ueber unwillkurliche Samenverluste*.

13. Larousse, *Grande dictionnaire*, "Masturbation," vol. 14, p. 165, col. 4. Five full columns are devoted to this entry; "Spermatorrhée" gets another two, in which onanism is credited as a cause of this disorder and cessation of reading, shows, and erotic reveries are suggested as parts of a cure.

14. Jameson, *The American domestick medicine*, p. 312.

15. Venette, *Conjugal Love*, p. 111.

16. Foucault, *History of Sexuality*.

17. Foucault, *History of Sexuality*, pp. xxx, 140, 102.

18. Hunter, *A Treatise on the Venereal Disease*, p. 200. The second, 1788 edition, the one microfilmed by the ESTC, leaves out these somewhat kindly claims about masturbation. The third 1810 edition, leaves them out but contains an argument by Hunter's son-in-law, the well-known surgeon Everard Hone, against them.

19. "Masturbation," vol. 10, col. 51–52.

20. Beddoes, *Hygeia: Or Essays Moral and Medical*, p. 48.

21. Quotes in Goldstein, *Console and Classify*, pp. 91–92; see pp. 90–105 on this point more generally.

22. Crichton, *Origins of Mental Derangement*, pp. 10–11.

23. Beddoes, *Hygeia: Or Essays Moral and Medical*, essay 3, p. 76; essay 4, p. 45.

24. Darnton, *The Great Cat Massacre*, pp. 243–47.

25. These quotes and those in the next paragraph are from Taylor, *Early Opposition to the English Novel*, pp. 53–69.

26. Rousseau, "Le Luxe, Le Commerce et Les Arts," pp. 517, 516–24 *passim*.

27. "The Dun" quoting de Casaux c. 1820. I am grateful to Catherine Gallagher for this quotation as well as for her criticisms of an earlier draft of this piece.

28. Hume, "My Own Life." The emphasis is in Hume's text.

MIRIAM SILVERBERG

Advertising Every Body: Images from the Japanese Modern Years

In a key text appearing in the February 1929 issue of the Japanese journal of political social commentary *Monthly Review*, popular commentator Oya Soichi defined "modern life" as "a form of consumer economy which aims at sensual gratification." (**See ad 1**.) This cultural critic, who was to become the leading archivist of pre– and post–World War II Japanese journalism culture, was point- ing to the new social life of commodities in Japan during the 1920s. Most likely he drew his conclusions from images of commodities within a visually oriented material culture desired and acquired by all classes in Japanese society by the middle of the decade. Commentators such as Oya conceived of Japanese modern life as fashioned by mores constituting a culture under construction. (**See ad 2**.) These producers of culture were implicated in a discourse about contemporary desires, which reworked cultural identity to take into account the unprecedented circulation and consumption of European- and U.S.-identified items and images of items. Their work defined the Japanese subject as female-Japanese or male- Japanese in a self-consciously "modern" (the term was **modan**) manner. The Japanese years of a cultural and socially experienced modernity spanned the decade following the great earthquake of 1923 and preceded the state consoli- dation of culture accompanying the military expansion onto the Chinese continent and into the so-called "Southern Pacific" region during the 1930s and early 1940s. Elsewhere I have discussed how Japanese cultural producers and consumers experienced the "modern" as defined by the process of culture-in-the- making, especially in the years of renovation following the destruction of the metropolitan center, Tokyo, in 1923. Here, my intent is to attempt to recapitulate how bodies were visually imagined in Japanese "modern" culture by differing cultural practitioners: the archivist (as choreographer of history), the capitalist (as photographer, advertiser, and caricature-producer), and the cartoonist (as choreographer of the affective body in history).[1]

My narrative of the imaging of the embodied and sometimes nationalized (but not necessarily racialized) Japanese men, women, girls, and boys relies on varied sources. I work from a 1938 primer for Japanese professional photographers, the writings of the leading modern Japanese cartoonist Okamoto Ippei, and the almanac of the leading prewar Japanese advertising agency, Mannensha, which published its annual advertising almanac in consistent format between 1925 and 1943. I also make use of advertisements from two leading Japanese magazines of the teens, twenties, and thirties aimed at a largely urban, male, nouveau riche set of intellectually inclined and, in the latter case, left-leaning readers: *Central Review* (**Chuo Koron**) and *Reconstruction* (**Kaizo**). Images of femininity are taken from advertisements in *Women's Arts* (**Nyonin Geijutsu**) during its years of publication, 1928–1932, when it led a contradictory existence as an avowedly chic commodity written and edited by women intellectuals and artists and aimed at sexual and political revolution.[2] Pictorial references from the three leading magazines are interspersed within this textual narrative (**see ad 3**) and are then reproduced in a second pictorial narrative of twenty-four chronologically ordered advertisements. The reader thus has the option to read my history of the advertising of "every Japanese body" both through my interpretation, moving back and forth between text and images from *Chuo Koron, Kaizo,* and *Nyonin Geijutsu* or solely via my ordering of pictorial images.

The interpretive narrative overview consists of two investigations and one concluding question. The first investigation, "Cultural Constitution of the Body," I divide into gendered parts, relying on two key terms from the teens and twenties in Japanese modern culture, "woman-likeness" and "man-likeness." These two uses of the suffix denoting "likeness" (**rashisa**) were in ubiquitous evidence during Japan's modern years, for this was a time when approximation was used to anchor uneasy definitions of femininity and masculinity, when women thronged the urban streets en route to work, play, and political demonstrations. At the same time, the masculinity (and authority) of the white-collar (ostensibly) patriarchal male was parodied in such songs as "My Wife Has a Moustache," and the Ozu Yasujiro film classic "I Was Born But," about the sons of an office worker who undertake a hunger strike in protest against their father's obsequious behavior toward his boss.

My second investigation traces the break away from the common notion of "modern life" (**modan seikatsu**) of the 1920s and early 1930s as this shift was articulated in representations of the Japanese body in advertisements. These images, consumed by Japanese readers from the middle of the 1920s into the Pacific war, are one record of the slide into wartime scarcity and consolidation of censorship controls necessary for the ultimate triumph of state hegemony in the media representations of the 1940s. I am curious to know how Japanese **modan** culture became wartime culture and presume that by lining up images familiar to those in the imperial and colonial metropoles of the Japanese empire, contours of a part of that experience can be traced.

My closing question, interrogating the privileged mode of representation in the advertisements of the modern years, is formalist, political, and historiographical. It calls into question the manner in which modern Japanese history was choreographed in the bodies in advertisements. By asking why caricature—what we might term cartooning in the West—was so predominant, my goal is to generate questions linking the images to synchronic and diachronic tradition, for ultimately these images have to be read within such dense relationships. The pictures of female and male belong within the context of Japanese traditions of representations of the body and of habitual practices, including Western traditions incorporated and reworked within pre–Pacific War Japan. These pictures must also be read synchronically because they were both produced and consumed in the culturally specific context of spectatorship of the Japanese modern years.

This essay is but one preliminary attempt to crack the Japan-specific cultural codes of Japanese identity during this era, codes not unrelated and not entirely different from those informing the (masculinist) modernism demarcated by Raymond Williams. Williams defined his modernism as determined by such border crossings as the movement of provincial immigrants to great imperial capitals that colonized "leisure, culture and the psyche" at a time when photography, cinema, radio, television, reproduction, and recording all made decisive advances and as the experiences of visual and linguistic strangeness were familiarized via such means as the integration of the "lonely, bitter, sardonic and skeptical hero." In the cultural modernism of Japan (as in Andreas Huyssen's vision of the feminized modern) it was the heroine who was more finely delineated, at a time when ads and ad-making strategies, including the techniques of the modern advertisement exposition, crossed borders from Europe and the United States into Modern Japan.[3]

Investigation I: Cultural Constitution of the Body: WOMAN-LIKENESS

In 1938, a portrait photography primer titled *Introduction to Studio Portraiture Photography* set forth the code for disciplining the female body for a properly gendered representation in a section titled "Woman," within a chapter devoted to "the actualities of photographing various types of people." The photographer, the author directed, was to express both the "external . . . soft beauty of the skin, the elegant limbs and the "internal **woman-like** gentleness and brightness"—"in other words, the female beauty related to male beauty—the beauty unique to woman." The author was careful to take into account variations on female beauty determined by social differences in class and vocation/occupation, while recognizing the most contemporary forms of eroticization catering to modern male fantasy: the lady was to be photographed lady-**like**, the madame, madame-**like**, and the likenesses of both geisha and movie star were to be presented "geisha-like" and "starlet-like." (The other types listed in the table of contents of the primer included "man" (who was listed first) and the ungendered "old person" and "child," along with the similarly undifferentiated "parent-child," "newlyweds," "groupings of two or three people," "the group," and the "home portrait."[4] The fact that there was no elaboration regarding the body language of lady, madame, geisha, or movie star in the section called "Woman" would seem to indicate the uniformity in the social imaginary of that time regarding the ideal for the first two categories—marked as proper and classed as privileged—and for the two latter categories of geisha and starlet. While the geisha had of course been eroticized since the early modern, feudal era, by the middle of the 1920s and through the 1930s the aspiring photographer studying the primer did not have to be told that in the popular imagination (fueled by the aggressively crossreferenced mass culture of magazines, films, and serialized novels) the film starlet (in kimono or in modern, Western costume) competed with the geisha as the ideal erotic female. The multivalence of the female ideal affirmed by the photography primer was evident in the Japanese illustrated mass media. See, for example, how the synchronicity of radically different feminized images belied a singular pictorial definition in advertisements for desirable women (and therefore, of course, commodities) in ads for Agfa film (**ad 4**), soy sauce (**ad 5**), a mini-mall of restaurants at a beach resort (**ad 6**), and the hit movie *Tokyo March* (**ad 7**).

The 1938 photography primer rejected any likeness of a female body that was too fat or too thin. While claiming that each individual woman should be found beautiful in differing, "non-artistic," and "ordinary" aspects, it then marked the aspects of the woman's body to be positioned as feminine through portraiture. The same body parts inventoried in the 1938 manual had been accounted for and advertised in the bulk of ad images in the decade following the earthquake of 1923, when Japanese modern culture had peaked. These were ordered in subheadings in the primer. The **neck** (not to be leaned backward, warned the primer, lest the photographer detract from the subject's "womanly" gentle grace) was followed by the **entire torso**. Setting aside those women "who were altogether too thin," no body was to face front, warned the primer. Fat women in particular were to take care to drop their shoulders, as this would affect the feel of the "body as an entire body." The **hands** were not to stand out—they need not be altogether hidden as in the past—but should be photographed in their "natural, womanly softness." A separate section, devoted to an elaboration of how the hands should be placed together in order to bring out a "well-bred eroticism," was followed by directions as to **seating** that conformed to the 1920s concern (backlash?) for denying the presence of the female buttocks. This concern was fetishized in such contemporary texts as an essay lamenting the fact that the kimono sash no longer functioned to hide that aspect of female anatomy.

Body and clothing placement were combined in the final sections on placement of **folds of parts of the kimono**, the tips of the **feet**, **legs**, Japanese-styled **hair**, and of Western clothing (which was denigrated as characterized by a simplistic use of color and of pattern, in contrast to kimono material). The author conceded, nonetheless, that those women who fancied Western clothes tended to be "modern young ladies" for whom a freeness in posing was often becoming (**ad 8**).[5]

Not listed in the 1938 manual were eyes, but woman's gaze was indeed present in the modern ads and thus must be taken into account. A largely female readership of *Women's Arts* saw almost no male bodies advertised nor images of women accompanied by men. Nor were women presented with men in most of the advertisements (and articles) in *Reconstruction* or *Central Review*. Did the female reader-spectator of the woman's magazine or of the male-oriented journals identify with a male spectator, seeing herself as an object of male desire? An application of Western theories of gendered spectatorship would not suffice to explicate how the woman reader fantasized her body and others'.[6]

And how was the male body masculinized/molded/enfolded? In the chapter on "Man" in the photography primer, the male body was apportioned without any reference to body type—man, apparently, in a Japanese example of the double standard upheld in the contemporary West, could be fat or thin. Moreover, there was much less emphasis on body parts.[7] The expression of man's beauty was to be sturdiness on the outside and dignity within. Gendered, imagined male types were the military man, the politician, and the dancer. The choreographed male body was divided into: **face and neck** (not to be "leaning too far forward in a feminine posture"), the **upper torso**, the **necktie**, the **pocket handkerchief** (to be photographed "after all pens and automatic pencils had been removed from the pocket"), the **hands** (often best positioned by asking the man to hold a pen and by then removing the pen from the posture), and the **legs**. Like the woman, the man in position was told how to adjust the collar of his kimono, but unlike the female subjects, he was given objects with which to express his "everyday life and hobbies" in a section that allowed him to hold a cigarette or place a book or magazine in his lap. (It should be noted that this was the era when state-affiliated scholars were encouraged to catalogue the leisure activities of workers. "Reading" was a common category on surveys of non–work-time "play," a new modern leisure activity analyzed at great length by the social scientists.) In a separate section, the photographer was told to accurately photograph the decorations and medals of civil and military officials. Men were also warned that in official dress, whether it be Western or Japanese, they should take care not to express a pose or expression drawing attention to themselves, for "unlike Western people, Japanese people were lacking in bodily expressiveness, and any expressions that stood out were considered low class."

The above statement disengaged the male body in a way not prescribed for either the high-class or the glamorized female. And in the case of this desensitized male beauty, attention to Western clothing in large part substituted for attention to physique. The modern male likeness in advertisements of the late twenties and early thirties was very much a disembodied variation on this theme of uniformed man at work and at play (**ad 9, ad 10**). There was, however, one formal variation in the themes of man at work plus man at sport (skiing, hiking, and diving were new, modern contenders with the bourgeois pleasure of golf). This was the use of caricature (**ad 11**). One substantive (if not substantial) exception to the avoidance of reference to the male physique was a much-repeated ad from the 1920s which prefigured an obsession of the late 1930s. The text accompanying this male crotch shot read, "Strength of the flesh, virility of spirit . . . forging of the abdomen" (**ad 12**). Aside from this exception, the absence of variety or ambiguity in representation of the often-eerily faceless male during the modern years of the late 1920s and early 1930s remains in marked contrast to representation of the Japanese woman's body and is one Japanese illustration of Rosalind Coward's insight that "women's bodies and the message which clothes can add, are the repository of the social definitions of sexuality. Men are neutral."[8]

If we transpose the term "culture" for sexuality—to presume that women's bodies and their clothing provided the repository of the social definition of culture, and attempt to pin down the social definition of culture in 1920s Japan as expressed by woman's body, we see that woman's contours are ambiguous regarding her cultural identity. Sometimes woman's gender identity was also ambiguous (**ad 13**).

Such pictures illustrate a predominant theme in turn of the 1920s print culture in Japan that I have discussed elsewhere—woman could cross both cultural and gender boundaries. The female body was glamorized as multivalent and crosscultural. Perhaps transcultural is a better term, and racial passing or crossing is a false notion when applied to the Japanese imaginary of the modern years, since distinctions documented in Kathy Piess's discussion of make-up advertisements aimed at different racial markets, for example, appear to have been absent from discussions of femininity and of the merchandising of femininity during this period. While the almanac of the leading advertising company of the pre–Pacific War years, for example, devoted extensive and separately organized space in each annual volume to the imagery and wording of advertisements in Japan, the Japanese colonies, and the West, no reference was made to inherent racial, biological difference among markets or consumers (**ad 14**).[9]

During the modern years, woman could become man-like, at which time she would be in Western garb, but man could not be feminized. Contours appear to have been, in the Japanese case of imagining bodies, and especially female bodies, more important than fixed content. Advertisements beginning in the mid-1930s indicate that such distinctions came undone with the imagery marking the shift I have termed "from body to every body."

Investigation II: From Body to Every Body

Vestiges of the contours of "modern life," including dining at Western restaurants and references to the **modan**, continued to be offered into the 1930s in advertisements in the three journals examined. However, the multivalent fashioning of pliable female bodies that could take on Japanese contours consistent with the recently canonized "tradition" of the Japanese "good wife and wise mother" (whose domesticity and nationality had been institutionalized along with the provisions of the early-twentieth-century civil code), while at the same time, in the same issue of the same magazine, assuming flapper and/or masculine trappings was abandoned. Male bodies in white face and gray suit also disappeared from the pages of the magazines aimed at men. What emerged during the 1930s (after the Japanese invasion and colonization of Manchuria in 1931 and after the invasion of China proper in 1937) was a new focus on **invigorating** (instead of fashioning) all bodies, but most specifically a male body in gender crisis (**ad 15**). By the early 1940s, the male body was no longer in crisis, nor was it even suited in the Anglophile fashions of the department store ads of the modern years. By the outset of the Pacific war, masculinity, not surprisingly, was linked even more strongly with physicality and with an essentially Japanese cultural/national identity.

Some aspects of the 1930s transition away from the modern are to be expected. In my analysis of the modern girl as militant, I argued that the media obsession with a modern woman represented as single (although not celibate) and active in public (as an apolitical consumer of leisure items and/or of the companionship of the male rendered passive and/or infantile) was a projection fantasized by media critics defending a perceived threat to the patriarchal state ideology. The fantasy, as is the case with all fantasies, was, of course, grounded in the social historical—young women in new, high, Western fashion. Although a very small percentage of the daughters of the nouveau riche and of the urban working poor, who fastidiously examined window displays, did promenade along the Ginza boulevard, which was lined with department stores, cafés, fruit parlors, and other emporiums catering to modern sensibilities. Moreover, in provincial cities, their imitators exhibited themselves in public places that were named "Ginza" after the Tokyo locus of the modern. Yet economic history and a study of surveys from the time make clear that most women could not afford to be consumers of modern material culture, except in pictorial form. Moreover, any notion of the ubiquity of the modern girl is challenged by an examination of advertisements from the final years of Japan's modern moment. For example, the representation of family was not totally absent even from the ostensibly "modern" image of the pairing of "modern girl" with "modern boy," which could, after all, have reproductive implications. One specific example can be found in the text for the ad for Hechima cologne, which offered Hechima cologne for every body: "for the male body, for the female body, and for the body of their beloved child" (**ad 16**). The fact that both male and female were off-balance suggests a recoding of both bodies, but there is no need to indulge in hermeneutic conjecture regarding gender advertisements à la Irving Goffman,[10] because we have the more bold images of the unquestionably Japanese family during the next several years (**ad 17**). A shift from focus on mores (*fuzoku*) to close-up on scenery (*fukei*) might be investigated during this transitional moment. Some ads show a family wherein the woman serves the man (and here, in an understandable reversal of the 1920s gendered faces, it is the woman who is faceless) (**ad 18**). Other advertisements assemble and rank family generations, thus displacing the 1920s images of pairings of mother and daughter or father and son en route to department store glamour and leisure. By the late 1930s, the health and welfare of every family body would be displaced by pictures pointing to the health of all male bodies within a masculinist hierarchy (**ad 19**).

The transition to an emphasis on patriarchy is not surprising. It represents the pictorial equivalent of the widely disseminated state documents celebrating Japanese difference, *Cardinal Principles of the National Entity of Japan* (**Kokutai no hongi**, 1937) and *The Way of the Subject* (**Shinmin no michi**, 1941).[11] But the ads reveal a surprise. What has hitherto **not** been discussed by historians of Japan is a gender ambiguity present in representations of the male body during the 1930s. According to the printed text for pomade that appeared in the January 1935 issue of *Central Review*, the hair cream could be used both by men and women. While the subheading reads, "for a new male beauty for 1935," the section of the text below the chin of the body is addressed "to the gentleman" and the section along the bust-line is addressed "to the lady" (**ad 20**). When added to a second image, advertising the same commodity in the same magazine two months later, male anxiety rather than androgyny emerges as the subtext of the moment. This ad is confident of its male subjectivity, as it challenges in a highly assertive male voice, "Look at my male beauty." Yet the image of a face and hand effeminate in features and gestures contests the text. The figure looks like a (female) male impersonator of the Takarazuka all-girls theater discussed by Jennifer Robertson, but I would argue that the image is male-identified, distinguishing it from the gender-bending described by Robertson. Here, there is an extra twist, for this is not an image of a masculine or male or man-like woman, but of an effeminate man. (From our perspective in the West we may be concerned that this is a woman dressed like a man, but my sense is that the Japanese readership for this advertisement did not imagine so.) Elsewhere, later in the 1930s, male hormones were presented to a reader in doubt of the articulation of his gender, and in other words, of his body and possibly, therefore, of his sexuality (**ad 21**).

By 1939, another picture pointed to the end of the modern moment in the advertisement of bodies: A round man seeking masculinizing energy is unquestionably both Japanese and associated with the land. Scenery as background as homeland (*fukei*) has overcome modern mores as customs or practices (*fuzoku*) associated with the modern years (**ad 22**).

By the 1940s the transition from the polymorphous/modern and into the masculinist/militarist era was complete, celebrated formally by the displacement of caricature by photographic mimesis. Aggression was heralded by advertisements using martial arts imagery and more contemporary icons of imperial warfare such as the bugle and the jeep, by dedication to the body mobilized for work (**ad 23**), and by increased cartooned images of Chinese women as documented in the 1940 volume of the Mannensha annual.[12] Moreover, advertisement texts were dominated by exclamatory imperatives. During the early 1940s, it would appear, all male bodies were to be invigorated by pills, vitamins, and potions to maximize energy for the Japanese effort. In contrast, during the final years of the Pacific war, there were almost no pictorial images of the body. Elsewhere I have discussed how Anglo-European bodies disappeared from film magazines after Pearl Harbor.[13] In the final issues of *Central Review* and *Reconstruction*, in part because there were no commodities to sell, there was no body.

Closing Question: Why the Caricature?

Clearly, Japanese producers of ad images rejected the American way of what has been called "capitalist realism."[14] Their alternative choices have major implications for reconceptualizing the pre–Pacific War Japanese technology of culture, which has largely been characterized, by Japanese and American writers, as enamored of symbols and commodities emerging from rationalized, American production (including fantasy production). This position was challenged during the modern years by Japanese critics such as the cartoonist Okamoto Ippei, inventor of the first "cartoon story" (**storii manga**) and author of what he termed "**movie**

novels." Okamoto Ippei saw European culture to be as dominant as the so-called "Americanism" associated with modernity in 1920s and 1930s Japan. My own position at the moment is that the impact of the visual culture of the European avant-garde, including the hard-edged graphics of the Constructivists and the montage methods of Surrealist photographers and Soviet filmmakers on Japanese mass culture counters any simple label of "Americanization." Nonetheless, while I have not noticed a critique of Taylorism reminiscent of Chaplin's critique of American culture of the modern in *Modern Times*, I am struck by the presence of most of the locales in the film *Modern Times* in Japanese representations of "the modern" in the mass culture of the 1920s and 1930s. See, for example, the ubiquity of the prison, the site of the worker's protest march, the factory, the department store, the fantasy home of the bourgeois nuclear family, and the café.

In modern Japan, the European Constructivist graphic appears to have won over the mimetic, photographic realism of the American ad of the same era, but there were similarities in the ads of Japan and the United States. For one, the Japanese body, like the American body, was marked off into parts, as discussed by Stuart Ewen, and woman's body in particular was manipulated (and often elongated as in the U.S. ads) as a symbol of modernity. The average male in both places was represented as a businessman. Moreover, part of the self-fetishing through fashioning was performed through the mirror's gaze. As the Mannensha annuals reveal, Japanese producers of advertisements were careful students of American ad psychology, history, and iconography and paid close attention to annual shifts in representation, to the secondary literature published in the United States, and to the professionalization of the advertising industry through annual expositions in the United States and Europe.[15]

Yet the contrast in visual style between the Japanese and American ad should not be ignored. The most important difference in form relates to the construction of the body of the ad. Instead of the conventionalized background, detailed vignettes of social life, and dramatic realism of the social tableaus documented by Roland Marchand in *Advertising the American Dream*, there is an absence of background.[16] Instead, all is foregrounded in what a Western viewer might (or might have) termed nonrealistic caricatures and contours of bodies or persons and things. Nor is there even a pretense at narrative. While early-twentieth-century Japanese newspaper ads did blur the ad and the editorial in the camouflaging technique noted by Marchand and described by Japanese historians and novelists, this blurring is absent from the magazine advertisements of the 1920s and especially the 1930s in Japan, when, as the Mannensha editors noted, "advertisement culture" came to be dominated by the magazine and not the newspaper.[17]

The question then becomes, if photography connoted authenticity, and authority, as has been argued by Marchand for the American case,[18] what did contouring mean in the Japanese modern case? One possible answer is provided by Oya Soichi, the archivist quoted at the outset of this essay. He stated that Japanese modernity was stimuli without emotions, morals or ideals—all contours and no content. Another archivist, artist Kishida Ryusei, did not agree. In his formulation of cultural relations, he subverted the power relationship of a Western modernity subsuming a Japanese tradition by claiming that a new culture was inevitable. In his terms, "all material culture [would] inevitably . . . Europeanize

Japan." And Kishida continued: "Once Japan was Europeanized to the most extreme extent—one would be able to see contours of a true Japan which was no longer Europeanized." Kishida's conception of a process of cultural restructuring, which he said was illustrated in the work of Futurists and Constructivists, is evident in the strategy of what I term the "contouring" employed in modern Japanese advertisements.

For the modern Japanese capitalist producer of advertisements who was fully aware of the ubiquity of photographic imagery in illustrated magazines, the strategic decision to represent outlines instead of filling in details by photograph (or by pen) was a Constructivist choice to focus on the historic experience of the structuring of culture. These producers made a conscious decision to use the cartoon form at a time when the relationship between people and things was being restructured within a capitalist economy not totally under the purview of the state. As part of my own project of considering how Japanese capitalist mass culture may have subverted the ideology of state authority during the modern years, it is worth considering how the caricature of contouring of social relationships of people to things, of woman to woman, of woman to man, and of Japanese consumer to her or his own body—as an alternative to a mimetic representation—could provide a counterpoint to the surety of the ideology and the visual representations of state authority.

A reading of the editorial essays in the annual advertising almanac of the Mannensha company from 1924 through 1941 documents the choreography of the industry by modern advertisers, who in 1924 saw advertisements as a means to "spread culture" via "scientific means." This was expressed as nationalist sentiment as early as 1929. The editors were open in their agenda of wielding "politics" by 1933 and in their sympathetic discussion of the "Manchurian Incident." By the time of their tenth anniversary issue, in 1935, the almanac was calling for censorship during the "emergency moment." According to the 1935 editorial analysis, the emergency was within Japanese capitalism, and the colonization of Manchuria was an appropriate move. By 1938, the empire was being discussed in an article relating the "China Incident" to the advertising world. The following year, the annual focus on such editorial categories as "cosmetics," "print items," and "household miscellaneous" disappeared. The editors instead chose to highlight commemorative advertisements for newly established state festivals celebrating the Japanese empire, along with the state's proclamation exhorting "restraint in consumption," which was faithfully reproduced by the Mannensha staff.

Let me suggest that during the 1920s, advertisements produced in contour form challenged the stereotypes projected by the state, which had reified gender and culture distinctions in official proclamation, school textbook, and other public pronouncements not discussed herein. The Constructivist figurations reminded the consumer that the world of things and the human body could be configured and were being assembled to act as culture (**ad 24**). By 1940, this project had ended—the leading annual advertising almanac was devoted to following strict state censorship laws. Moreover, for the first time, the almanac devoted extensive space to discussions of rules regarding representations of sexuality.[19] To recapitulate the narrative evident in the advertisements reproduced herein and in the concerns expressed by the Mannensha annuals, during the modern period advertising was being choreographed by the advertising industry, with an eye to Western content, but with a Japan-specific form of representing bodies. By the end of the modern years, ads were produced or "choreographed" in the most rigid sense, according to strict guidelines mandated by state authorities.

Returning to my original distinction among archivist, capitalist, and cartoonist, I would call Oya Soichi an archivist who had a need to choreograph history but whose definition of Japanese modernity did not take into account the shaping by Japanese people of their own actions. The capitalist ad men did choreograph bodies, but were constrained first by their need to follow the rules of the Western marketplace within which Japanese capitalism was implicated. It was the cartoonist Okamoto Ippei who was a choreographer in the freest sense. His discussion of what cartoons meant during Japan's modern years sheds light on why the advertising capitalists chose the cartoon form during their relatively autonomous years and why photography as a form entered advertising after the transitional, crisis years of the mid-1930s.

Okamoto's discussion of his work as a producer of **manga** (cartoons) fleshes out the history of the Japanese cartoon for us by inserting the modern years into our existing English language narrative. The history of the Japanese **manga** or cartoon has been discussed most extensively in English as originating in the pre-modern era and then appearing ubiquitously in the form of the now-highly pornographic cartoon novels. Okamoto sketches out how the cartoon was a form that could choreograph how men and women shaped their own practices in pre–Pacific War, modern Japan.[20] According to Ippei (who is so well-known in modern Japanese cultural history that his given name rather than his patronym must be used in reference to the cartoonist) **manga** was more mimetic than a detailed representation. Moreover, the cartoon was grounded neither in the past nor in the future. (This, I would say, separated him from the nostalgic concerns of the archivist and the future-oriented concern of the capitalist.) Okamoto, like other ethnographers of the time, respected the rapid cultural changes around him in the present. For him, the task of the cartoon was to "address the [social] human being of the present via grasping the living mores by which this person of the present live[d]." Distinguishing between satire and cynicism, Okamoto likened cynicism to rice curry—which became a modern Japanese food served at the new mass eateries catering to workers and other urbanites on Sunday outings during the 1920s—cooked without the spice.[21]

Okamoto's conception of portraiture was different from the rigid choreography of the portrait photography manual discussed at the outset of this essay. According to his directions, the structure of the human being had to be grasped before clothing or flesh could be added. Like the author of the photography manual, he isolated parts of the body—for him the neck, shoulders, chest, legs, and hands were important and were gendered. He also referred to types—men fell into such categories as "bureaucrat," "petty bureaucrat," "white collar worker," "petty merchant," "soldier," and "worker." Okamoto explained to his readers that women were embodied, in new, modern times, in such unprecedented categories as "family oriented wife," "woman educator," "actress," "cafe waitress," and "maid." Like the photography manual, Okamoto made allowances for Japanese versus foreign body language when in his writing he emphasized the cultural positioning of the body in such motions as the hunching of shoulders. But Okamoto's view of choreographing the body through cartooning was a very different form of advertising of the body from that produced by the other professionals of the modern years. This view affirmed the creative agency in the Japanese experience of the modern.

Unlike the archivist Oya (who dismissed Japanese emotions as inauthentic), the photography manual (which denied the existence of affective expression in Japan), or the ad industry editorial writers (who were openly interested in creating and controlling emotions), Okamoto wanted to give form to "the shape of emotions," seen, for example, in different types of laughter, as inextricably linked with the body in motion. He saw the human beings around him as actively engaged in a process of choreography. The cartoon was important within this process, he explained, because it implied movement in space, in Japan, in the present.

Okamoto explained the prevalence of the **manga** in the Japanese advertising business materially and psychologically. Cartoons gave work to advertisers because they made advertisements work and the reason contouring was so effective was because "they quieted the screaming of the ad page." In other words, according to Okamoto, they gave readers a focus because in Japan cartoons were linked, very carefully, with everyday practices of the contemporary reader. The cartoonist made note of the double standard in Japanese advertisements, which resulted in the drawing of the bodies of women and of the clothing of men, in his comment about changes in cartoons mirroring changes in modern culture: "the legs of Modern Girls were thicker and the pants of Modern boys wider than before." But his central concern was not to differentiate treatment of male from treatment of female. Instead he sought the specifically Japanese content of the cartoon form. His conclusion was that Japan **manga** included humor but were different from both the funny pictures in the United States and from the cartoons drawn in the cool British style.

Japanese modern culture, according to Okamoto, was different from its European and American variants because men and women constantly made choices as to how they would feel and act. This was not a racialized theory in any way. For this Japanese cartoonist, as for the Japanese producers of advertisements, the difference from the West was cultural and not physiological. The Japanese body was in motion and emotion. And when the cartoonist set out to capture the motion and the emotion, he was to begin with the face. What is clear from Okamoto's primer-like directions to his readers is that this was not a nationalized face, but could be the face of any body. To illustrate his premise to the cartoonist-in-training who was learning to draw the male figure, Okamoto chose contrasting famous faces: the leading modern novelist of the early twentieth century, Natsume Soseki, and Woodrow Wilson ("of the United States"). Special characteristics (such as Wilson's pince-nez) were to be added to the bodies to make the choreographing complete. Otherwise, the bodies were the same— defined by the shapes of each and every body (such as six types of eye shape undifferentiated by any form of ethnicizing difference) and the positions into which they moved. During Japan's modern years, bodies moved not within a Japanese nation, but within the moment.

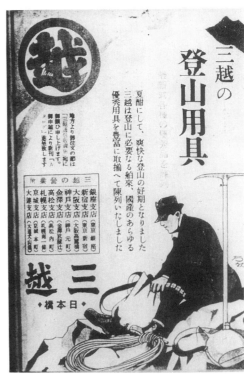

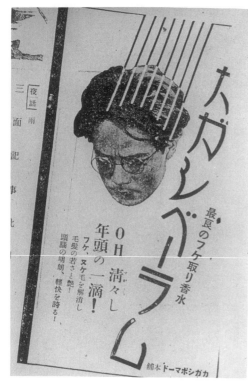

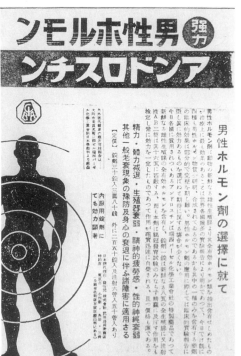

NOTES

1. For a more extensive discussion of this phenomenon, see Miriam Silverberg, "Constructing the Japanese Ethnography of Modernity," pp. 30–54. For a discussion of the access of different classes to the mass culture of the 1920s and 1930s in Japan, see my "History of Modern Japan," pp. 61–89. See also Baudrillard, *Political Economy of the Sign*, pp. 37, 63, 66.

2. Regarding *Women's Arts*, see Silverberg, "The Modern Girl as Militant," pp. 239–66. The almanacs have been republished. See Taketoshi, *Mannensha Kokoku Nenpan*.

3. On Modern Japanese movie magazine imagery, see my "Remembering Pearl Harbor," pp. 24–76. For Raymond Williams on modernism, see *The Politics of Modernism*, pp. 31–35. For Huyssen's discussion of the feminization of modern mass culture, see *After the Great Divide*, pp. 44–62.

4. Kiyoshi, *Shajo jinbutsu satsuei nyumon*, pp. 185–215. In the best-selling media the starlet did not face off against the geisha as a new form of glamour to be sold, perhaps because the starlet was marketed to the male and female audience. Rather, the geisha competed with the figure of the café waitress. See, for example, the best-selling serialized novel of 1928–1929, *Tokyo koshinkyoku*, which was almost immediately rechoreographed into film and song. A famous variation—the trope of eroticized womanhood in the "modern" jazz culture versus staid, domestic womanhood clad in kimono—provides the tension in Japan's first mass-marketed talkie, *Madamu to nyobo* (The Madam and the Wife), 1931.

5. For a reference to the "absent buttocks" fetish and more discussion on the representation of the body of the "modern girl," see Silverberg, "Modern Girl as Militant," pp. 239–66.

6. Here, I am thinking of the work of Laura Mulvey, Maryanne Doane, Annette Kuhn, and others (including those who have recognized that the flaneuse must be placed into Benjamin's formulations of urban adventuring). I also defer to Abigail Solomon-Godeau, who makes a point of distinguishing film from photography criticism, and others who have revised Mulvey's focus on the male as spectator. See Mulvey, "Visual Pleasure and Narrative Cinema"; Doane, "Film and the Masquerade"; Kuhn, *The Power of the Image*; Gammand and Marshment, eds., *The Female Gaze*; and Solomon-Godeau.

For an example of a recent revision of Mulvey in regard to Japanese film, see the discussion of the position of the Mizoguchi heroine, Oharu, as "the subject whose look objectifies the man," through reverse shots in *The Life of Oharu* in Cohen's "Why does Oharu Faint?" p. 37.

One of the complexities of thinking of Japanese spectatorship and reader response to film and non-moving images is the issue of what we in the West have called race in popular, scientist presumptions that bodies are colored and shaped in forms that can be typologically ordered. My own research in progress, as reflected in my essay "Forgetting Pearl Harbor," indicates that bodies have not been imagined in a comparable way during the course of modern Japanese history. For work that corroborates my conclusion, see essays such as Robertson, "The Politics of Androgyny in Japan," pp. 1–24, along with her recent work on "cross-ethniking."

7. Ezaki, *Shajo*, pp. 172–84.

8. Coward, "Female Desires," p. 30.

9. See Peiss, "Making Faces," pp. 143–69. See Taketoshi, *Mannensha Kokoku Nenpan*, 1924–1941.

The question of how race/ethnicity/national identity has been conceptualized during the course of modern Japanese history is complex. I am purposefully setting aside an elaboration on this issue and have chosen for purposes of my discussion to appropriate the notion of "cultural" difference used by the Japanese conservative ideologues, who called for an "overcoming" of the modern in Japanese society in terms of the claims of the Japanese cultural distinctiveness. I am also setting aside the occasional advertisements of Africans in Japanese advertisements of the 1920s and 1930s, not because they were irrelevant, but because they deserve separate, detailed treatment in order to better come to terms with contemporary Japanese exoticized racism aimed at Africans and African Americans. For scholarship on Japanese representations of Africans and African Americans, see the work of John Russell.

10. Goffman, *Gender Advertisements*.

11. For an English language overview of both documents, see Dower, *War without Mercy*, pp. 221–22, 280.

12. The 1940 Mannensha pictorial ad samples (available in each volume beginning in 1925) are striking for their overt reference to "the China Incident" (p. 38) and for the unprecedented two-page spread of ads representing a Chinese-looking man, women, and boy child. It should be noted that this spread of figures in Chinese clothing also included the modern icon of the Glico caramel (ethnically ambiguous but highly masculine) athlete running to the finish-line and the modern emblem of the Matsuda light-bulb. See Taketoshi, *Mannensha Kokoku Nenpan*, vol 16, pp. 38, 44–45.

13. Silverberg, "Remembering Pearl Harbor," pp. 24–76.

14. For a discussion of "capitalist realism" see Schudson, *Advertising*, pp. 209–233.

15. One of Okamoto Ippei's "story novels" for children was titled "Heiki no Heitaro" (a title implying that nothing would bother the boy hero). See Okamoto, *Ippei Zenshu*, vol. 13. The first volume of the Mannensha annual almanac offered a glossary of advertising terms, listing such words as the Japanese terms for advertising agency, Futurism, and market research, and defining the Japanese word for "advertisement" (*senden*) as the translation for "propaganda" (*puropoganda*). Examples of works from the United States advertised in the Mannensha manual were Adams, *Advertising and Its Mental Laws*; Calkins, *The Advertising Man*; Eaton, *How to Advertise a Bank* and *How to Make Advertisement Pay*.

16. Marchand, *Advertising the American Dream*, pp. 164–205. To underscore the Japanese advertising establishment's rejection of the American style of representation, I cite an article in *Mannensha* that dismisses as pedestrian an ad that would seem to fit Marchand's description of the ad incorporating a narrative text.

17. Much of the Mannensha almanac space was devoted to the analysis of newspaper advertising, but the shift to an emphasis on magazines was identified. For a discussion of the history of Japanese advertising that analyzes the relationship of graphics to text, see Taketoshi, *Kokoku no shakaishi*; and Silverberg, *Changing Song*.

18. Marchand, *Advertising the American Dream*, pp. 149–150, 153.

19. A close reading of the essay, "The Recent Japanese Advertising World," found at the beginning of each volume, is revealing. See Taketoshi, *Mannensha Kokoku Nenpan*.

20. For a representative narrative history of the Japanese cartoon, see Buckley, "Penguin in Bondage," pp. 164–71.

21. Okamoto, *Ippei Zenshu*, pp. 7–229.

JOSEPH ROACH

Bodies of Doctrine: Headshots, Jane Austen, and the Black Indians of Mardi Gras

You grab the girl by the wrist. "Enough of these disguises, Lotaria! How long are you going to continue letting yourself be exploited by a police regime?"

This time Sheila-Ingrid-Corinna cannot conceal a certain uneasiness. She frees her wrist from your grasp. "I don't understand who you're accusing, I don't know anything about our stories. I follow a very clear strategy. The counterpower must infiltrate the mechanisms of power in order to overthrow it."

"And then reproduce it, identically! It's no use your camouflaging yourself, Lotaria! If you unbutton one uniform, there's always another uniform underneath!"

Sheila looks at you with an air of challenge. "Unbutton . . . ? Just you try. . . . "

Now that you have decided to fight, you can't draw back. With a frantic hand you unbutton the white smock of Sheila the programmer and you discover the police uniform of Alfonsina; you rip Alfonsina's gold buttons and you find Corinna's anorak; you pull the zipper of Corinna and you see the chevrons of Ingrid. . . .

It is she herself who tears off the clothes that remain on her. A pair of breasts appear, firm, melon-shaped, a slightly concave stomach, the full hips of a *fausse maigre*, a proud pubes, two long and solid thighs.

"And this? Is this a uniform?" Sheila exclaims.

You have remained upset. "No, this no. . . ." you murmur.

"Yet, it is!" Sheila cries. "The body is a uniform! The body is armed militia! The body is violent action! The body claims power! The body is at war! The body declares itself subject! The body is an end and not a means! The body signifies! Communicates! Shouts! Protests! Subverts!"

—Italo Calvino, *If on a winter's night a traveler*

First, let's quibble. To speak of *the* body, as if there were only one, effaces the particularity of bodies, of which there are, of course, many different kinds. Look around. From the wanton couplings of nature and artifice come gendered bodies, classed bodies, and cultured bodies. From the plenitude of historic representations descend period bodies, modern bodies, and postmodern bodies. From the rubble of the contemporary urbanscape emerge bodies categorized by varied forms of violent incompletion—dislocation, dismemberment, and homelessness—which lie sprawled across the paths of the nicely differentiated bodies of the privileged. *The* body stands still, like a statue, or lies in repose, like a corpse. As a metaphysical abstraction or a bracketed phenomenon, its essence transcends its action, its color, its features, its history, its desire, its transactions, and its pain. A plenitude of bodies, by contrast, suggests multiple possibilities of movement, interaction, combination, circulation, and exchange. Just to begin to make the list of the diversity and the reciprocity of bodies is to question the totality of *the* body.

The interdisciplinary centrality of dance and theater studies, it seems to me, resides in their exploration of the intensified meanings of particular bodies in motion. An awareness of the specificity of bodily movements combined with methods of interpreting their significance works against the temptation to totalize the body as general, trans-historical, solitary, and inert.

For the temptations of totality, Michel Foucault gets perhaps too much of the blame. If an interdisciplinary study of bodies has matured in the recent proliferation of cultural studies, then *Discipline and Punish* and *The History of Sexuality* at least must be recognized as two of its problematic but foundational texts. Feminists and others have criticized the absence of the politics of gender from Foucault's explication of the modern production of docile bodies.[1] At the same time, however, the reigning discursive vocabulary, which enables practitioners to imagine issues of power and knowledge in corporeal terms, has developed so conspicuously from Foucault's work, while the important statements he made on the politics of gay sexuality have been so perplexingly slow to come to the fore,[2] that any attempt to describe an interdiscipline in the name of *the* body must begin by scrutinizing its (mis)understandings of Foucault.

Italo Calvino's nesting doll, performing her paramilitary striptease, suggests several opportunities for ways in which Foucault might be reapplied, shifting the ground from the metaphysic of the body to the performative practices of bodies.[3] I have divided this territory into three zones, understanding not only that there may be significant overlap between the categories, but also that these categories do not begin to exhaust or even to index the variety of ways in which the discourse of *the* body might be pluralized. The categories are: (1) performing bodies, (2) textual bodies, and (3) ethnographic bodies. To these categories I offer three corresponding examples: (1) actors' commercial "headshots," or resume photos, as juxtaposed to drag and/or transsexual striptease; (2) the choreography of implied stage directions in a scene from Jane Austen's *Emma*; and (3) the Black Indians of Mardi Gras, "tribes" of African Americans who dress as Native Americans and parade through the streets at carnival time in New Orleans.

That these examples encompass gender, class, and race should not suggest that I regard that oft-invoked trinity as the only schema of human difference.

They do exemplify three cultural tactics, however, that I want to illustrate here by looking at the ways in which bodies enter into representation. I call these "tactics" because "strategies" would attribute a too general, motivated, and deliberate consciousness to behaviors that are mainly local, automatized, and contingent—"second nature," in a manner of speaking—while calling them simply "behaviors" would invest them with an innocence that would efface their degree of agency and invention. The first tactic is subtraction, the performative act of publicly taking away something, whether it be clothing, organs, or personality traits; the second is subordination, or social choreography, the process whereby bodies sort themselves into hierarchical taxonomies; the third is substitution, bodies standing in for one another as surrogates. All three tactics may be deduced from such Ovidian metamorphoses as Calvino's mutation of Corinna's zipper into Ingrid's chevrons, but I want to draw attention to a cornucopia of possible transformations by sketching in the performance-rich instances that follow.

Performing Bodies: Subtraction

The Foucauldian dimensions of current performance theory and practice are argued concisely by Judith Butler in *Gender Trouble: Feminism and the Subversion of Identity*. Contesting the received dichotomy of truth between "inner" and "outer," "body" and "soul," Butler concludes that "the gendered body is performative" in the sense that actions, gestures, and postures combine to fabricate an illusion of a "psychological 'core.'" This leads her to syllogize: "If the inner truth of gender is a fabrication and if a true gender is a fantasy instituted and inscribed on the surface of bodies, then it seems that genders can be neither true nor false, but are only produced as the truth effects of a discourse of primary and stable identity."[4] In such a discourse, performance is the most tangible manifestation of either subversion or assent.

Butler, following Esther Newton, cites the role of bodies in drag shows to illustrate the potentialities of subversion. Drag parodies not an original but the very idea that a stable original can exist: "*In imitating gender, drag implicitly reveals the imitative structure of gender itself—as well as its contingency.*"[5] The same train of thought runs through the mind of the reader of Calvino's text. By shouting that "the body is a uniform," Sheila (or the same manikin by another name) dissents from the dichotomy of physical exterior and essential psychological core. Beneath her thin veneer is a thin veneer. Her naked body, with its vegetable boobs and metallic tummy, showcases yet another collage of stage properties.

The emphatic constructedness of the fleshly uniform brings to mind Morris Meyer's recent finding about the postsurgical, show-biz career paths of male transsexuals. Significant numbers give (drag?) performances as striptease artists or chorus girls.[6] Transsexuals, after all, like female characters in the works of male novelists, have the advantage of bodies made to order by men: "The body is an end and not a means!" Transsexuals, however, participate as agents in their own (re)construction. Skeptics would perhaps reply that their agency predicates itself on a painfully limited menu of performative choices. Even within these limits, however, the omniform possibilities of bodies, as opposed to the pre-designated essence of *the* body, are affirmed by the disruptive layering of selves within selves, a core-less casting off of shells dramatized by the surgical striptease itself: "Take it off. Take it *all* off."

Transsexual striptease brings to mind the historic commonplace of gender studies that all women are to some extent female impersonators. As a profession, the theater trades on this sort of legerdemain, which may be demonstrated in the conventions of resume production, a specialized genre of autobiographical fiction familiar to all those who have either auditioned or held auditions for parts in plays or films. "Headshots" dominate this genre. They enable actors, actresses, and models to circulate representations of their faces as synecdochical mementos of their bodies. On the backs of their eight-by-ten glossies, they staple their summaries and vital statistics—height, weight, hair and eye color, (and for

(*Left*) The three-quarter body shot, currently in fashion. Photo by Dan Daby.

(*Below, left*) A classic headshot, made slightly unconventional through its inclusion of the hands. Photo by Susanna Gold.

(*Below, right*) A more dramatic and sultry look. Photo by Gerard Barnier.

models) bust, waist, dress and shoe size. Most headshots present one view of the subject, and most actresses, regardless of age and experience, go with the in-genue-style headshot. This type is characterized by an ear-to-ear smile exposing bleached teeth (figure 1), which may or may not be vaselined (to prevent the lips from sticking in a spastic grimace when the smiling muscles become paralyzed from over-use during a long photo session), or by an indescribable glow radiating principally from the eyes and suffusing the whole visage with a lambent, airbrushed phosphorescence (figures 2 and 3).

When photographer and subject connect, the result is supposed to be a "dynamite" headshot. In theory, this dazzling image will burn itself into the mind of the beholder, creating a readily retrievable memory, a poignant associative trace, like a whiff of perfume, which will lead inexorably back to a uniquely employable persona. A repertoire of subliminal persuaders supplement this tactic, such as leaving the image of the photographer's flash reflected in the retinas of the subject, an electromechanical simulation of vivacity.

Dynamite headshots, however, come about largely by subtraction. They blow people away. As in transsexual striptease, identity emerges as elements disappear from it: the airbrush peels off the surfaces, stripping the image not only of zits, but of ambiguities. Under all the other layers, there is that special look; the face is a marker holding open an empty place, not of anonymity but of essence, not of nothing but of zero. The photographic image, created in a performative moment, records the effects of many rehearsals, retakes, and preparations. The headshot thus records a long-running performance, the creation of a fictive persona, cleansed of superfluities, the special residue that many call a life.

This approach draws on Richard Schechner's encompassing definition of performance as "restored" or "twice-behaved" behavior—behavior that is repeated, reinstated, and rehearsed. Such a concept embraces theatrical performances, sacred and secular rituals, and social displays of many kinds, from sporting events to shamanism.[7] The centrality of bodies in performance studies stems naturally from the ancient verity that the bodies of the performers are the media of performance. Performance studies predicates its concept of behavior on the experience of active bodies undergoing intensely physical trials and exhibitions—carnivals, sacraments, parades, and the like. The clarifying definition of performance as restored (or restorable) behavior opens for exploration the historical dimension of performance, its recordability as well as its transmittability through time.

Textual Bodies: Subordination

For purposes of debate about "choreographing history," we might define literature as the archive of restored behaviors. Literature captures its own special version of those quotidian rituals that leave their residual traces in texts as they recede from the customary usages of social life, passing through nostalgia and mystification on their way to incomprehensibility and oblivion.

The *drame bourgeois* and the eighteenth-century novel, which staged cognate scenes of nuptial possibility, provide one such notarial repository of restored behavior. In the staging of such dramas as *Le Père de la famille* (1761), for instance,

Denis Diderot sought to transform the "bienséance cruelle" of neoclassical theater, in which a lineup of tragic nobles under the downstage chandelier dominated the stage picture, into a series of well-regulated tableaux, in which distinctive groupings, expressing the passions appropriate to their compositional units and social stations, arranged well-differentiated bodies according to principles of subordination. Showing bodies in meticulously studied proxemic relationship to one another displays and records (if the performance is documented) the restored behavior of deference and degree (figure 4).

Theatrical representation of this kind creates pictures through many hours of rehearsal. William Hogarth's ironic view of the rehearsal process in "Strolling Actresses Dressing in a Barn" (1738) shows the principles of subtraction and subordination at work (figure 5). The scene is a working-class Olympus. While the actress playing Diana, goddess of chastity (center), loses her dress, the cat to her left loses another segment of its tail (to supply realistic stage blood) and while the actress playing Juno loses herself in rehearsing her part, her monkey voids into her helmet (lower right). The teeming chaos of life depicted here will be refined, is being refined before our eyes through rehearsal into a more orderly pattern of specialized roles and relationships, but clearly this company will fall far short of the bourgeois cleanliness on view in the tidy domestic space of Diderot's *drame*. The ironic substitution of sluts for deities signifies Hogarth's carnivalesque inversion of class hierarchy, a "topsy-turvydom" that tends ultimately to reinforce the attractions of the official order, returning the subordinates to their proper places (that is, the barn).

In the eighteenth century, subordination through the analysis and refinement of movement attained a high degree of perfection. The dissemination of a workable system of dance notation enhanced the ability of professional dancing masters to teach the members of the middle and upper classes how to move, not only in the steps of particular dances, but also in the decorous motions of daily gracious living. To be excluded from this kind of kinesthetic literacy was to be socially located and judged. John Weaver, one of the foremost English dancing masters and the person who introduced Feuillet dance notation from France, explains what was at stake:

> From the Regular or Irregular Position, and Motion of the Body, we distinguish the handsome Presence, and Deportment of the fine Gentleman, from the awkward Behaviour of the unpolish'd Peasant; we discover the graceful Mien of a young Lady, from the ungainly Carriage of her Maid; and this Regulation even stamps Impressions on the Mind, which we receive from the outward Figure of the Body; for as the Soul is inform'd from the external Objects of Sensation, how careful ought we to be, to give the most agreeable Impressions, which cannot be affected without this Regularity; and how commendable, how advantageous is it, for a gentleman, or Lady, to be Adroit at every Step, and, that every Motion, and Action of the Body, be consonant to Symmetry and Grace.[8]

Such appeals to the anxieties of the elite move from writing to notated movements, from notated movements to bodily ones, and from physical bodies—

Diderot's *Le Père de la famille*. Courtesy Comédie Française.

William Hogarth's "Strolling Actresses Dressing in a Barn."

nerves, sinews, motions, and memories—back again to textual bodies in the archive of restored behavior.

I cannot be the only reader to have been struck by the similarity between the precise movement patterns in Jane Austen's fictional courtships and eighteenth-century dance notation (figure 6). Her plots, like Feuillet's meticulous jots and dashes, inscribe the trajectories of marriageable bodies, passing through the most scrupulously regulated social spaces, seeking their erotic fates. Their movements play out in notated steps of subordination. As the title character in Austen's *Emma* gazes down the main street in her village, for instance, the scene comes to life as choreography:

> Much could not be hoped from the traffic of even the busiest part of Highbury;—Mr. Perry walking hastily by, Mr. William Cox letting himself in at the office door, Mr. Cole's carriage horses returning from exercise, or a stray letter-boy on an obstinate mule, were the liveliest objects she could presume to expect; and when her eyes fell only on the butcher with his tray, a tidy old woman traveling homewards from shop with her full basket, two curs quarreling over a dirty bone, and a string of dawdling children round the baker's little bow-window eyeing the gingerbread, she knew she had no reason to complain, and was amused enough; quite enough still to stand at the door. A mind lively and at ease, can do with seeing nothing, and can see nothing that does not answer.
>
> She looked down the Randalls road. The scene enlarged; two persons appeared; Mrs. Weston and her son-in-law; they were walking into Highbury;—to Hartfield of course. They were stopping, however, in the first place at Mrs. Bates's; whose house was a little nearer Randalls than Ford's; and had all but knocked, when Emma caught their eye.—Immediately they crossed the road and came forward to her; and the agreeableness of yesterday's engagement seemed to give fresh pleasure to the present meeting.[9]

Jane Austen's novel provides useful materials toward the reconstruction of a ballet of provincial social life, a kind of Regency *Sacre du Printemps*. In the middle distance, the figures of the picturesque genre scene, the Hogarthian workers and lower-class children described unblinkingly by Austen as "objects" or as "nothing," are painted on the scenery. The character dancers briefly enact the named but inconsequential comic roles of tradesmen and professionals. When the marriageable gentry enter on their diurnal rounds, however, the scene enlarges. They alone exist as "persons." Their movements are purposive, their destinations sure, and their social as well as physical mastery complete. Taking the stage, they fill Emma's vision and the reader's imagination with movement and meaning, while the novel itself, taking down steps, notates a social performance, the restored behavior of hierarchical selection.

Interdisciplinary research devoted to textual bodies might investigate what I call "genealogies of performance," the historical transmission and dissemination of cultural practices through collective representations. For this formulation, I am indebted to Jonathan Arac's definition, revising Nietzsche and Foucault, of a "critical genealogy" that "aims to excavate the past that is necessary to account for how

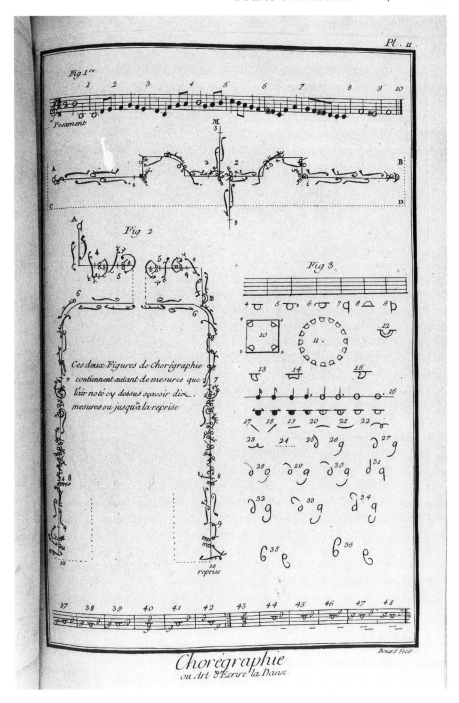

Diderot and d'Alembert, *Encyclopédie.* Courtesy of Special Collections, Northwestern University Library.

we got here and the past that is useful for conceiving alternatives to our present condition."[10] A genealogy of texted dance performance, for instance, from the ballet to the striptease, might disclose certain continuities in the narrative and stylistic strategies for making the effects of subtraction and subordination vivid in the bodies of the characters and thereby kinesthetically felt in the bodies of the readers. Performance genealogy documents the heirlooms of a history of the present.[11] I do not imagine that Jane Austen would ever have expressed herself in anything like Italo Calvino's words, but she did understand the corporeality of performance sufficiently well to have recognized that her work had a place in the genealogy of Sheila the programmer's declaration: "The body declares itself subject!"

Ethnographic Bodies: Substitution

Ethnography operates on the cusp of text and performance; indeed, "writing culture" might be thought of as a process of turning performances into texts. Yet at the same time, as performance ethnographer Dwight Conquergood explains, "ethnography's distinctive research method, participant-observation field work, privileges the body as a site of knowing." Probing the singular intimacies and immediacies of field work, which eschews the passive spectatorship of both the reader and the theatrical voyeur, Conquergood concludes: "The return of the body as a recognized method for attaining 'vividly felt insight into the life of other people'[12] shifts the emphasis from space to time, from sight and vision to sound and voice, from text to performance, from authority to vulnerability."[13] In other words, these experiences derive not from a textual archive of restored behaviors like Jane Austen's *Emma*, but from living bodies in the present. Yet the motions of these living bodies restore behaviors with roots as deep as cultural tradition itself: Like texts, bodies carry messages, posted in the historical past, but continuously arriving in the present, delivered by the performers themselves.

My current research is along these lines, and it specifically concerns the symbolic role of bodies in contemporary American urban street violence, which I term "the performance of waste." This performance predominates in carnival, especially in the former slave cultures along the circum-Caribbean rim, including the residents of America's "Third Coast," who often have either very much or very little material wealth to expend. I believe that so-called "senseless" violence, like carnival, is a way to consume and spend symbolically; in this case, however, bodies and lives are substituted for other kinds of wealth. By defining violence as the performance of waste, I assume three corollaries: first, that violence is meaningful, never "senseless," because violence in human cultures always, one way or another, serves to make a point; second, that all violence is excessive, because to be fully demonstrative, to make its point, it must *spend* things—material objects, blood, environments—in acts of what Veblen called "conspicuous consumption"; and third, that all violence is performative, for the simple reason that it must have an audience—even if that audience is only the victim, even if that audience is only God.

The "Black Indian" parades in New Orleans feature "tribes" or "gangs" of working-class African Americans who masquerade as Native Americans. The genealogy of their performance is in their speech and in their movements, which must be experienced in the streets of New Orleans on Mardi Gras, St. Joseph's Day, or the climactic "Super Sunday" in late March. The call and response chants and the percussive "Second Line" of supporters, quoting West African and Afro-Caribbean performance traditions, accompany the Indians through the neighborhoods, a brilliant human wave of music, feathers, and festivity. As the procession of warriors uncoils through the streets, it claims the space through which it moves by sound and gesture, imaginatively reversing manifest destiny, the Amerindian genocide, and the African diaspora by pushing white people and their culture to the peripheries.

Some of the Mardi Gras Indian songs carry an explicit message of territory repossessed. In material gathered by the W.P.A. Louisiana Writers' Project, there is a transcription of one of the most famous songs, in the version sung by the "Red, White, and Blue" tribe (c. 1930). Between the lines, the refrain "Tu-way-pa-ka-way" eludes translation, but it could express a message in creolized French (*tué*) and African (Ilunga) dialect (*mpaka*) to the effect that "you're dead if you don't bow down." It could also be a corruption of Creole slang, *tuez bas qu'on est*, "kill who's over there," or *tu n'as pas couilles*, "you ain't got no balls."[14] As it was explained to me by Larry Bannock, big chief of the Golden Star Hunters,[15] it means "You go this-a-way, I go that-a-way":

> Oh, the Little Red, White and Blues,
> Tu-way-pa-ka-way,
> Bravest Indians in the land,
> Tu-way-pa-ka-way,
> They are on the march today.
> Tu-way-pa-ka-way,
> If you should get in their way,
> Tu-way-pa-ka-way,
> Be prepared to die.
> Tu-way-pa-ka-way,
> Oowa-a-a!
> Oowa-a-a![16]

More recently, hapless motorists, including me, in search of Mardi Gras Indian parades, have experienced "foot percussion" provided gratis by the Second Line dancing on top of their cars. But the high drama is reserved for the ritualized meetings of rival tribes.

In the not-so-distant past, confrontations between heavily armed "chiefs" led to mayhem and death when the gangs met on contested turf. Now the competition—to make the rival chiefs "bow down"—turns on the contest of magnificent, hand-sewn costumes, feathered and beaded masterpieces called "suits," in which Indians such as Bo Dollis, big chief of the Wild Magnolias, appear before their followers at dawn on Mardi Gras (figure 7). The Indian who triumphs is he who is judged most "purdy."

It is no accident that competitive stitchery, bead-work, and opulent adornment have edged out bodily violence in the confrontation between rival gangs.

Bo Dollis, big chief of the Wild Magnolias. Photo by Michael P. Smith.

At carnival everyone wants to be seen in acts of conspicuous consumption and expenditure. Violence is one such act, for which the Mardi Gras Indian suits offer a kind of sacred substitution. In the year of exhaustive labor that it takes to make them, sewing each bead on separately, their designers "sweat blood."[17] The same costume must not be worn two years in a row. After Super Sunday, the Mardi Gras Indians take them apart, piece by piece, so that the materials (often thousands of dollars' worth) may be re-used. Their destruction doubles the sacrifice of living bodies in that vast American spectacle—the performance of waste—but with the miraculous transformation of blood into feathers. The substitution of Native American costumes for African ones enacts a complex history of Louisianian *métissage*, a kind of intercultural surrogation, predicated on the alliance of escaped slaves and Native Americans against the Euro-American regimes of enslavement and deportation.[18] The bodies of the Mardi Gras Indians, adorned to evoke the Ghost Dancers from two tortured continents, rise Phoenix-like out of the ashes of diaspora and genocide, offering a powerful alternative of regeneration to the death-spiral of American urban violence.

Theirs is not the only version of the performance of waste, however, and the tactics of subtraction, subordination, and substitution also shape urban cultures in which blood, not beadwork, answers for blood. Surrogation need not require a year's labor at the sewing table. New Orleans rivals Washington, D.C., Atlanta, and St. Louis for the record in murders of young men by their peers. For inner-city youth, as for Calvino's doll, inside one costume there is apparently always another one to rend: "The body is violent action! The body claims power! The body's at war!"

NOTES

1. Diamond and Quinby, *Feminism and Foucault.*
2. Cohen, "Foucauldian Necrologies," pp. 87–101.
3. Fraser, "Foucault's Body Language," pp. 55–70. I am indebted to Fraser for the reference to Calvino.
4. Butler, *Gender Trouble*, p. 136.
5. Butler, *Gender Trouble*, p. 137, Butler's emphasis. More recently, Butler has qualified and made more stringent her presentation of gendered performance, including drag. See Butler, *Bodies that Matter*, especially pp. 124–37.
6. Meyer, "Transsexual Striptease as Scientific Display," pp. 25–42.
7. Schechner, *Between Theater and Anthropology.*
8. Weaver, *Works*, pp. 867–68.
9. Austen, *Emma*, pp. 209–210.
10. Arac, *Critical Genealogies*, p. 2.
11. Roach, "Power's Body," pp. 99–118.
12. Trinh, *Women, Native, Other*, p. 123.
13. Conquergood, "Rethinking Ethnography," pp. 180, 183.
14. Berry, Foose, and Jones, *New Orleans Music*, p. 218.
15. Conversation with Larry Bannock, chief of the Golden Star Hunters, November 7, 1991.
16. Saxon, Dreyer, and Tallant, *Gumbo-Ya-Ya*, p. 20.
17. Conversation with Larry Bannock.
18. Smith, *Mardi Gras Indians.*

Historians as
Bodies in Motion

SUSAN A. MANNING

Modern Dance in the Third Reich: Six Positions and a Coda

It is a curious fact that interdisciplinary surveys of the arts often exclude dance. The reasons for this exclusion interest me less than how the inclusion of dance might alter the scripting of the cultural record. Once dance is written into the history of the arts, how will the narratives governing that history shift in response? For me, this is the provocative question. Not that I deny the validity of asking why cultural history has ignored dance, but the answers seem self-evident.[1]

In terms of my own research, what concerns me is not why most historians of German culture have overlooked the development of *Ausdruckstanz* ("dance of expression"), as modern dance was known during the interwar years, but rather how the history of *Ausdruckstanz* counters the standard narratives and periodization of Weimar culture. Survey after survey reiterates the familiar tale of Weimar modernism cut short by the rise of National Socialism in 1933. The now-standard studies of Weimar culture by Peter Gay, Walter Laqueur, John Willett, and Bärbel Schrader and Jürgen Schebera look at literature, theater, painting, film, music, architecture, design, even popular entertainment and mass media, but not *Ausdruckstanz*.[2] The omission is significant: Were modern dance included, then the notion that the National Socialists branded all manifestations of artistic modernism as "degenerate" would no longer hold. For in contrast to the other arts, where a majority of leading modernists either went into exile or stopped working after 1933, only a minority of self-proclaimed modernists in dance emigrated. The majority of modern dancers remained in Germany after Hitler came to power and, in varying ways, came to terms with the Third Reich.[3]

Only recently have dancers, critics, and scholars begun to probe the alliance between *Ausdruckstanz* and National Socialism. To date, their discussion has sketched five positions from which to view the dancers' collaboration. All five perspectives implicitly theorize the relations between ideology and form, and this essay begins by uncovering and articulating the differing assumptions underlying each viewpoint. Three of the five positions assume one-to-one correspondences between ideology and form, investing the form of *Ausdruckstanz* or the form of its antagonist, ballet, with persistent ideological imports. In contrast, many of the dancers who lived through the Third Reich have adopted an ambivalent, even paradoxical, stance, asserting both the independence of artistic form from political ideology *and* the corruption of artistic form by National Socialism. Finally, some critics have formalized the dancers' position, believing that form remains independent of ideology except in cases of clear political manipulation.[4]

My own explanation for the collaboration of modern dancers with the Third Reich forms the sixth position outlined in this essay. My account assumes neither the independence of ideology and form nor their one-to-one correspondence. Rather, my explanation foregrounds the shifting relations between ideology and form over time and the multiple contexts—socioeconomic, political, institutional, performative—that inflect these changes. In my model, although such contexts are not necessarily determinative, they are absolutely necessary for understanding the alliance between *Ausdruckstanz* and National Socialism.

Yet my theorization also has its limitations, which I attempt to elucidate in the coda to this essay. The coda describes Anna Halprin's *EarthDance*, a "dance ritual" staged as part of the Choreographing History conference at the University of California–Riverside in February 1992. From my perspective, *EarthDance* recalled the "movement choirs" staged during the Weimar and Nazi years, and the resemblance challenges my model of the relations between ideology and form shifting in response to context. Thus my essay subjects not only the writings of colleagues but also my own position to scrutiny.

In my catalog of possible explanations for the alliance between *Ausdruckstanz* and National Socialism, the first position is that taken by the two Marxist scholars who have paid attention to modern dance, namely Jost Hermand and Frank Trommler. In their encyclopedic overview, *Die Kultur der Weimarer Republik*, Hermand and Trommler note the "mysticism and irrationalism" of *Ausdruckstanz* and imply that these traits allowed for the "relative ease" with which the National Socialists appropriated the form.[5] Although they never use the term "protofascist" in relation to Weimar dance, the suggestion is clear. Implicit in their brief comments is the notion that any form possesses innate qualities that can be read as an intrinsic ideology and that the passage of *Ausdruckstanz* from Weimar to the Third Reich only clarified the ideology inherent in the form. In their retrospective reading, the fascist appropriation of the form rendered it "protofascist" during the Weimar period.

Hermand and Trommler's suspicion of any form that promotes "mysticism" reveals their debt to the expressionist debate that took place among German émigrés in the thirties.[6] According to Georg Lukacs, the antirational dimensions of expressionism paralleled and in some way facilitated the rise of fascism. Lukacs held realism to be the more fail-safe vehicle for the revolutionary consciousness of Marxism. Reversing Lukacs's claims, Ernst Bloch argued that realism worked to uphold the status quo of the bourgeois order, while expressionism worked to destabilize that status quo and thus aided the revolutionary movement in Weimar Germany, a movement that the émigrés pursued in exile.

In assessing *Ausdruckstanz*, Hermand and Trommler implicitly take sides with Lukacs rather than with Bloch. Positing a link between *Ausdruckstanz* and expressionism and between expressionism and fascism, Hermand and Trommler simplify and rigidify the relations between ideology and form. Like Lukacs (and like Bloch, for the two antagonists made similar assumptions regarding the relations of ideology and form, however divergent their conclusions), the two scholars of Weimar culture assume that any form embodies a single and unchanging ideology. Their perspective does not allow for the possibility that as form changes over time, so too does its ideological import. For Hermand and Trommler, the form of *Ausdruckstanz*—and its ideological import—moved relatively intact from one cultural situation to another.

Many of the dancers who lived through the twenties and thirties vehemently disagree. From their perspective, the National Socialists' appropriation of *Ausdruckstanz* altered the form beyond recognition. Many of the dancers' memoirs imply that the practice of *Ausdruckstanz* changed radically as it moved from one cultural situation to another. As Mary Wigman, one of the leading choreographers during the twenties and a figurehead of German Dance during the thirties, wrote:

> The cultural dictatorship of the Third Reich kept German creativity bogged down as if by a rock around the German neck; it particularly crippled the German dance. I cannot resist recalling the slogan of the time, a slogan which determined the end of the development of dance in Middle Europe: "Schmissiges Ballett und zackige Erotik" ("dashing ballet and bold eroticism"). It is hardly necessary to comment on it. In these words are expressed the finality of misunderstanding of dance. In them are the utmost in contempt of the ethical and spiritual values we truly find in dance. By negation of its spiritual and moral content, dance was debased to the level on which it could function, if at all, purely as entertainment.[7]

During the twenties, modern dancers had struggled to define their practice as "art" rather than "entertainment." When the National Socialists came to power, they introduced ballet technique as part of the curriculum for modern dancers and advocated a less "philosophical" form that displayed "beautiful women's bodies," to quote comments made by Joseph Goebbels in 1937.[8] Mary Wigman resented the dance policy pursued by Goebbels, and in her postwar memoirs she presents German Dance, as *Ausdruckstanz* was renamed, as a debased version of its earlier form, a form that had changed utterly from Weimar to the Third Reich.

However, Wigman's memoirs undercut her assertion of the mutability of *Ausdruckstanz* by presenting her own practice of the form as resistant. Her memoirs claim the status of "degenerate artist," an artist whose works challenged the prescribed aesthetic of Goebbels's Cultural Ministry.[9] Wigman's claim raises complicated issues, for although the choreographer did register some disagreement with National Socialist dance policy, neither her life nor her livelihood were ever endangered during the Third Reich. Focusing solely on her gestures of nonconformity, her memoirs omit mention of her acts of compliance: accepting commissions from Goebbels's Cultural Ministry to create group works in 1934, 1935, and 1936; reorganizing her school curriculum to accord with official directives, including the requirement for classes to be offered in ballet and in National Socialist *Weltanschauung*; and publishing *Deutsche Tanzkunst*, a statement of support for fascist aesthetics.[10] In the postwar period, Wigman saw herself as a victim of Nazi policy, not as an artist complicit in her own victimization—and the victimization of others.

The choreographer's claim to the status of "degenerate artist" thus undermines her implicit theorization of the mutability of *Ausdruckstanz*. For in believing her own continued practice subversive, she presents the form as capable of carrying its ideological import from the Weimar period into the Third Reich. In effect, she considered her own practice unchanged, even while insisting that the form itself had changed radically. Oral history with students at her school during the Nazi period supports her paradoxical claim, for they believed her practice after 1933 to have been as "liberating" and as individually empowering as her practice before 1933. Even some of her Jewish students who later emigrated defend her and remember the school as a "haven" from the pervasive anti-Semitism of the time.[11]

Over the last few decades, German dance critics and scholars have grappled with the seemingly contradictory claims made by Wigman and many of her colleagues. Is it possible that artists who chose not to emigrate managed to resist the fascist order even as they overtly conformed? Is it possible for the ideological import of a form to change and yet not to change as it moves from one cultural situation to another? In their attempts to explain the alliance between *Ausdruckstanz* and the Third Reich, German critics have staked out positions that recast the claims buried in Wigman's memoirs.

In a two-part article published in the early seventies that broke the taboo within the German dance world against sustained discussion of the Third Reich, Horst Koegler presented an alternate explanation for why *Ausdruckstanz* went soft, so to speak, during the Nazi period. According to Koegler, the form had reached a point of exhaustion before 1933. Its working method of structured improvisation could take choreographers only so far, and the second generation—students of Wigman and Laban such as Kurt Jooss and Yvonne Georgi—felt the need for a more secure technical basis. They rejected what they perceived as the amateurism of the first generation—critiquing not necessarily the leaders but certainly many of their followers. But before the second generation could pursue their vision of an integration between *Ausdruckstanz* and ballet, the National Socialists intervened. Proponents of *Ausdruckstanz* had no choice except, in Koegler's words, to "compliantly conform to the Nazi ideology of blood and soil with its dream of a new festival culture."[12]

Narrating the history of German dance, Koegler writes as a critical advocate of the ballet boom that dominated the German dance stage in the fifties and sixties. In his telling, the ballet boom reinvigorated the incipient ballet movement that National Socialism had cut short with its appropriation of *Ausdruckstanz*. As an international form free of the fascist taint of *Ausdruckstanz*, ballet reestablished the necessary distance between art and politics that National Socialism had subverted. This narrative implicitly posits ballet as a form above or without ideology, in contrast to *Ausdruckstanz*, a form that took its ideology from its historical context, progressive before 1933, reactionary after. In other words, Koegler invests ballet with what scholars have come to call the "ideology of the aesthetic."[13]

A decade after Koegler broke the taboo against discussion of dance in the Third Reich, Hedwig Müller and Norbert Servos authored an alternate explanation for the alliance between *Ausdruckstanz* and National Socialism. The two critics wrote as advocates of *Tanztheater*, a dance form that appeared in the seventies and took *Ausdruckstanz* as precedent for its assault on ballet. Like Koegler, Müller and Servos pen a historical narrative that functions as critical apology for contemporary practice.

While Koegler viewed the *Ausdruckstanz* impulse as exhausted before 1933, the two younger critics saw modern dance as still viable at the end of the Weimar Republic. According to Koegler, the National Socialists imposed their vision of German Dance on the dancers, who had lost their own sense of mission. According to Müller and Servos, the National Socialists exploited the protofascist tendencies within *Ausdruckstanz*—its implicit irrationalism—and thus deformed the movement. Partly for this reason, *Ausdruckstanz* became subordinate to ballet in the immediate postwar period. However, the *Ausdruckstanz* impulse resurfaced in *Tanztheater* as it recovered those dimensions of modern dance that had remained resistant to National Socialist appropriation. As Müller and Servos summarized their argument:

> One cannot underestimate the momentum which *Ausdruckstanz* set in motion for the development of a free dance form enduring through to the era of Modern Dance, despite the mythical-mystical elements which could later so easily be subverted. It is no less than propagandist Leni Riefenstahl's contribution to the development of the documentary film—a double-edged, perhaps vexing fact, but one which cannot be ignored.[14]

In other essays, Servos pursued the theoretical implications of this position and reversed Koegler's privileging of ballet over modern dance. In the introduction to his 1984 monograph *Pina Bausch Wuppertal Dance Theater*, Servos cites Ernst Bloch and Norbert Elias, arguing that ballet exemplifies the constraints placed on the body by industrial society, while modern dance demonstrates the resistance of the body to such disciplining. From Servos's perspective, ballet inscribes the internalization of discipline that Elias defines as characteristic of modernity, while modern dance inscribes the body's rejection of the fundamental illusion of modernity—control masked as freedom. Thus, modern dance fulfills Bloch's understanding of the utopian potential of art. Like Bloch (and like Lukacs), Servos posits a simple and direct relation between ideology and form.

Strikingly, the one scholarly study to date on the relations between *Ausdruckstanz* and National Socialism backs away from examining the relations between form and ideology. In a 1988 dissertation subtitled "the effects of the Nazi regime on the German modern dance," Suzan Moss explains the dancers' collaboration in terms reminiscent of their own attempts at explanation. In fact, oral history formed an important source for her research. Moss writes:

> The years spent under the auspices of National Socialism do not negate [the] achievements [of Wigman, Laban, and others]. Similarly, these achievements

do not negate the fact that for a brief but terrible time, some of these dancers were blinded by their devotion to their creative work, and ignored the deeper implications of their actions. Their passion for creating new dances and furthering the development of their art eclipsed their awareness of their role as cultural propagandists for National Socialism.[15]

Assessing the reasons why some dancers collaborated while others emigrated, Moss posits the independence of art and politics. As she summarizes her underlying assumption, "modern dance, . . . like any art form, is politically neutral in and of itself, until it is utilized for political objectives."[16]

My own explanation for the alliance between *Ausdruckstanz* and National Socialism rejects Moss's assumption of the typical separation of ideology and form as well as the reductive equations of ideology and form underlying the arguments of Hermand and Trommler, Koegler, and Servos. From my perspective, these accounts fail because all assume a static and unchanging relation between ideology and form, whether that relation is dependent or independent. Rather than assume such a static relation, my argument posits a complex and shifting interplay between ideology and form in response to the changing social, economic, and political organization of the dance world. To summarize my argument: *Ausdruckstanz* underwent an institutional crisis around 1930, a crisis resolved by the National Socialist "reorganization" (*Gleichschaltung*) of cultural life. In my telling, this is what led so many modern dancers to collaborate with the Third Reich.[17]

During the 1920s, *Ausdruckstanz* drew its patronage from amateur students devoted to *Tanz-Gymnastik* ("dance gymnastics"), as popular in Germany then as aerobics were in the United States during the eighties. This popularity meant that the artistic project of *Ausdruckstanz* was tied to the mass cultural interest in physical culture and sport. Indeed, the improvisational methods of *Ausdruckstanz* blurred the distinction between professional and amateur dance, for concert dancers deployed the same methods as amateur devotees of *Tanz-Gymnastik*. Amateur students not only flocked to the private studios opened by Wigman, Laban, and their followers but also provided a ready audience for the dancers and dance groups that toured from city to city.

Amateur dancers also formed the constituency for the movement choir (*Bewegungschor*), a form innovated by Rudolf Laban and disseminated by his many followers. As conceived by Laban, the movement choir involved anywhere from fifty to more than five hundred participants. During the 1920s, movement choirs were founded in association with dance studios and municipal theaters, with unions and political parties (in particular the Social Democratic Party and the Communist Party), and with Catholic Church organizations. The notation system that Laban developed during the twenties was linked to the requirements of the movement choir, for small groups could learn the dance from notated scores and then come together for the final performance.

A provocative conjunction between art and physical culture defined Weimar dance. However, by 1930 this convergence threatened to come apart. As an oversupply of trained dancers encountered an undersupply of new students, dancers began to look elsewhere for patronage and came up with radically different sources. Some dancers managed to find positions in opera houses, which meant that they had to modify the improvisational techniques of *Ausdruckstanz* and acquire ballet training. Other dancers applied to schools and social organizations to offer their services as physical education instructors, which usually meant that they had to de-emphasize the artistic and develop the gymnastic components of *Tanz-Gymnastik*. The onset of economic depression only reinforced the economic straits of many dancers and intensified their search for new forms of patronage.

When the National Socialists came to power in 1933, they supplied the new institutional support, in effect substituting the patronage of the state for the patronage of amateur students. As they did for the country as a whole, the National Socialists put the dancers back to work—in the opera house, in mass spectacles, in physical education programs, and in leisure organizations. Responsibility for reorganizing German dance was divided between Goebbels's Cultural Ministry, which credentialed professional dancers, and Alfred Rosenberg's Fighting League for German Culture, which oversaw a massive physical education program. Significantly, this bureaucratic compartmentalization resulted in the segregation of stage dance from physical culture.

The transformation of dance patronage under the Third Reich did not happen all at once. Nor was National Socialist dance policy necessarily monolithic or consistent. In the early years of the regime, the Cultural Ministry and the Fighting League for German Culture cooperated in the production of *Thingspiel*, open-air spectacles that drew on German history and legend for subject matter. As Henning Eichberg has demonstrated, the *Thingspiel* borrowed and adapted the form of the movement choir from Weimar dance. However, for reasons that are not entirely clear, the national government withdrew its support from the *Thingspiel* after 1936, even though local municipalities continued to patronize the form. From this point, the portfolios of the Cultural Ministry and the Fighting League for German Culture significantly diverged. Whereas the Cultural Ministry sponsored dance concerts as an entertaining diversion, the Fighting League trained physical education instructors to staff the League of German Girls, the female counterpart to the Hitler Youth. "Art" and physical culture went their separate ways, as they continued to do after the fall of the Third Reich.

How did changing patronage structures and institutional affiliations mark the form of *Ausdruckstanz*? Consider the example of the movement choir. During the Weimar period, the movement choir emphasized the participation of all who were present at the event. Thus, the form functioned to intensify each member's sense of individual self-awareness and to heighten all the members' sense of group solidarity—whether the group was composed of amateur students enrolled in a private dance studio or members of a Catholic youth organization or workers at a Communist Party rally. Like many other theatrical innovations of the Weimar period, the movement choir broke down the distinction between performer and spectator necessitated by the proscenium theater. However, when redeployed as part of the *Thingspiel*, the movement choir became the basis for a large-scale spectacle that reinstated the separation of performer and spectator. In the open-air theaters specially built for *Thingspiel*, several thousand spectators would watch the precision patterns executed by the hundred or more members of the movement choir. Thus the form dramatized the individual's subordination to the group. As the political and performative contexts for the movement choir changed, so too did the form and its ideological import. Thus, my model conceptualizes form as variously mutable across time and space and as deceptively mobile from one ideological context to another.

Or so I held until participating in a "dance ritual" staged by Anna Halprin as part of the Choreographing History conference in February 1992. Although Halprin, a senior member of the American avant-garde, would never call her form a "movement choir," it fits the definition—a form of large-group dance that does not require professional performers and that emphasizes group involvement over individual authority or expression. Or, more accurately, a dance form designed to minimize the potential for conflict between the leader's authority, individualized expressivity, and group affiliation. The program for "Dancers/Scholars/Ritual," part of an ongoing work titled *EarthDance*, carried the dedication:

> In this moment of crisis in the life of the Earth, we will join together to perform the EarthDance as a prayer to deepen our commitment to and enact our faith in the survival of our planet, of each other and all of life.[18]

The "participatory event" began with a procession from the dance studio that was serving as a conference hall to another building. Before we set out—well over a hundred strong and accompanied by several drummers—Halprin instructed us to become aware of our selves and our environment as we walked—to note the rhythm of our steps, the swing of our arms, the feel of the damp air outside, and the presence of others in the long, straggling procession. Once we arrived in the adjacent building, we were instructed to take off our shoes and place them in an anteroom, then find a place to sit in a large room where crayons and pieces of drawing paper were spread out on the floor. Halprin then instructed us to draw an image of ourselves—not thinking too much about it, just doing it. (We turned over the paper and drew a second self-portrait at the end of the performance event.)

The central part of *EarthDance* took place outdoors. It was an overcast day and the ground was quite muddy from incessant rain. Having put our shoes back on as we headed out the door, we formed long lines holding hands and, linked in this way, danced in a large open grassy space for the better part of an hour—with lines breaking and reforming, circling and snaking, crossing and parting. It's hard to say who or what determined the patterns. The drummers set a basic rhythm. Halprin made some gestures as we began, instructing us to hold hands and form a large circle, and as we ended, instructing us to gather on a small rise to one side of the field. Otherwise I don't remember seeing her, but responding only to the people immediately around me, letting the movement of the line dictate my movement and only once breaking away and taking up the leadership role myself. Otherwise I just held on tight to an old friend on one side, a new acquaintance on the other, and attempted to not get knocked down as we careened through the space.

After Halprin's signal to gather on the knoll had passed through the group, we came together and everyone took a still position, either crouching or standing. (Sitting was not an option, given how muddy the ground was.) Again clearly directed by Halprin, everyone took a single note and held it—an "oom" sound—and built up a texture of overlapping tones. And then at a certain point Halprin gave the signal that this part of the ritual was over and that it was time to go back indoors and draw another self-portrait. (Not surprisingly, while my first drawing revealed my usual self-conception as an intellectual—distinct lines outlining the face only—my second drawing used vague lines to suggest the feel of the body in motion.)

According to the model proposed in my research, the ideological import of a movement choir staged in 1992 California necessarily differs from the import of a movement choir staged in 1920s Germany or in the Third Reich, for as the contexts for the performance event shift, so too do the relations of ideology and form. To a certain extent, my model held, for Halprin's *EarthDance* exuded a New Age spirituality and an ecological politics in keeping with its time and place. Yet participants and spectators surely judged the context and the symmetry (or asymmetry) of event and context differently. For some, the "dance ritual" seemed anachronistic, for others, visionary. For some, the "dance ritual" had little to do with life in California in 1992; for others, it confirmed a stereotype of West Coast culture. This variation in response did not surprise me. Indeed, in my own research I have attempted to integrate such predictable variability in response— for instance, between younger and older, German and non-German spectators of Wigman's dances—within a model that highlights context as the crucial variable for understanding the relations between ideology and form.

What did surprise me was the moment when I experienced the immutability of the form of the movement choir, a seemingly direct connection between its use in Nazi spectacle and in *EarthDance*. At one point someone ahead of me in line broke away and headed toward one of the few trees in the open field, pulling others along. I remember that we dropped hands and raced in a pack toward the direction we were headed. It was when the group gathered around the base of the tree and reached up to touch its bark that I pulled back, attempting to drag a friend with me. The association with Nazi nature worship—all those groups of Hitler Youth camping out together—seemed so direct that I couldn't remain part of the event. I did later continue, mostly because in that moment of pulling back I had begun to meditate on exactly how mutable was the form of the movement choir.

Does form too have a history and a memory? So Susan Sontag implies in her 1975 critique of Leni Riefenstahl titled "Fascinating Fascism." According to Sontag, spectators still respond to Riefenstahl's films because the "fascist ideal" persists "in such diverse modes of cultural dissidence and propaganda for new forms of community as the youth/rock culture, primal therapy, Laing's antipsychiatry, Third World camp-following, and belief in gurus and the occult."[19] Does Halprin's *EarthDance* comprise part of the survival, in Sontag's terms, of the "fascist ideal"?

Or is it the memory of the spectator that determines response, not the history of the form? Was it my own history—my years of grappling with the issue of modern dance in the Third Reich—that determined my response to *EarthDance*? How profoundly the history of the spectator or participant informs the reading of a work was suggested by two colleagues' responses right after we stopped intoning "oom." A new acquaintance, a musicologist around fifty years old, remarked that the "dance ritual" took him back to the seventies, when he often participated in such events, and that it reminded him of how much he then had enjoyed directing a choir in the open air. Another friend related quite a different experience. She, like me, was too young to have experienced the full force of the sixties' counterculture. But two days earlier, she had learned that a close friend of her family had died, and in the rush of preparation for the conference had never had a moment to mourn—until crouched down on the knoll she began to sob audibly.

That three participant-observers had three such different experiences of the same event underscores that interpretation is not monolithic or even subject to predictable variation. Social, political, economic, and institutional contexts surely inform the relations of ideology and form, but so too does the unpredictable range of spectatorship. This is where the limitations of my theorization of modern dance in the Third Reich became apparent. For my model could not do justice to the variability, much less the range, of possible responses to performance.

In retrospect, I realized that my model assumed a single, fixed position from which the spectator (or historian) could follow the constantly evolving dance of ideology, form, and context. In the course of my research I had constructed such an idealized spectator as a necessary fiction in order to explain the passage of *Ausdruckstanz* from Weimar to the Third Reich. Yet it goes without saying that no such idealized spectator exists. And now that I have completed my inquiry, it seems time to revise my model. The model I envision would set in motion not only the relations between ideology and form but also the viewing perspective of the historian. With both the observer and the observed changing places, what a complicated dance would result!

What would my revised model look like? It would assume multiple spectators (and multiple historians), but in a less schematic way than does my opening catalog of possible explanations for the collaboration of modern dancers with the Third Reich. It would take into account the binary oppositions that structure so much of contemporary discourse about performance and would speculate on the differences between male and female, gay and straight, black and white spectatorship. Yet it would not apply such binary oppositions reductively. I would like to leave open the question of whether spectatorship can be a transformative experience, that is, whether performance gives spectators access to viewing perspectives other than those conditioned by their race, class, gender, national identity, and sexual preference.

My memory goes back to my experience of Halprin's *EarthDance*. In this instance, it seemed possible to collate a difference in response with a difference in generation. Other differences among us—in terms of gender, sexual preference, and national origin—seemed not to matter or, at least, not to matter in ways that could generate clear correspondences between social identity and spectatorial response. And equally difficult to figure were the ways that our shared racial and professional identities shaped our responses—not to mention our divergent personal histories, including the histories of our physical selves.

Add all these variables to the shifting interplay between ideology and form in response to the multiple contexts of patronage and politics: Is it even possible for the historian to record, much less fathom, what results? I'm not sure, though I would hope this essay makes a first, awkward step toward learning that complicated dance.[20]

NOTES

1. To any reader for whom the reasons are not obvious, I offer the following catalog: the Judeo-Christian privileging of *logos* over *corpus*: the association between dance and the female body and the preponderance of women as participants, spectators, and scholars in the field; the absence of a common notation system such as Western music developed around 1600, which suggests an awkward fit between the oral and kinesthetic transmission of dance and the dynamics of a print culture; and the consequent methodological challenges of recovering historical dance practice. However, it must be noted that although reconstructing Western theater dance is difficult, it is no more difficult than reconstructing the staging of ancient Greek tragedy or Shakespearean drama.

2. Gay, *Weimar Culture*; Laqueur, *Weimar: A Cultural History*; Willett, *Art and Politics*; Schrader and Schebera, *The "Golden" Twenties*.

3. Although no scholar has yet undertaken a census of all the dancers involved, it is possible to compile informal statistics on the leading dancers. In 1930, more than one thousand choreographers, performers, teachers, and critics gathered in Munich for the Third Dancers Congress. Altogether, forty German choreographers presented their works on ten programs, along with thirty-five younger dancers who shared a single program and presented a solo apiece. (A twelfth program was dedicated to guest artists from abroad.) Of the forty established choreographers who presented their works, I have been able to trace the subsequent careers of thirty-one. While two died before the National Socialists came to power (Heinrich Kröller and Vera Skoronel), another two had established careers abroad for other reasons before 1933 (Corrie Hartong and Käthe Wulff). Of the remaining choreographers whose careers I have been able to trace, twice as many remained in Germany and collaborated with the National Socialists as did not. Altogether, eighteen of the leading choreographers in 1930 came to terms with the National Socialists: Rosalia Chladek, Dorothee Güthner, Günther Hess, Jens Keith, Jutta Klamt, Albrecht Knust, Rudolf Kölling, Valerial Kratina, Manda von Kreibig, Else Lang, Maja Lex, Lissie Maudrik, Rudolf von Laban, Frances Metz, Gret Palucca, Gertrud Wienecke, Mary Wigman, and Heide Woog. The remaining nine choreographers either emigrated after 1933 or stopped working in the dance field for reasons related to the rise of National Socialism: Olga Brandt-Knack, Jenny Gertz, Kurt Jooss, Gertrud Kraus, Sigurd Leeder, Ruth Loeser, Martin Gleisner, Oskar Schlemmer, and Margarethe Wallmann. Laban ultimately did emigrate, but only after he fell out of favor with Joseph Goebbels. See Preston-Dunlop, "Laban and the Nazis."

It is important to note that the division between dancers who collaborated and dancers who emigrated did not necessarily result from differing ethnic origins. Of the nine leading dancers who left Germany or stopped working after the Nazis came to power, I have been able to ascertain that only two (Gertrud Kraus and Margarethe Wallmann) acted primarily on the basis of their Jewish identity. The others were censored for their leftist or Communist politics. Whether or not they were "Jewish," I do not know. In any case, to search out which dancers had Jewish grandparents strikes me as too close to Nazi precedent for comfort.

4. It is important to note that this essay does not intend a comprehensive review of the literature but rather an overview of the differing theorizations buried in the extant literature. None of the writers surveyed explicitly comment on the relations of ideology and form. Rather, their personal memoirs and narrative chronicles rely on unstated assumptions, which my readings attempt to excavate.

5. Hermand and Trommler, *Die Kultur der Weimarer Republik*, pp. 217–18.

6. The primary documents in the debate are collected in Bloch et al., *Aesthetics and Politics*.

7. Sorell, *The Mary Wigman Book*, p. 164.

8. Goebbels, *Die Tagebücher*, p. 187.

9. Wigman's many apologists, including Walter Sorell, have reiterated this claim. Presumably it was Sorell who Gisela d'Andrea took as an authority when she wrote: "(After 1936) Wigman was still allowed to perform, but it was not long before her themes were considered too morbid. She was also eventually declared degenerate, non-German, and eastern. Her school was taken away from her and she was relegated to obscurity." See d'Andrea, "The New German Dance in the Weimar Republic," p. 97.

10. Wigman, *Deutsche Tanzkunst*.

11. That I focus on Wigman reflects my own extensive research into her career. However, her claims seem paradigmatic of those made by many of her students and colleagues in the postwar period.

12. This comment appears in Koegler's 1973 obituary for Mary Wigman, published the same year as the second part of his article on dance in the Third Reich. The English-language version of Koegler's research, published in *Dance Perspectives*, (p. 4) does not reveal his interpretive bias as clearly as do the German-language sources noted in the bibliography.

13. See Roach, "Theatre History," for a provocative analysis of the "ideology of the aesthetic" in eighteenth-century ballet, an analysis that accords with the view of ballet put forward by Hedwig Müller and Norbert Servos, Koegler's antagonists and successors.

14. Müller and Servos, "From Isadora Duncan to Leni Riefenstahl," p. 23.

15. Moss, "Spinning through the Weltanschauung," pp. 348–49.

16. Moss, "Spinning through the Weltanschauung," p. 345.

17. What follows summarizes the argument put forward in my book, *Ecstasy and the Demon*.

18. Halprin has been staging *EarthDance* in various locales for more than a decade. In 1955, Halprin founded the San Francisco Dancers Workshop, which became an important center for avant-garde dance in the sixties. By 1975, she had moved away from experimental concert dance to dance as a vehicle for individual self-realization, community development, and planetary survival.

19. Sontag, "Fascinating Fascism," p. 30.

20. I would like to thank Tracy Davis, Helen Deutsch, Laura Hein, and Sandra Richards for their comments on earlier drafts of this essay.

CYNTHIA J. NOVACK

The Body's Endeavors as Cultural Practices

In thinking about how to discuss the body's endeavors as cultural practices, I am moved to consider conceptions of the body among those who study it.

I count myself a member of three groups of people with proprietary interest in the subject: dancers and choreographers, people in the field of dance studies, and people in other academic fields who have interdisciplinary inclinations. As a dancer/choreographer and writer about dance, I would like to relate my comments about studying the body to the study of dance, and, as an anthropologist, I'd like to suggest relationships between developments in anthropology and those in dance studies.

Some brief ethnographic examples serve to introduce my discussion. The first case, Anna Halprin's *EarthDance*, was an event created for the Choreographing History Conference in 1992. At the scheduled time for this event, Halprin appeared and informed the gathering that in contemporary society, we have lost our ritual connections to the earth. Therefore, she explained, she was going to direct us in a "spontaneous ritual" to help reestablish these connections. Her first instruction was to cease all talking and join a procession to another building, focusing on sensations of our bodies as we walked. Once we had arrived and removed our shoes as directed, we were told to use the paper and crayons scattered on the floor to "draw how you feel" quickly, without thought.

How was bodily endeavor being defined as cultural practice in this sequence of events? All of the instructions requested attention to the body and emotions as linked, occurring in the absence of thought or speech. Such attention, it was proposed, would bring us greater harmony with the natural world, restoring something akin to an earlier, more integrated social order. At the same time, the procession was not monitored, and each individual could choose exactly how to follow the instructions—a number of people chatted and joked, while others were more contemplative. As I strolled along the pathway, music playing, I felt exhilarated after sitting in the same room all morning. As we congregated for the next part of the event, it seemed that most people felt enthusiastic or at least curious about what might come next.

Halprin spoke to the group of over a hundred people about her decision that we were to move outside to an open field and allow the spontaneous ritual to occur. "Don't think about what you should do," Halprin admonished us. "Let the earth speak to you through your body. The earth will tell you what to do." She suggested, however, that we might begin by all holding hands.

As we tugged our shoes back on, a historian whispered to me that I must feel confident of how to behave, since I was a dancer, whereas he, an academic who liked to dance socially, was quite nervous. Another dancer/dance historian next to us reassured him that she, too, had no idea what was going on. I felt that in fact Halprin had made many people anxious by her mystical introduction. Yet she also had set up an implicit, foolproof structure for the event, which both my companions would be able to join as soon as they stepped outside. Halprin had established herself as the director, the one who was allowed to speak and to give instructions, even as she reiterated the concepts of spontaneity and directionlessness. By providing musicians playing rhythmic music and organizing people in lines holding hands—the simplest and most flexible formation for a large, connected group—Halprin established an inevitable choreography of walking and running in lines, intertwining, breaking off, and regrouping. Halprin was identified as the source of guidance for anyone in the crowd who needed it, and thus she and her assistants could help steer people into an ending activity and location. Finally, Halprin had ensured an aerobic component of the ritual so that people would become physically invigorated, and she had conjured potent images of relationships to the earth, nature, and each other. Without question, most people would feel greater well-being afterwards and would make a second drawing that reflected a changed state.

I do not mean to imply that had Halprin said nothing, spontaneity would have prevailed. Indeed, spontaneity and organization would seem to be necessary complements of any social/choreographic event, without which either chaos or rigidity results. Nor do I think there's anything wrong with running around in a field and not talking—in fact, I believe passionately that moving about with others can be a unique, resonant, meaningful experience. Undoubtedly, Halprin's ritual was just that for many participants.

What has continued to disturb me about this event are the discrepancies between what was claimed and what occurred. For a conference examining writing about the body and the choreography of history, the unreflexive ritual struck an odd chord, one that promoted a particular view of movement and choreography without making that view explicit. Halprin's implicit assumption of bodily knowledge as essential, mindless truth, and of dancing as a spontaneous expression, devoid of choreographic intent or inspiration, exemplifies a particular construction of the body and self popularized in countercultural events in the United States beginning in the fifties and sixties, what I have called "the responsive body."[1] This construction has contributed to the development of avant-garde American theater and dance, therapeutic ventures, and social movements, in which the underlying wisdom of the natural body is thought to be recognized and followed, freed of dominance by the artificial mind.

The notion of the responsive body articulates a profound truth in the experience of many American dancers, and as such, it might be an important topic of discussion for those seeking to understand dance and culture—hence, my disappointment that this construction of the body remained at the level of implied content of Halprin's highly orchestrated happening. Subsequently, the conference participants never formally discussed the "spontaneous ritual" in which so many of us had participated. At an afternoon session about "the body's endeavors as cultural practices," in which I proposed such an exchange, Halprin stepped forward to request that people speak about "how they felt," reinforcing (whether consciously or not) the perspectives she had tried to create in the ritual event itself. A few people volunteered their reactions, but no one, including myself, offered a response that was analytical. Halprin, miffed by the lengthy discussion in which few people mentioned her ritual, declared (just before her conspicuous departure) that the people gathered there wanted to talk only about their thoughts and not about their feelings. Once again, Halprin's language was permeated with the view of body/emotion and mind as separate and antagonistic.

While Halprin's comments raised the ire of some conference participants who felt insulted and condescended to, others defended Halprin on several grounds. One was that Halprin, as an elder, deserved greater attention than she had been granted. Another was that Halprin had identified the central problem of the entire conference and that she represented the truth of the body (and, according to one person I spoke with, the feminine) against the endless, intellectual (masculine) talk that predominated. For me, the ritual and subsequent discussion illuminated recurring, all-too-familiar themes of opposition between mind and body/emotion in American culture, which set the course of debate riding in predictable directions.

These themes are by no means unique to dancers; they permeate scholarly views as well. To some degree, the justification of Halprin's behavior derives from the absence of body in most academic study, a condition that tends to trigger a defensive response from those who focus on the body in practice and consequently feel excluded. The relatively powerless position of dancers and dance scholars outside of academic institutions creates resentment of more established scholars who wield greater power and yet seem quite ignorant of dance studies and its possibilities for informing investigations of the body. Polarization thus results from social positions, as well as from opposite resolutions to the same body-mind constructions.

A second ethnographic example further explains my point. A call for papers several years ago for an American Ethnological Society meeting titled "The Body in Culture and Society" (1990) announced academic attention to the often-ignored body. However, virtually all the categories listed in the notice posited the body as an object, manipulated by external forces in the service of something: religion (the body as icon), the state (the discipline of the body), gender (the feminine body), and so on. Of course these categories do articulate part of social experience, but if they are taken to represent the entire experience, functionalism reigns and the body becomes simply a composite "result" of a series of more significant "causes." What about body as subject or body as an aspect of the creation of meaning? What about bodies of particular people in time and space who act, as well as react?

Furthermore, the AES notice listed categories of the body without questioning the positivist assertion of the body itself. A more historically and anthropologically sound approach would say that bodies, while ever-present for all human beings, are not necessarily conceived of similarly nor are they experienced or perceived similarly. If we do not assume that we know what body is, then we have to proceed with the understanding that people think, feel, move, imagine, and act through bodies/minds/selves/social groups that are variously organized in different historical periods and cultural settings.

Both tendencies noted here—the academic predilection for reducing lived experience to theoretical abstraction and the reactive, dancerly impulse to posit movement and bodily knowledge as privileged over all other knowledge—represent responses to virtually the same construction of the person in American culture. In this construction, "body" constitutes a biological absolute, a purely physical reality (sometimes with emotion and desire attached), and a separate realm of experience. The differences result from interpretations of the significance of this isolated body and what one might know or not know from one's experience of it. Those in dance studies may perceive that theirs is a minority view and believe that the relatively greater marginalization of dance studies makes it all the more important for the body's knowledge and independent agency to be noted. Yet if scholars of dance studies speak from the same framework as those who would objectify or reduce the body, little may be resolved. The scholarly mission should not be to figure out what to do with "the body"—abstract it, feel it, universalize it, forget it, worship it; rather we should be able to take a step back and consider whose body we're talking about in any given instance, how that person or people are experiencing their bodies, and whether or not "the body" is even at issue.

The difficulties of trying to understand the body, movement, or dance as culture are, as I mentioned earlier, embedded in institutions and social relations as well as in ideology. Scholars trained in using theories of culture, semiotics, or feminist analysis normally practice their theorizing in academic institutions that compartmentalize and marginalize bodily practices, artistic practices, and, certainly, the fields that combine the two—dance, music, and theater performance. American schools teach that thinking occurs while sitting still in a chair, that "physical education" exists apart from "real" education, and that the practices of singing, dancing, acting, storytelling, drawing, even "creative" writing are diverting entertainments. Students often have few opportunities for serious study of performance in a scholarly setting, and, without at least an introductory knowledge of, for example, how different people dance or how certain dance genres have developed historically, perceptive theorizing about dance becomes unlikely and difficult.

On the other hand, those who study dance practices rarely encounter the kind of "theory" sought after in the academy. The dance study that exists in studios and conservatories, particularly since World War II, has tended to promote technical analyses; alternative forms of dance study developing more recently (since the sixties) have relied largely on theories of movement analysis, kinesiology, psychology, the martial arts, and a transcendentalist/New Age American spiritualism. All of these theories tend to be both hermetic and hermeneutic, centrally important in an investigation of American culture but hardly in themselves articulating relationships between dance and culture.

Although cultural studies have attained a degree of status in the university, they have rarely included dance. Models for the relationships between dance and culture have been advanced primarily by independent dance historians and critics, philosophers, dance anthropologists, and teachers in dance departments of liberal arts colleges. Their models have often been vague, uncritical, and/or simplistic, a result in part of the painstaking and usually haphazard way in which knowledge and experience of dance tends to be acquired.

Yet the creation of more subtle, complex models of dance and culture has also been emerging over the past twenty years, as those in the field of dance studies have become increasingly cognizant of cultural questions, of potential contributions of dance studies to other fields, and of related investigations in other disciplines. These models do not rely on a single verb for functionally describing the relationship of dance and culture (dance "reflects," dance "integrates," dance "divides"), but rather approach dance as a complicated, multivocalic practice. Dance may reflect *and* resist cultural values simultaneously (the ballerina, who embodies and enacts stereotypes of the feminine while she interprets a role with commanding skill, agency, and a subtlety that denies stereotype). The same dance form may generate different meanings as its setting, participants, and institutional frameworks change (lindy hoppers at the Savoy Ballroom in the thirties as opposed to contemporary dancers who are reviving the form at the Cat Club) or as its audience changes (break dance in the seventies performed by adolescent boys for their peers on a Bronx street corner and break dance performed for an arts audience by these same boys at the Kitchen, a center for avant-garde music in Manhattan).

Groups of people may, through dancing, construct and separate themselves from others—their dance becomes associated with gender and age (as break dance was with teenage boys, for example), ethnic identity or national heritage (a huge variety of "folk dances" and national ballet companies), and/or political movements (rock dance in the sixties or Cambodian refugees recreating their court dance in America as protest of events in their homeland). People otherwise in conflict may find a temporary meeting ground in the experience of a dance event or a kind of dancing. Large institutions, such as schools, mass media, and governmental organizations, necessarily shape and constrain the frameworks through which people learn about, participate in, create, and produce dancing.

In short, artistic/bodily endeavors must be subject to the same historicizing and contextualizing as any other human endeavors. To study dance, we must take into account the "art" (the choreographic structures, movement styles, and techniques of dance), the institutions (local, national, global) in which it is practiced and performed, and the people who participate in it as performers, producers, spectators, and commentators. With this scope, dance studies have the potential to inform us about the history of fluctuating events and how to re-search and write about them. Dance studies can illuminate knowledge created through bodies, movement, artistic ideas, and choreographic interactions. It can participate in dialogues about theory and practice and about the most personal articulations of political forces and social power.

Such developments and possibilities in the field of dance studies, of course, have been growing out of larger methodological and theoretical concerns that have affected many fields. It is no accident that dance studies have burgeoned during a period of transformation in a number of disciplines. The field of anthro-pology, for example, has witnessed growing emphasis on self-reflexiveness by authors—conscious articulation of their relationship to the subjects of their field-work and to the methods and styles of their ethnographic writing. Many anthropologists have also become increasingly concerned with the role of the individual actor in society (rejecting a more abstract, static notion of social struc-ture), and with discerning the nature of experience and action by individuals within the restraints and conflicts of larger institutions.[2] These changes within the discipline have supported the emergence of dance studies in anthropology because of the fit between these concerns and the particular qualities of dance—its inherent interplay between performer and spectator, observer and observed; its ephemeral existence in space and time and its constant (re)creation and trans-mission through action; and its necessarily dual nature as a personal, individual, creative act and as a social, culturally defined occurrence.

The study of dance within anthropology is a relatively recent phenomenon. Early twentieth-century ethnographies that included dance operated largely on the functionalist model that dance simply reflects the social structure or an aspect of it. While some anthropologists wrote interesting narrative accounts, they produced few systematic descriptions that analyze a range of movement and choreographic features.[3] Beginning in the late forties and fifties, Gertrude Kurath tried to develop what she called a "dance ethnology" that would take into ac-count the particular features of the dance, its relationship to music, and how "dance and its music express other cultural aspects." Kurath, whose training in modern dance and in music provided her with technical analytical models, pro-duced a body of descriptive and notated records that established dance as an observable category in fieldwork. Yet the anthropological theory Kurath tried to apply, ideas of environmental influences and acculturation, did little to illumi-nate how dance might be seen as part of culture.[4]

The generation of dance anthropologists after Kurath began to investigate other theoretical sources, including ethnomusicology, linguistics, and symbolic anthropology.[5] Such explorations, in conjunction with the emerging critical con-cerns in the field of anthropology mentioned above, launched a new stage in writings about dance and culture. These and other dance anthropologists have continued to develop their work, while some anthropologists not previously con-cerned with dance have begun to venture into this area.[6] And more recently, extended ethnographies that investigate dance as a complex cultural practice have appeared, including Jane Cowan's analysis of gender in the dance of a Greek community, Margaret Drewal's study of Yoruba ritual, Sally Ness's ethnography about three versions of Philippine dance, and my own ethnohistory of contact improvisation viewed in the context of American culture.[7] These books reveal the influence not only of anthropological theory but also of structuralist and post-structuralist thought, performance theory, and "new" historicism. At the same time, they carry on dialogues with other recent interdisciplinary books about dance, music, and the body. The territory becomes more complicated and intriguing all the time.

Finally, to return to the initial question of this essay, the recent work on dance, in anthropology and in other fields, clearly indicates the necessity to problematize "the body." Body must be understood as a constructed category susceptible to analysis, and it should be considered both from vantage points within the experiences of the actors in any given event and from the perspective(s) of the scholar. To see bodily endeavors as cultural practices requires critical consideration of conceptions of the body in any given circumstance and determination of the relative importance of those conceptions.

To give one brief example, contemporary "traditional" dance in Ghana, by the accounts of its teachers and performers, has more to do with a combination of musical/movement ideas and social ethics than with "the body" as an isolated entity. Ghanaian dance forms share rhythmic patterns and compositional structures with the drums, and this interrelationship of dancers and musicians constitutes both the aesthetic and social core of the event. While certainly the use of the body and the movement style of Ghanaian dance could be analyzed, a conception of "the body" as a distinct part of the person might not be relevant in this case, as it would be for most American dance forms. With Ghanaian dance, one needs to consider how the dancing shapes the perception of individuals as meaningful only when they are in a particular relation to a group, and how sound and movement weave together as separate yet interlocking units. To do so calls for models other than "the body." This caution against automatic transference of our own cultural categories should be exercised as well for other cultures and times.

It is easy to observe that most Americans share a conception of the mind and body as separate and opposed. It is harder, however, to perceive how these themes are embedded in language, action, identifications, and allegiances so familiar as to become natural and unrecognizable. However, if we do not carefully examine how it is we understand "the body" and make use of the term, our discussions of the body's endeavors as cultural practices fail to ask the most important questions. And if we wish to entertain other frameworks, we will have to make conscious, articulated efforts to do so.

NOTES

1. Novack, *Sharing the Dance*, pp. 183–89.
2. Sherry Ortner has written a concise summary of anthropological theory since the sixties in which she suggests that the eighties might be characterized by attention to

two concerns: practice (or praxis, action, interaction, activity, experience, performance) and agent (or actor, person, self, individual, subject). See Ortner, "Theory in Anthropology," p. 144. See also Clifford, *The Predicament of Culture*, and Clifford and Marcus, *Writing Culture*, for discussions of ethnographic writing.

3. Some interesting early examples of anthropological writing about dance include Radcliffe-Brown, *The Andaman Islanders*; Fergusson, *Dancing Gods*; and essays in Boas, *The Function of Dance in Human Society*; and Belo, *Traditional Balinese Culture*.

4. Kurath's articles have been collected in one volume, *Half a Century of Dance Research*. Her numerous books include an extensive analysis of Tewa dance written with Antonio Garcia. See Kurath and Garcia, *Music and Dances*.

5. Kealiinohomoku, "Theory and Methods"; Kaeppler, "Method and Theory"; Youngerman, "Shaking Is No Foolish Play"; and Sweet, *Dances of the Tewa*.

6. See, for example, Spencer's *Society and the Dance*, a collection of essays by British social anthropologists on dance, and the anthology edited by sociologist Helen Thomas.

7. Cowan, *Dance and the Body*; Drewal, *Yoruba Ritual*; Ness, *Body, Movement and Culture*; Novack, *Sharing the Dance*.

LENA HAMMERGREN

Different Personas:
A History of One's Own?

If we turn our interest "inwards," or toward the self of the historian, we can reflect on the idea of different personas as a knowledge-making device for writing history.

The concept of persona is usually linked to the theories of C. G. Jung, who used the term to distinguish between wo/man's masques or roles (personas) and her/his inner self. Jung's persona (note the singular form) is conceived as a relativistic subject in dialogue with its socio-cultural context, expressing itself by means of a language filled with stereotyped phrases (in contrast to the language of dreams and thoughts).

Although we may take issue with Jung's conception of the persona as riddled with clichés and even with his opposition between the persona and a true, inner and unconscious self, we may retain his sense of the persona as a relativistic subject. We can expand on this context-specific notion of the persona using the English author Virginia Woolf. It has been said of Woolf that she conceptualized the individual identity as being in a constant flow, every moment changing its character in reaction to the surrounding forces. The "I" is continuously shaped and reshaped, and the past, in which the identity of the present rests, is never fixed in one form but is as changeable as the mind that recalls it.[1] In other words, Jung's singular, relativistic subject can swiftly be turned into changeable, pluralistic personas.

Different Personas as a Narrative Mode

To use different personas as a narrative mode has a tradition of its own, at least within some literary genres.[2] In this tradition we can distinguish two distinct categories of use: either the different personas are used, by the same author, in different kinds of texts, or the multiple perspectives engendered by the different personas appear within a single text.

A ROMANTIC ANALYST

The former line of action is exemplified by the French nineteenth-century critic and author Théophile Gautier. In his criticism, which is usually referred to as being solely romantic and empathetic in nature, we find an analytic-minded persona when writing about theater performances and quite another when indulging in the erotic atmosphere of beautiful necks and enticing smiles found in ballet performances.[3] To Gautier, the choice of narrative personas was probably axiomatic in nature, where one "simply followed" the implications of existing attitudes closely tied to different modes of art, thereby acknowledging theater as different from dance as painting is from sculpture. Following this line of reasoning, we could speak of each art form having inherent possibilities and limitations concerning the attitude toward them and language used to comment on them and hence the personas capable of interpreting them.

ALTERNATIVE VOICES OR NO SELF

In contrast to Gautier, Virginia Woolf used mobile and pluralistic viewpoints within each specific text. The motive behind this can be interpreted, as Toril Moi has suggested, as a refusal to let herself (Woolf) be identified with any of the many personas in her works.[4] Even her own self is, as in the autobiography *Moments of Being*, divided into at least two: the present and the past selves. She acknowledges these two while trying to find meaning in the past, a meaning that could not have been obvious for the "I" who experienced it.

THE ETHNOGRAPHER'S SELF

Studies of ethnography from the 1960s and 1970s opened up a discussion concerning the role of the researcher and how this role is to be presented in the written account of the research process and its results. Works by ethnographers, for example, Malinowski, show the separation of personas that have traditionally been a characteristic of ethnographers. In a diary, Malinowski reveals his personal antipathy for his informants, a dislike that is absent from his scientific texts.[5] These separated personas, the scientist and the private person, are to a high degree brought together in contemporary ethnography. But ethnographers argue that this union often results in *anxiety* since, in the process of overlapping between the role of the observer and the empathy with the ones observed, the limits of the ego are threatened.[6] This, I would argue, is consonant with looking on the self of the author as a kind of fixed and absolute referential system, a system that engenders anxiety as soon as its harmonious "oneness" is questioned. Problems with research ethics, the Other and the self, are often ventilated in relation to the researcher's existential image of possessing a singular persona that, as in a therapeutical process, struggles toward a fuller understanding of itself. The readers of these texts are thereby presented with a firm perspective from which to judge the world, however obvious it is that the author is struggling with his/her self-reflexivity, often in an almost confessional manner.[7]

This same critique could also be applied to efforts of writing in collaboration, which I would argue typically replicate the image of a unified self. These collaborations often demonstrate that the individual is capable of only one interpretation. Either the authors try to reach a consensus or they each present their version as a complete world within a universe of incompletion. It seems to be up to the reader to personify the miraculous human being who could grasp the juxtaposed views and find meaning in a contradictory world in a manner in which the individual author fails.

Multiple Personas: Viewing the Dancer

Consonant with the discussion above, I want to argue for a new approach to historical research, for an attitude where we put ourselves in the reader's place and try to share with him or her the burden of "putting it all together," while, at the same time, accepting multiple perspectives. How can we, as researchers, picture ourselves changing our personas without faking our point of view and thereby giving an "untrue" interpretation of the historical project at hand? And, even more difficult, how do we let different personas simultaneously form a single account of our results? If not as an answer, at least as inspiration, we can turn toward the dance itself, or rather the dancer as a figure that could guide a response. The very nature of performing as a dancer or of watching a dancer perform, is multidimensional in character and can be used as an image to form a "strategy" for the use of different personas. I look on the "strategy" not so much in terms of a method, but more as a state of mind, a way of inspiring us in reaching out of entrapments imposed on us by the image of a unitary self.

Viewing dance, I accept simultaneously the dancer as a specific person (for example, Anna Pavlova), as a dancer by profession (whose craftsmanship I admire), and as a dying swan (that is, a performance persona), not to mention the images of other "dying swans" that come to my mind. In a successful performance, these personas are united into a whole, but only on one level. At times we do separate these personas—be it tacitly or consciously. But we don't merely separate them, we also simultaneously keep them together. In other words, we accept several dimensions of the dancer without losing track of a possible meaning concerning the phenomenon as such.

Past and Present Personas

Placing the image of the dancer and the viewer alongside Virginia Woolf's concept of the persona, I would suggest that they share a constantly changing series of referential systems, systems that shape and reshape points of view. If we can leave behind our fear of losing control over our subjectivity (and our objectivity) and at the same time forget Jung's singular, relativistic subject, we instead find pluralistic and mobile personas sensitive to the referential systems that surround and confront us. So how can a dance historian turn this into a useful perspective? With a few examples from my own research project on Isadora Duncan and her performances in Sweden, I will highlight some aspects of the use of different personas.

We are dealing here with a period of time during which a certain individual is forming a career that later will be characterized in terms of its pioneering instincts, its originality, and its break with traditional artistic as well as social and moral rules. The individual's name, Isadora Duncan, immediately triggers an awareness of individual genius, of selectedness, of sensing the beginning of a gigantic moment in the history of dance—at the beginning of the flow of events that we call the twentieth-century modern dance tradition. It is not by chance that I've chosen Duncan to support my reasoning. In writing about her I have to face an individual who has already become distinctly located in the history of dance, whose accomplishments have acquired the status of facts, and whose existence in the historical record to date is defined by two kinds of analysis: the chronology of accumulated data concerning her life and work and the eulogistic appraisal of her reputation, emphasizing her influence on hitherto unnoticed dancers. This characterization may appear too limited, but it seems to me to inform the basic options with which I could write about Duncan. In stating the when and where of her appearances in Sweden, I would do no more than accumulate so-called data, out of which the conventional telling of the results (that is, influences) could be used to introduce and publicize a Swedish dance community unknown to the rest of the world. But what if, instead, I "use her" as the starting point for reflections of a historiographical nature involving past and present personas.

INTIMACY AND DISTANCE

Most historians who have written about Duncan—her beliefs, loves, work, and influence on others—share an awareness of her as someone who has played an outstanding role in the history of dance. They assume a perspective in which the "I" of their analytical attitude (and of their texts) is placed at a distance from the historical moment they are interpreting. Well, isn't this always the case in writing history? *We* are of another time than *they* are, and the difference in time gives us access to answers, solutions, effects, etc. If, however, we look into the research process itself, we discover how we occasionally try to free ourselves from the "now" in order to move to the core of how it "was" or could have been. The act of trying to leave our "now" behind us places the "I" of the researcher in an intimate relation to the historical moment.

Applying this to Duncan, I could write about her by assuming the persona of the viewer watching her perform in Östermalmsteatern (the theater at Östermalm) in Stockholm during the spring of 1906.[8] As a result of assuming this interpretive position, I might disregard anything happening after that particular evening, especially insofar as it concerns the notion of Duncan as an imperative influence on the future. This orientation would break with a teleological historical view, where the end justifies the means in reconstructing history. The persona acknowledging Duncan's imperative power can move backwards and forwards in time, with an underlying credo of knowing the direction the events point toward. With this approach it becomes inevitable that each event will be analyzed in order to fit the evaluative frame that is constructed from the very beginning.

Historians have sometimes tried to tack back and forth between perspectives of intimacy and distance in an attempt to mediate between past and present, but this has typically resulted in the distancing approach overshadowing the one of intimacy. There are numerous examples of this in dance research. In reconstructing historical dances, dance researchers have appealed to corsets, voluminous wigs, and textiles made using historical weaving techniques in order to help the dancer shift into another persona. This persona, with the help of these tactile "tools," can experience the movement style of a specifically restricted body. Later, the impressionistic result of this shift is used in order to help form a chronological account of changes in dancing techniques (where the dominant perspective is one of distance). These research projects are of great interest, but do not preclude other ways of presenting the research process and its results: ways in which the shifting of personas is used to comment as much upon what the historian presents as how it is presented, thereby chronologizing the kinds of "I's" involved in the interpretive process.

Juxtaposed Selves

And what if we allow the different personas to remain juxtaposed against one another with no attempt to reconcile them? In such a text, the reader would shift among different kinds of approaches and accept whatever ambiguities surface. The ambiguities would immediately signal problems concerning the coherence of the history being written. After Foucault, we are, however, able to speak of "events" or of histories as displacing one another like chains of epistemic islands, but what about our-*selves* as they become involved in mapping out these islands? By asking this question, we can begin to reach new understandings of what coherency means, the different shapes it can and should be allowed to take.

In my own research on Duncan, one of the most intriguing ambiguities to surface has framed the issue of individual identity in terms of national versus international personas. Both Duncan and Gordon Craig (who followed her on the Scandinavian tour) tried repeatedly to invite the Swedish author August Strindberg to watch her perform, but he refused, stating that he would not be involved in any seductive attempts from Duncan. Her offer to place him in a latticed box and her appeal that he look at her with a man's eye were described by Strindberg as a rape, a violent action where the gender roles were reversed.[9] As encountered by an international persona, this story registers merely as a funny anecdote of secondary importance, perhaps emphasizing the image of Strindberg's misogynist character rather than reflecting on Duncan and her behavior. From a national persona's perspective, Strindberg's manners could be contextualized as a reaction to audience responses in Copenhagen, where the male viewers left their wives at home and brought their opera glasses to take a closer look at Duncan.[10] To a Swede, this is both an important "meeting," a confrontation between two, equally important historical celebrities, and an event highlighting differences in regard to gender, art forms, cultural and moral values, Swedish and foreign temperament, ideas of the body, etc. It is obvious to me that the national perspective gives reason to deal with a different set of components than the international perspective, and that this is obvious because I juxtapose the two. The point is that with this interpretative attitude we accept that this particular event becomes *both* peripheral and crucial to the story.

My Duncan project could perhaps become surrealistic. It could separate things that belong together, it could unite disparate events, use temporal movements, and mix "fact and fiction," that is, consciously juxtapose different narrative strategies. Using the perspectives of juxtaposing different personas, I could allow myself a genuinely positivistic approach, describing in detail the place where she was performing, and I could also adopt a more phenomenological approach that would enable me to account for how I, in this particular place, experience her body and movements in relation to an image of my own body and movement "personifying" the spectator of that time. (This strategy becomes more dramatic when one is confronted with architectural, costuming, or technological elements of dance productions as foreign to us as those of the authentic eighteenth-century court theater at Drottningholm on the outskirts of Stockholm. To enter this space, with its harmonious unity of auditorium and stage and its soft, flickering and equally spread lights, gives one a distinct kinesthetic feeling of how one can move and how one can experience one's own body as well as others; the distinctiveness of this kinesthetic surrounding in comparison with the space of a contemporary theater is enormous.) To assume this past persona involves trying to discern the bodily disposition of the viewer, especially insofar as it helps form attitudes toward the feminine body. When I first started this line of investigation, I thought that I would find a more or less outspoken conflict between the restricted body in the auditorium and the liberated body on stage (with regard to costume, social etiquette, style of ballroom and theatrical dancing, movement conventions in theater performances, the disciplining kinesthetics of the auditorium, etc.)[11] But the conflict was more ambiguous than I had expected. The male journalist Boo Hjärne found Duncan's dancing beautiful, but, as he wrote, so pure and chaste that a poor sinner longed for some sensuousness, without which dance becomes too monotonous.[12] A group of young women from the Swedish school of physical education were enthusiastic, but did not, as far as Duncan thought, grasp the deeper meaning of the dancing, trained as they were to use a static and objectified body aiming toward a bodily fitness.[13] Neither party seemed to commune with her about the idea of the body as a vibrating source of energies where nudity becomes neither erotic/exotic nor a sign of a healthy mind in a healthy body.[14] But Duncan herself is ambiguous with regard to her "true" approach to the dancing body. Her biography tells a different story than her "sexist" appeal to Strindberg, which can be interpreted as if she was trying to exchange services with him through the means of her art, that is, her body (and by so doing giving her lover Craig a better chance to meet with Strindberg, with whom he wanted to work). So, in effect, my idea of a liberated body on stage seems to take on different meanings with every new perspective I encounter.

Acknowledging differences as the focus and starting with the notion of Duncan as a pioneer, I could juxtapose this attitude with a "deconstructive" approach, where her "winning" originality becomes reinterpreted as conflicting ideas of feminine and masculine images and of theatrical and social conventions. Here there might be no winners at all, except the ones who are supposed to indulge in pastries during intermissions and those who puff on their pipes and drink Swedish punch. During this time we often find both sexes enjoying themselves socially during intermissions, but in separate theater cafés (indeed, a change from the late-nineteenth-century conventions, when men could relax, drink beer, and eat sandwiches, while women stayed in their seats and listened to entr'acte music). The ways in which intermissions are spent might get a more prominent position than Duncan's dancing in this part of the Duncan history. This raises questions concerning how we are to understand Duncan as a phenomenon, reflecting back on our needs to give her different roles. If we still need to consider her a pioneer, is it as an innovator of dancing techniques; a clever "cross-gendered" manipulator; an example of a radically new femininity; an innocent "prisoner" confined in a web of habits, discourses, social and economical relationships; or simply an ideal for those of us who can't resist cream teas (since she was rather plump when performing in Stockholm)?

The perspective of different personas can make us understand that, even for so-called scientific research, the past and the present continuously and actively insinuate themselves into one another, resulting in an elusive identity both in regard to the "I" of the text and to the history of which it is speaking. In accepting this elusiveness and the multiplicity of our personas, we can also get a different sense of context-oriented studies, where it becomes not only a question of which context we choose to examine, but also of how *we change* together with the context. Discerning, and perhaps even disciplining, these changes reveals the false nature of a binary opposition between objective and subjective perspectives, an opposition founded on perceiving the author as being either the authority of a text or completely absent from it. In an intriguing fashion we are both and thereby neither. The making of history is and yet is not our "own" doing.

NOTES

1. See Woolf, *Ögonblick av Liv* (*Moments of Being*). These comments are made by Jeanne Schulkind in the postscript.

2. An extreme version of this is when we have a multi-authored text being attributed to an individual. See Montaigne, *Journal de voyage*, where two personas join together under the name of Montaigne. About half of the text is written by an anonymous scribe who refers to Montaigne in the third person. Cf. the unidentified authors of Domenica da Piacenza's *De arte saltandi et choreas ducendi* (from about 1416). In *The Alexandria Quartet*, Lawrence Durrell expands his story by introducing different personas, each giving their version of and changing the story. In an essay on theater autobiographies, Thomas Postlewait has remarked that the narrative "I" can be divided into three different personas. He also notes that the earlier self may well be a stranger to the author, who is trying to unify and make coherent the development of his or her own career. See Postlewait, "Autobiography and Theatre History," pp. 248–72.

3. Robert Snell remarks that although Gautier's prose embodies accurate descriptions and contains the seeds of a scientific, positivistic, documentary approach, "it was for the aptness and wit of his more subjective, poetic responses" that he became famous

among his contemporary readers. See Snell, *Théophile Gautier*, p. 213. A close reading of Gautier's theater and dance criticism certainly suggests varying approaches instead of a single subjective and evocative modus operandi. See, for example, Gautier's *Histoire de l'Art Dramatique*.

4. Moi, *Sexual/Textual Politics*, p. 8. In Moi's opinion, it's also clear that Woolf's rejection of a unified self has led to difficulties among feminist critics to appreciate her writing because they can't transform her works into singularly feminist texts.

5. Malinowski, *Diary in the Strict Sense*. Several ethnographers have staged this personality "split" by writing conventional dissertations and later publishing texts where they comment on their professional and personal personas. See, for example, works by Jean-Paul Dumont and Manda Cesara (the latter a pseudonym).

6. See Devereux, *From Anxiety to Method*.

7. The firm perspective does not necessarily have to be a more or less outspoken unity. It can just as well be a fixed duality between the scientific and the personal, manifested, for example, in questioning the scientific character of one's own text. An example of this is Barbara Myerhoff, who worries about her oscillation between being scholarly and personal in *Number Our Days*.

8. Using such a persona wouldn't mean giving way to "total subjectivism." Within reception theory with a historical orientation, one speaks of finding a specific disposition of an audience, which is thought possible to determine empirically. See Carlson, "Theatre Audiences," pp. 82–98.

9. Engström, *August Strindberg och Jag* (*August Strindberg and Myself*), pp. 39–40.

10. Mørk, "Husk Mig for Min Kunst," (*Remember Me for My Art*).

11. The kinesthetic effects that the Östermalmsteatern in particular provides are sketchy, since the theater burned down in 1913. The theater was built in a contemporary fashion and situated within an Oriental-like circus building. The framing of one's expectations might have been that of pleasure tinged with exoticism, but still restricted if one bears in mind how one would enter the narrow aisles while keeping the arms close to the body and sit down close together in strictly arranged rows. Contrary to this, the open space on the other side of the proscenium arch will be filled with flowing arm movements, soft body curves, a woman skipping around and lunging down—movement patterns foreign to a "natural" social etiquette and even to the contemporary conventions of the different theatrical genres.

12. Hjärne, "Isadora Duncan," p. 6.

13. Duncan, *Mitt Liv*, p. 154.

14. Duncan, *Mitt Liv*, p. 154.

Embodying Theory

SUE-ELLEN CASE

Meditations on the Patriarchal Pythagorean Pratfall and the Lesbian Siamesian Two-Step

Quem quaeritis?

The *Quem quaeritis* is often figured as the site for the rebirth of theater in the medieval period in Europe. It is from the Easter morning service, which opens with those lines "Whom seek ye?" asked by the priest to choirboys representing the three Marys who have come for Christ in his tomb. Institutional theater, then, reemerges, after church censorship for several centuries, at the site of the vanished body—the empty tomb, where women remain to seek the male body that is now beyond bodily limits. The permission for performance is granted at the site of an interrogation that registers the transcendence of the male body into bodiless meaning meaning and where women wait, seek, and watch—women represented by young, singing boys. This was, then, and remains, a trope for performance itself. The sublime male body vanishes and in its vanishing becomes transcendent, while the bodies that perform are somehow displayed, and depreciated at once: caught up in sleights of cross-gender gestures in which women are also absent, but represented as remaining.

"Whom seek ye?" is an appropriate question for the stage, along with what that empty tomb represents. The dying body, which provokes intimations of immortality, haunts Eurocentric performance and philosophical systems from the dying Socrates through Christ, through Senecan death sentiments which continue into the Renaissance, through the body in pain in the Jacobean era, through Samuel Beckett's works to (here I beg your indulgence for a few pages) Jerry Lewis. The trope trick remains pretty much the same as in the *Quem quaeritis*. In her article "Therefore, Socrates Is Immortal," Nicole Loraux works it out as the dynamic between Plato's interested account of Socrates's death and the Platonic insistence upon essences:

> But if we have thereby been led to the paradox of a body rejected, depreciated
> and banished, yet more present than ever. . . . If it is Socrates' memorable

body that also constitutes a memorial, that makes us believe in the survival of his soul. . . . what are we to do with that body of Socrates. . . . the soul is immortal, but that immortality is upheld chiefly by the memorial that was Socrates' unforgettable body.[1]

This is what Herbert Blau, in his book on performance and meaning, calls Blooded Thought. The representation of the body in pain, the body representing the agonizing limits of the body, incites abstract meaning. Death is performed as the interrogation of life. Where the body gives way to abstraction, yet reinscribes itself in its swan song of corporeal semiosis, is where the inscription of the meaning of performance occurs. Blau notes that not only is meaning inscribed in performance through the representation of the dying body, but also in the actual dying of the "live" performer as [he] acts: "When we speak of what Stanislavski called Presence in acting, we must also speak of its Absence, the dimensionality of time through the actor, the fact that he who is performing can die there in front of your eyes; is in fact doing so."[2] "Live" performers move through "real time" toward their deaths as they perform, in contradistinction to performance in film or other technological media. Thus, Blau asks: "What is the theatre but the body's long initiation in the mystery of its vanishings?" (p. 299). He reiterates the priestly incantation of *Quem quaeritis* in hermeneutic language.

Habeas Corpus

If dying is represented and transcendent absence is the catalyst of meaning, how does the body perform it? What are the disciplines of the body for such production and how are they meaningful? This performance technique might be called the pathos of the patriarchal Pythagorean. Pythagoras, if not providing an originary moment, at least provides an enduring metaphor: the use of the taut string to sound out music and meaning at once. Pythagoras is the figure of plucking the taut string to yield sound, dividing the string to display the octave, to produce ratio, and thereby the sciences of harmonics and mathematics while performing music—all culled from the taut string. In other words, the taut line, when divided, is a discipline that will yield art and science at once. The taut line is the vehicle of abstraction in performance which provides the technique required to render death and transcendence. Nietzsche wrote the *agon* for the Apollonian lyre against the Dionysian *aulos* in his *Birth of Tragedy*: stringed sense against blown ecstasy. The taut line of meaning extends metaphorically into the body in the taut muscle, the sense that muscles *work* to produce meaning. Hence, the effective male, or more precisely (though contingent) the masculine muscular body, represents effective work. Pumping iron to get "in shape" to perform.

Likewise, the lines of blocking, given to the actors from the director, chart the meaning of the text into the placement of gesture and motion through the abstraction of line. Bertolt Brecht saw blocking as locus of the social, political sense of the drama. The body, then, producing through muscles, following the blocking (or choreography) "projects" (as it is called) meaning. The performing, masculine body is caught in a web of lines that comprises a safety net: the net holds it safely over the extreme of dying, suspends it *en abyme*. This is the high-wire act of semiosis.

In the twentieth century, this act becomes the patriarchal Pythagorean prat-fall. The overdetermination of the cultural codes of masculinity, playing along with the tortured ambivalences of value determination, have created the con-torted body that displays the excruciating convections of the Pythagorean lines. As the lines pierce the body and intersect there, body and meaning become locked in a fierce struggle to produce what might be a stillborn semiosis. For ex-ample, the contorted body in Expressionist acting: Think of Caligari in *The Cabinet of Dr. Caligari*, with the turned-in feet and knees, the restricted steps, the taut neck, or in Kokoschka's *Job*, with his head twisted agonizingly to one side. Lines are painted on the actors' faces, proliferate in the *Mise-en-scène*. Meaning is inscribed everywhere on the diagonal, in the twisted line—as if it will not yield, or is so conflicted in its modes of production that it cannot yield (meaning). As Samuel Beckett wrote it, meaning might or might not eventually come (GODOT) in a performance tradition where the pratfall lasts forever. Beckett's characters constantly fail to produce masculinity or meaning and are the victims of lines that shoot through them from the outside to contort them into a near-stasis. They move agonizingly, but get nowhere. His first novel, *Watt*, begins with a long description of the walk of the title character:

> Watt's way of advancing due east, for example, was to turn his bust as far as possible towards the north and at the same time fling out his right leg as far as possible to the south, and then turn his bust as far as possible towards the south and at the same time fling out his left leg as far as possible towards the north. . . .

Watt's comic double is Jerry Lewis, or the postmodern Lewis, Pee Wee Herman, with the strained, high voice, turned-in feet and knees: the contorted masculine body. The strained muscles turn against themselves, break down, fail to produce meaning/masculinity. When the body fails to produce the requisite transcendence it remains a feminized presence, like the choir boys as Marys or the lipsticked, powder-faced Pee Wee.

Insofar as women's bodies are represented and read in this economy of the production of performance meaning, they are cross-gender cast, either literally, as in the *Quem quaeritis*, classical Greek theater, Shakespeare, or figuratively, as Teresa de Lauretis has written it as sexual (in)difference in representation. De Lauretis, working off David Halperin, allies the production of women by men in the system of representation with the production of sexual difference and hetero-sexuality.[3] The lesbian body in performance can neither transcend nor take the pratfall. Although she can't altogether escape the Pythagorean net, she isn't strung out on it. She refuses to wait for the sublime, male body at the tomb. "Whom do you seek?" is here replaced with "What do lesbians do together?" with the full effect of that question, which implies "what could they possibly do?" Permission to perform not granted. As de Lauretis configures her, the lesbian body in representation is invisible, or only shimmers in visibility before her masculine, heterosexual contradiction. As I have argued elsewhere, hers is the vampire body, visible only through the precision of its proscription.[4] The question remains: How can this body perform when it has no permission?

We Are Siamese If You Don't Please

The lesbian body, defined by its desire, is always two bodies. Ulrike Ottinger's lesbian film *Freak Orlando* is ridden with twins. It concludes with Siamese sisters as the love object. They share their bodily systems. Biologically, they image mutual penetration in an enduring way. These are bodies that do not project, but simultaneously interject into one another. Perhaps this provides a further development of Susan McClary's idea of the chromatic crunch as the sexual in *Carmen*[5]—too close for diatonic comfort. These bodies represent a kind of Siamesian semiosis.

Monique Wittig imaged this mutual penetration in a more violent way in her novel *The Lesbian Body*. Although her j/e, shot through with the diagonal, seems to suggest the Expressionist *agon* described above, it is more like the Siamese twins in Ottinger. The pleasures of interpenetration yield a body that means in the internal organs—subcutaneously read:

THE AREOLAS THE ECCHYMOSES
THE WOUNDS THE FOLDS THE
GRAZES THE WRINKLES THE
BLISTERS THE FISSURES THE
SWELLINGS THE SUNBURN THE
BEAUTY-SPOTS THE BLACKHEADS. . . .
NERVE NETWORKS THE NERVE-
ROOTS THE BUNDLES THE
BRANCHES THE PLEXUSES THE
MOTOR NERVES THE SENSORY THE
CERVICAL THE PNEUMOGASTRIC (53)

What does this imply, then, about the old taut string? The body that projects? Of course, one might see the presumption of an audience, for which this is all necessary, a primarily patriarchal assumption. What earlier lesbian feminists configured as the intimacy of the domestic becomes the intimacy of the interpenetrated body. Who's performing and who's the recipient?

I foresee a kind of *Road Warrior*–version of performance in the future: The patriarchal body will have technologically transcended into what is called virtual reality, or cyberspace, completely digitally abstracted and scopically surrounded. All systems GO. Meanwhile, back below the shredding ozone, in which space cannot be defined as performance space/stage/the-marked-off because the atmosphere itself is unstable and polluted, two bag l/adies, joined at the ————, alone together, in a world in which reading and writing went down when the

VDTs went dark, do, what, when my mother used to yell at me in my bedroom "Sue-Ellen, what are you and Judith doing in there," I would answer "nothing."

NOTES

1. Loraux, "Therefore, Socrates Is Immortal," pp. 38–39.
2. Blau, *Take up the Bodies*, p. 83.
3. See de Lauretis, "Sexual Indifference and Lesbian Representation," pp. 17–39.
4. See my "Tracking the Vampire," pp. 1–17.
5. McClary, *Feminine Endings*, pp. 56–57.

PEGGY PHELAN

Thirteen Ways of Looking at *Choreographing Writing*

Preface: What are the forms of writing that will allow us to hold the moving body? The moving body is always fading from our eyes. Historical bodies and bodies moving on stage fascinate us because they fade. Our own duration is measured by our ability to witness this fading; writing is one way of measuring that duration.[1]

Language contains within it an intimate anthropomorphism. Buried within our most routine speech is a quiet anatomy of the body. Always uncertain about the boundaries of bodies we bury and revive in a constant dance of mapping (cartography), e-rasing (holography), and re-membering (scenography). This text highlights the ways in which we do and do not face these bodies. "Thirteen Ways" graphs some of the point(e)s around which figurations of physical, lexical, and historical bodies are composed.

About-face: (Nietzsche: "The most essential question of any text is its back question.")

In the tiny space created between the back and the face, the slender spine holds the book of writing. Its location has a built-in blind spot: It is as impossible to write oneself as it is to see oneself. Writing allows one to name others but the writer seeks always some other voice to call her name, later—after her face and hand have faded. (This is the premise of the Christian Bible. If the Book of Life includes your name, you'll be in heaven. Otherwise, it's off to hell. Hell is name-lessness, and eternal pain is defined as perpetual suspension between a signifier and a referent. That's why, as Christopher Marlowe, Mel Brooks, and Jacques Derrida all conclude, this life is hell.) Writing the names of others, one hopes others will read, someday, one's own name. History writing trembles and travels around the asymmetry of temporality: The historian writes of the past for a future reader. (Economies of time, of psychic desire, and of knowledge are never reciprocal, one-to-one arrangements; exchanges between two subjects always involve the agency of a third. This is immediately clear in the founding principle of credit card companies.)

To write of "choreographing history" then is to consider again the agency of this "third"—the currency through which the exchange takes place. This third is the field of graphing, the field of writing. Like any graph, it is composed of numbers and signs. Implicit within the graph is a code of reading, a way of pre/ perceiving the relation between the value and interest of each term. The numbers of this graph can be mapped horizontally and vertically, north and south, in Roman headers and Arabic footnotes.

I. Photo-graphy

Face To Face: In the presence of one another, direct communication, they say, is possible.

Portrait photography writes the image of the body with light. After the camera takes its shot, the model's body disappears into the negative. What gets exposed after the chemical bath is the visual "prop" of the model's body: This prop stands in for the "real" body and defines it as a visual property—his and hers. We recognize Cindy Sherman by her disguise; the thin black whip snaking out of the print is how we know Robert Mapplethorpe.

Proposition one: the corporeal body can only be represented through the prop, the hook where the viewer's eye interprets the image as body, an image "owned" by the being, who, in turn, is said to "own" that body. (Roland Barthes: "If only Photography could give me a neutral, anatomic body, a body which signifies nothing! Alas I am doomed by (well-meaning) Photography to have an expression: my body never finds its zero degree. . .")[2] Precisely because bodies cannot have zero-degrees they are inscribed in an economy of exchange whose root value is registered in the syntax of possession. From pornographic prose ("I lent him my body") to sacred scripture ("This is my body, take and eat"), writing the body presupposes a vocabulary of secure possession, an ethics of choice (if only to register the violence of its betrayal), and a solid line that securely connects bodies and beings.

Like the physical body, the textual body also always registers an expression. Borrowing the words of others and other words, writers (re)produce documents that bear the proper name of the author(s). Rummaging through the history of other people's language—what scholars call research, citations, footnotes, and bibliographies—historians interpret history. The soil of used words which stains the page compose the author's prop/er name. Brockett's Theater History, Foucault's History of Sexuality, Shakespeare's Histories as Interpretations of Holinshed's *Chronicles*, Ernest Jones's and Peter Gay's Histories of Freud, Linda Brent's and Frederick Douglass's Histories of Slavery. The proper name, like the proper subject and the proper body, needs to be continually rewritten. If the link between names and referents, beings and bodies, were certain, writing and representation would be redundant. In writing of Freud, perhaps Gay hoped to see how Freud might have written (of) him. In my writing of Gay, perhaps he sees how he might be read. Such textual-temporal layering, like the achronological layering of psychic time, involves a model of writing that can be read both forward and backward, face to back, up and down. As Gregory Ulmer put it, "The model for a writing which goes beyond juxtaposition to superimposition is not collage but photography."[3] Such graphing knows that all development (psychic, historical, stylistic, sexual) requires a good negative.

The void in the center of the most vital eye is portrait photography's truest model. As Susan Sontag and Roland Barthes everywhere remind us, the photograph, in developing the image of the model, shows us the moment that has faded, the death and disappearance of that particular configuration of subjectivity frozen by the camera. The moment effaced and washed in the chemical bath frames the passage of time's measured light across the surface of the print. When the light stops the image is arrested, fixed, fully developed. No longer fluid and moving, the image "dies" in order to be seen. Writing "dies" when it is bound in books, revised, proofed, and published. To push against this arrest, writing needs to expose again the movement of the negative. Writing, like photography, covers over and thereby recovers what is not there—historically, psychically, imagistically, performatively.

II. Autobio-graphy

Inter/Face: *In sewing, the disappearing prop which holds the collar stiff.*

Q: What do you know about choreography?

A: I almost went to the International Dance Conference in Hong Kong to speak about cross-cultural dance. But then I couldn't. I was ill. An infection in my left eye passed the blood-brain barrier. A threshold crossing. Every hour for eight days I was asked who the president was. If I had been in Eastern Europe, I would have flunked. But since the answer is always the same in the United States, I passed. On the third attempt to save my eye, the doctor placed a small piece of porcine tissue on the surface of my cornea. He wore gloves and pushed the pig skin in while I lay on the bed, both eyes open. On his forehead he wore a big bright light, like a miner. His illuminated eye squinted into my blind eye. An eye for an eye: The Bible does not list the curative properties of pig skin. Peggy's eye glued together with/in a pig's eye.

The doctors told me I could not go to Hong Kong. They were uncertain about what the change in the air pressure in the airplanes would do to my eye. They could not tell what I would be able to see. They wanted to watch me see what I could see close to home. I stayed to save my eye. And so I did not watch the Hong Kong dance go by.[4]

Proposition two: Doctors are the contemporary critics of the undecidable body-text. They read symptoms that often can only be measured through disappearance, the vanishing visual field, for example, the way historians read traces of presence in ruins. Doctors measure symptoms through recourse to histories—histories of the rate of the disease's progress in many bodies, not the patient's "own." Employing those histories as their frame, they look at the current patient's body. This medicalized body (the doctor's body) is composed of separate organs, tissues, bones, and blood, whereas the patient's body (her "own" body) is composed of pains, pleasures, and peaceful pauses from each.

For doctors, bodies are "typical," or "atypical." For patients, bodies are unstable but deeply desired possessions which, like erotic relations, are given to betrayals and failures. Contemporary diseases are progressive, and again like erotic relations, often subject to retreats, remissions, repetitions. Doctors use medical histories the way butchers use scales. But since the human living body is closer to the quantum than to a dead pig, these measurements, historical and projected, can only be uncertain.

Q: What about the body is uncertain?

A: Its health.

III. Sceno-graphy

Facetious: Jocular and playful. *In my memory, her face seems to me always facetious.*

> Comic [to me] interlude: Yesterday in New York walking down Mercer, near N.Y.U. A large man with a deep voice, leather jacket, bald head says to his thin, shivering, younger companion. "There's a biography of Heisenberg called *Uncertainty*." Long pause, shivering companion waits silently. Older man continues, "It's very detailed."

Proposition three: Uncertainty is detailed, absolutely—this much is certain. As we know from crime, medicine, and history, details increase uncertainty. The relation between her body and her being is uncertain, subject to doubt. (Lacan: "Doubt is a defense against the Real.") Just as we have learned to speak so easily about "the hole in the signifier," the failure of language to convey meaning exactly, we are beginning to learn to speak of "the hole in the body," the failure of corporeality to convey being exactly. But living as if one's body is not continuous with one's being is more painful than living as if one's words are only approximations of meaning. (Blanchot: "The danger [is] that the disaster acquire meaning instead of body.")[5]

Q: Is the body meaningless? Why does Blanchot say "meaning **instead of** body"?

A: We cannot know *what* the body means—but that does not mean the body is meaningless. It does mean that there is always mistranslation, misrecognition, misalignment, between meanings and bodies, between beings and bodies.

Q: What is uncertain about the body?

A: Its relation to its home/owner.

IV. Holo-graphy

Face-Off: In knock-hockey and ice hockey the game begins when the puck is released between two opposing players.

Q: What does this have to do with choreographing history?

A: I hate direct questions. Can I tell a story instead?

Q: I'm afraid not. The time is almost up.

A: I'll be very brief.

Q: I'm sorry, but we really do need to conclude and you have not offered an answer to the question.

A: Lacan says we can only offer what we do not have. We mime for the other what we think the other wants, so that the other will show us what we desire. Our desire is always the other's interpretation of it.

Q: I only want an answer to the question at hand.

A: Turn it over? Lacan would say you want my answer only to confirm your own. So perhaps, in the interest of time, you should just say what your answer is.

Q: I think the answer has something to do with finding a way to write that mirrors the subject of history, the subject of the always-moving body in always-moving history.

A: But mirroring is a term from mimetic theory, from a notion of the real—as in the "realist" novels of Flaubert; the "realism" of plays like *The Heidi Chronicles* or *Lost in Yonkers;* the cinema verité of *Daughter-Rite*. It comes from Aristotle for heaven's sake! Realism has often been associated with conservative politics, with consolidating the normative theater of "everyday life." (Sue-Ellen Case: "Cast the realism aside—its consequences for women are deadly.")[6] Are you sure you want historiography to find a way to *mirror* its subject?

Proposition four: The one who questions often invokes the rules of the institution (the state, the university, the magazine policy, the clock) as a way to accent the apparently unequal power relations operative between the speaker/questioner, the interviewed/interviewer. While appearing to be subordinate to the one who answers, interrogators are almost always in positions of enormous, although often concealed, power. The invocation of rules, as here about the limited time, function as theatrical props that index the real through which the illusionary drama is judged.

V. Steno-graphy

Bold Face: A printer's term to describe dramatic **type** face. A courageous speech act might be called a bold-faced lie.

Q: Look, I'm not sure of anything. I was just offering an answer to see if I could discover yours. Besides, mirroring has been used as a subversive form of mimicry. Michele Wallace suggests that African Americans use mimicry as a way of transvaluing racial oppositions; Irigaray argues that women within phallocentric culture and language can use mimicry as a way of resisting the reproduction of the Self-Same, the *homo-sexual* labor of metaphor and cultural exchange.[7]

A: But now we've lost the relation to choreographing history, haven't we?

Q: I'm not sure. I thought you were going to speak about the invisible, unmarked kernel of the body's identity, and of the misrecognitions that compose history (and) writing. But I guess you are sick of making these arguments by now?

A: An accelerated and exhausted version: In all forms of representations of the body—from portrait photography to historical dance reconstructions—the body in question seems to make an appearance, then it definitely disappears, and is then re-presented. History and writing are constituted from and by that disappearance. Moreover, this disappearance *suspends* the proprietary relation between body and being. In its journey from disappearance to representation, the body does not "belong" to the subject who wears it, who dances in and through it, who is sick within and through it, who models within and through it. Rather the represented body comes into Being as it is apprehended within the frame of the representation. In that apprehension, the prop of the body (the "supplement"), is seized/seen and taken *to be* "the body." These props in dance are called "movement signatures," in portraiture "characteristic gestures," in medicine "the progress of the disease," in psychoanalysis "revealing symptoms" which define subjectivity. History writing traces the motivations, technologies, and discursive possibilities that inform these apprehensions.

Proposition five: The suspension of the proprietary relation between body and being allows us to see the noncontinuity of the body's history itself. Insofar as all apprehension of the body is representational, this suspended separation is inevitable—but often unbearable. The job of (historical) interpretation is to secure and reestablish the proprietary relation between beings and bodies. Such interpretations can only be contingent and impermanent because the suspension is reframed each time a new technological or discursive possibility emerges. This is why we keep writing histories of the same periods . . . and also why psychoanalysis, erotic relations, and historiography can never be said to end, to possess a terminal point. In this sense, all three write against the sentence's dying fall . . .

VI. Historio-graphy

Efface: To erase or obliterate someone or something. Women, they say, often efface themselves in the presence of men. Some say men often efface women. Historically, on the face of it, both appear to be true. Effacement, this fading, is integral to history's movement. It is woven into the movement syntax of history's choreography.

Q: In writing history, one engages in a restaging of the disappeared. But what has disappeared is both "the subject" of history (for example, World War I) and the historical subject's relation to that history. Historians offer their writing as compensation for that loss. Words can be accepted as substitutes for missing bodies because words are themselves the shells of missing bodies. What they convey is the disappearance of the thing they re-present. Naturally, this is all unbearable.

Proposition six: The traditional psycho-political burden of history writing has been to efface the double disappearance signaled by both history and writing as such. This is accomplished by reestablishing a proprietary relation to the historical subject—"Blanchot's history of disaster"—in which both the historian and the historical subject exist in a representational frame that can be apprehended, possessed, understood. What disappears is the uncertainty and doubt about the possibility of such possession. What disappears is the devastating force of disappearance.[8]

A: So we can see then that traditional history writing resuscitates the proprietary desire lurking in all representation *and* continually rewrites *that*.

Q: I'm not sure I understand. It seems terribly abstract.

A: Perhaps now I can tell my story?

Q: OK. Maybe we'll just push the time a little bit.

VII. Choreo-graphy

Multi-faceted: Having many faces and aspects.

A: Good. Now, of course, it's not really *my* story. It's Yvonne Rainer's. In the late sixties she and other members of the Grand Union were trying to present dance as *neutral* movement, trying to create spectacles of movement rather than shrines to display movers. The Grand Union made dances in which people literally moved mattresses across a loft and dances in which people simply walked. In 1975, however, Rainer, reflecting on her history, recognized something that had faded from her earlier eyes: "I wrote that one can't 'do' a *grand jeté,* one has to 'dance' it. Well, neither can one 'do' a walk without investing it with character. One of the reasons [Steve Paxton's] walking people were so effective was that the walk was so simply and astonishingly 'expressive of self.'"[9]

I like the story because it insists that the representational frame, "dance," always invites an interpretation of the activity, "moving," "walking." Just as Barthes discovers no photograph can free him of expression and frame his body at zero degree, so too does Rainer discover that there is no such thing as a "neutral," expressionless movement *within* the frame of dance. The fact that modern Western dance is always indexed back to the dancer is more than the logical proof of the intractability of Yeats's echoing questioning, "O body swayed to music, O brightening glance, / How can we know the dancer from the dance?" and more a symptom of the desire to use the body of the other as a mirror *and* a screen for one's own g/lancing body. And my own clichéd repetition of Yeats's poem is another index of the past's inability to stay there.

Q: What do you mean when you say "the desire to use the body of the other as a mirror and a screen"?

A: Oh, that's Lacan again, accelerated.

Q: What does it mean?

A: One must detour through the eyes of the other to see oneself. (This is the commonplace explanation of the desire for history writing.) Self-seeing can only be accomplished through seeing the other in terms of the self and through seeing the self in terms of the other. Thus, self-seeing is always misrecognition, distortion, nonmimetic. That's why I was so impatient with your idea about thinking of historiography as an attempt to mirror the subject transparently. Historiography employs the other subject/time in order both to mirror AND screen the contemporary subject/time.

Proposition seven: But writers can only be "external" to the written narrative, which creates other problems—psychic, political, and historical.

VIII. Ethno-graphy

Face Up To: To confront bravely something one would rather not.

Q: How can you propose that the writer can only be "external" to the written text? That's not true at all. There has been an extraordinary amount of new writing that explicitly locates the writer within the account—especially in ethnography and anthropology.

A: The "self-reflexive" pose in contemporary ethnographic and anthropological writing attempts to equalize the inequitable power-knowledge relation that adheres between the object and subject of knowledge. But it cannot be equal. It must be faced.

Proposition eight: The writer cannot be her own subject because she writes seeking a response to what her subjectivity *is*. There is no secure subjectivity from which writing (or movement) emerges.[10]

A: This new writing disguises and distracts one from the central dilemma.

Q: Which is?

IX. Holo-graphy Redux

Face Out: To endure until the end.

A: The gaze cannot see the one who employs it; the gaze promises mastery but shows the world without oneself. The radically progressive project, then, is not the pursuit of some "reflexive" dialogue, but rather the admission of the failure of self-seeing and the absolute *contingency* that such a central failure implies for a relation to the representational—which is to say, for a relation to the Real.[11] The point is not where to "locate" the writer, but rather to admit that the writer cannot be located within the other subject s/he seeks. This is the radical challenge facing contemporary historians.

Q: Oh God, this is standard Lacanian stuff. I didn't know you were so invested in him—a dead, white, European man?

A: I am and I am not. As for the fact that Lacan is a dead, white, European man—surely this is a ridiculous barometer to measure the political utility of someone's ideas. If the back-face of your question betrays impatience with psychoanalysis as a critical method, I can only suggest that we face the question directly. Psychoanalysis is one method among many: It has a reputation for being "totalizing" and "ahistorical" but it is, precisely, the opposite.

Proposition nine: The very notion of an unconscious makes psychoanalysis incapable of making a totalizing claim about anything: The unconscious ensures the failure of absolute claims to knowledge (including its own claims about the unconscious). Similarly, the possibility of "knowing" or "recovering" individual and collective history is everywhere interrogated by psychoanalysis. Psychoanalytic history proceeds from the belief that the distinction between imagined events and empirically verifiable events is a false one. The force of the primal scene is not dependent on a distinction between ocularly witnessing or "merely" imagining it. Additionally, psychoanalysis makes apparent the impossibility of "having a body" separate from the community in which desire to "possess" it— libidinally, syntactically, psychically—circulates.

X. Chrono-graphy

Facial: The application of cosmetics to the visage, often accompanied by a massage.

Q: Why are you so tired?

A: I can't work out duration.

Q: What do you mean?

A: I have no idea how to sustain anything, so I never know if something is just beginning or if it is fading away. When you suggest that Lacan is useless because he's a dead, white, European man, I think I couldn't have said anything in all this time talking. It's all random. Not even numbering the points gives us a way to count our progress. Like Hansel and Gretel with their bread crumbs: The numbers aren't mapping our progress—they just are measuring the time vanishing.

Q: Oh, come on. You are being a bit melodramatic, aren't you?

A: Maybe. Melodrama is underrated. Characters in melodrama seem to understand duration; I envy them that. And they enjoy repetition, as I do, except when I'm exhausted.

Q: But I can't see *why* you are so tired.

A: It's as if I'm at the airport but they've announced that the plane is indefinitely delayed. So I'm waiting and I don't know if I've traveled anywhere or am about to. I have a ticket and I can see the plane but we're not attached. I'm not sure if the waiting counts as travel time or not. I can hear the clocks moving and I can see the numbers piling up, but I'm not sure if they have anything to do with me or if I'm outside the time loop altogether since if we do climb into the sky the hours will get renumbered anyway. So this is another form of suspension, a paralytic pause in time that my body cannot map. My being feels lost.

Q: Why do you always have to speak in allegories and metaphors? You seem angry with me—somehow I think I've repeated a question you don't like. You seemed to get tired when I asked you about your relation to Lacan's work.

A: The evaluative question that needs to be asked about Lacan's or any other theorist's work is: What can these ideas do and what can't they do and for whom? Lacan's work is useful when it is employed politically—the way Zizek does in *The Sublime Object of Ideology*—but it is deadening when it is used, often by film theorists, to resurrect a utopian Imaginary, a pre-Oedipal heaven.

Q: But isn't the body itself somewhere between the Symbolic and the Imaginary?

A: No. The body is Symbolic. Perhaps one's relation to one's own body is Imaginary insofar as one fantasizes that one's body and being are continuous.[12] We live in bodies and bodies live in us—but we do not "have" bodies in the way we "have" clothes or money. The relation between body and being is not self-identical. Precisely because it is not, we need the representational frame to see, and to secure, what the body is, and whose is whose. The frame of dance, for example, works to solidify the insecure and noncontinuous relation between walking and "Steve Paxton."

Q: What do you mean: "We live in bodies and bodies live in us—but we do not have bodies in the way we have money or clothes?"

Proposition ten: We have multiple bodies in the way we now speak of multiple identities.

XI. Carto-graphy

Facade: From architecture, the face of a building, especially one that is elaborately decorated. These decorations bridge the architectural meaning with the vernacular one of a false front.

A: I'd agree with your proposition, except I want to note that the accent in the U.S. version points the wrong way. The body is nonsingular because of loss, not because of wealth and freedom, as many people in the United States like to think. In the face of grief and loss, the subject internalizes the object of loss and thus imaginatively possesses even more deeply that which is gone. The history writer experiences a similar form of introjection, which s/he in turn maps for the reader. Such introjection both disavows the loss and deepens the cut. Judith Butler has recently argued that this internalization happens across genders—in other words, when the girl child "loses" the beloved father she internalizes him. After this internalization, her own gender can no longer be self-identical, but is rather "doubled." Same for boys and mothers.[13]

Proposition eleven: There is no singular gender in any/body. There is no singular body.

XII. Choreo-graphy Redux

Aborti**fac**ient: A chemical injection used to induce abortion.

Proposition twelve: Our "own" body is the one we have and the history of the ones we've lost. Our body is both internal and external, invisible and visible, sick and well, living and dead. Full of jerks and rears, the body moves like an awkward dancer trying to partner someone she can never see or lay full hold of. Her deaf ears (cheek to phantom) are not soothed by the smooth music of time's rolling rhythms. She keeps waiting to hear someone call her by her proper name. The hole in her body whistles, and history is the story of his attempt to fill it. They were failing. And they were going to fail.[14] It was December all February. He missed her and the music didn't care.

XIII. Bio-graphies

Prima Facie: At first sight—the face is an eye, I, for the first time, see.

Proposition thirteen: History writing and choreography reflect and reproduce bodies whose names we long to learn to read and write. Our wager is if we can re-call and revive these fading forms, our own may be recalled by others who will need us to protect themselves from fading. This repetitious dance assures our continual presence: We are the characters who are always there disappearing.

Peggy Phelan.[15]

NOTES

1. Sex is another.

"I know,
you touch so blissfully because the caress preserves, because the place you so
tenderly cover

>   does not vanish; because underneath it
>   you feel pure duration. So you promise eternity, almost, from the embrace."

—Rilke, *Selected Poetry*, p. 159. The hiccup behind that "almost" is what makes erotic historiography (more or less the impetus of the eighteenth-century English novel) endlessly fascinating.

2. Barthes, *Camera Lucida*, p. 12.

3. Ulmer, *Object of Post-Criticism*, p. 91.

4. A question about my authority as a writer about dance solicits an account of dance I did not see. The history of what I've missed fuels the anxiety that authoritative prose seeks to overwrite.

5. Blanchot, *The Writing of the Disaster*, p. 41.

6. Case, "Toward a Butch-Femme Aesthetic," p. 297.

7. Wallace, *Invisibility Blues*; Irigaray, *Speculum of the Other Woman*.

8. Although in the case of Blanchot, it is precisely history's disappearance which gives historiography its intimate relation to disasters.

9. "Interview with Yvonne Rainer," p. 78. Steve Paxton, a choreographer and dancer in Grand Union, had created a dance in which the choreography consisted of nothing but "neutral" walking.

10. This may also be why point of view is such a slippery concept in history writing. The "naturalized" point of view is unmarked and the "reflexive" point of view is marked, but neither faces the failure to *see* what one's point of view *is*. One is so busy "having" it or "naming" it that one can't actually observe it "as in itself it really is." (One cannot both observe observation and observe its "content.")

11. Jean Baudrillard argues in *Simulations* that for postmodern culture the representational has become the real. There are many problems with this proposition, and yet it attains a kernel of truth. For a fuller response to Baudrillard's argument, see my *Unmarked: The Politics of Performance*, especially chapters one and eight.

12. It is this fantasy of oneness which is betrayed by the routine language of possession. To maintain the intimate subjectivity of one's body one quickly resorts to inane constructions such as "Don't forget, Doctor, I am in this body"—thereby rendering one's body an object of possession and defeating the desire to convey that this very body is who one is. The difficulty stems partially from the fact that bodies both exceed and curtail the being that language seeks to locate in bodies.

13. Butler, "Gender Insubordination."

14. The intertext/interface of this text is Wallace Stevens's poem "Thirteen Ways of Looking at a Blackbird." His thirteenth stanza reads:

>   It was evening all afternoon.
>   It was snowing
>   And it was going to snow.
>   The blackbird sat
>   In the cedar-limbs.

The equivocations elaborated by Stevens are here "mirrored" in order to suggest that criticism's uncertainties are much the same as poets'—the difference, as ever, is in the details.

15. Academic convention requires the "proper name" of the author here as the signature. So I offer it precisely because it stands in for what I cannot name or write. The reader is more **prop**erly the author of this measured graphing. The "failing" audible in the off-rhyme of my sur name (his name) registers the fading of "my" identity even as it seeks to hold her name.

SHARON TRAWEEK

Bodies of Evidence: Law and Order, Sexy Machines, and the Erotics of Fieldwork among Physicists

Some anthropologists do not study human communities as discrete, bounded, holistic, and atemporal; we do not play the mythical role of distanced, privileged, neutral, bodiless observers of mythically naive natives in our fieldwork, and we do not write ethnographies in that rhetorical mode. We also do not write confessional stories about finding our own distinctive subjectivity as we grope about in some bush with nameless, but generic, natives. Whatever our subjects make of us and how they make use of us is continuously negotiated with what we make of them and how we make use of them; any stabilities are temporary and local. It is in these highly situated encounters that we all are producing knowledges; we are both subject and object to each other, neither subjective nor objective.

It is on this middle ground that I learn about the moral laws, aesthetic order, and erotics of physicists. (It is also where I learn about the moral laws, aesthetic order, and erotics of anthropologists.) There is an elaborate aesthetic and moral discourse among high energy physicists. Key words in this vocabulary are trustworthy, good, and reliable; beauty, charm, sexy, and cute; economical and expensive; law, constant, and order; risk, stability, and commitment. They use these words to talk about equipment, experiments, data, laboratories, colleagues, students, directors, pedagogy, the public, and funding. I will give you some examples.

Sexy and Cute

It turns out that what is sexy and what is cute are machines and software, but not all machines and software can be called sexy or cute. I have been told by old men and young men in the lab that crawling around inside a detector (a room-sized piece of research equipment) and rearranging the detector according to the latest change in theory is "a very powerful sexual experience." Sexy machines and software can be reconfigured whenever these physicists change their minds. Cute machines and software have a clever arrangement of details.

These same people speak of other pleasures. They like uniformities, regularities, stabilities, hierarchies, taxonomies, and laws. Once I watched a group of physicists gazing at a book of images of fractals; with each turn of the page came a soft chorus of pleasured sounds. When I asked why they like them so much, they seemed surprised at the question. One said, "it's the same everywhere you look"; the others nodded. I had to explain that I come from a place where we like difference everywhere we look. I could tell they were appalled. The fractals and the detectors give them real aesthetic pleasure, the pleasure of law and order, of certainty. In their desire for order and for sameness, there is no pleasure in ambiguity. Ambiguity just means error.

Most scientists find beauty in simplicity. There are always a few who prefer the sublime: complexity, instabilities, variation, transformations, irregularities, and diversity. They find pleasure in spaces where everything appears to be different; they do not seem attracted to sexy reconfigurable machines and cute software with amusing details. The proportion of scientists who prefer the sublime seems very low in high energy physics, but higher in some other fields.

Inexplicable difference is a problem for the physicists I study.[1] I found that the American members of an international collaboration of physicists based at a lab in Japan were disturbed about Japanese modes of measuring the ambient radiation in the research areas. Americans calculate the risk of exposure to discrete body parts over one year; the Japanese measure the risk of exposing a whole body over a person's lifetime. American research scientists tend not to trust or even respect the safety experts in their own labs; the Japanese scientists see their lab radiation specialists as trustworthy fellow scientists. The Americans demanded that radiation counters with visible meters be placed in their research area; some Japanese commented that sometimes Americans seemed like people from a Third World country: They do not believe what they cannot see. Some Americans threatened to get counters from a Japanese group opposed to nuclear energy.

At about that point in their debate I told the physicists I was pregnant; I continued coming to the lab. Some Americans thought I was voting for the Japanese with my body. I soon began to have health problems; I gained fifty pounds in a small number of months and I lost some hair, so everyone could see I was ill. I got recommendations from doctors in the United States for doctors at the local, nationally known medical school hospital; I was diagnosed and eventually hospitalized and treated; I also lost the pregnancy. My recovery, as predicted, was gradual, but steady. After leaving the hospital, I encountered two reactions to my experience. Most of my fellow aliens at the lab thought that I had shown very bad judgment, first by coming to the lab when they had already questioned the radiation monitoring procedures, and second by not returning to the United States, where they thought I could have gotten more expert care. I lost standing with these people.

The Japanese scientists were clearly aware of those aliens' opinions and they asked me how I had made my decision to stay in Japan and continue coming to the lab. I replied that I had felt I had Japanese friends who would help me if I needed it and I had confidence in my doctors and their diagnostic procedures, so I preferred to stay and continue my work. They said, "You really trusted Japanese doctors and Japanese hospitals!" Surprised, I replied, "Sure. Don't you?" "Of course, but you are the first foreigner we've seen who did," was the answer. I told them that I actually had never seriously thought about leaving and they said they knew that. My standing with them had clearly risen.

National scientific communities are no longer in the margins when their scientists' findings are accepted as a matter of fact and without replication. A Thai mycologist has told me that she must send her samples along with her classification and analysis to some major lab like Kew Gardens if she wants her papers to be taken seriously. Fortunately, she has an extensive international network from having gone to graduate school in the United States, so she can at least get her samples and papers looked at. The American scientific community reached that point in the 1930s and 1940s, but the Japanese are still in that transition period. If I had not been ill, I am not sure if I would have heard the aliens' stories of suspicion about Japanese science and the Japanese scientists' awareness of their foreign colleagues' lack of confidence in their work. It was a charged subject: The Japanese needed the aliens for the lab to gain credibility in the international high energy physics community; the foreigners were afraid they were losing status by even being there. They joked a lot about their "high risk, high gain" situation. At a party, one told me that no one who was really good would have to take the risk of being so far from the center of the action.

In the last forty-five years, Japan has changed from an exceedingly poor country to a very rich one. During the past fifteen years, the Japanese government has faced a lot of pressure from other rich countries to assume the international responsibilities appropriate to its wealth. The government leaders, quite conservative members of the party which had been in power for the last forty-five years, posed the question: What would be a Japanese way for Japan to assume an international role, rather than an English or American or Russian way? What followed was a resurgence of an old genre. This literature takes two forms: *nihonjinron*, essays on Japaneseness, and *nihonbunkaron*, essays on Japanese culture.[2] The former is considered déclassé by readers of the latter; the physicists I studied seemed to read the former. When I was discussing with a Japanese physicist the differences between the way Americans and Japanese lead groups of experimentalists, he proceeded to explain to me the importance in Japan of *harage*, leadership from the force of one's will or, more literally, from one's lower stomach. He explained that a good Japanese leader listens and then conveys his position powerfully, but nonverbally. He contrasted this to Americans, who lead from the mouth by talking all the time. I have noticed over the five years I have been studying a group led jointly by an American and a Japanese that the American is talking in formal meetings less and less; he is increasingly regarded as a good leader by the Japanese.

Law and Order

Japanese bodies and their distinctiveness are an important theme in both *nihonjinron* and *nihonbunkaron*. I was often asked by the Japanese physicists to explain to the Americans these issues; they assumed that because I was an anthropologist I was knowledgeable about such matters. (Some Japanese anthropologists have become quite successful as experts who are proponents of these nativist ideas.) Whenever I explained that American cultural anthropologists had concluded several decades ago that race was a political notion (and hence not scientific), they clearly thought that this had been a political move on the part of American cultural anthropologists. When I would counter that most physical and medical anthropologists now agreed with the cultural anthropologists, they would just laugh. One evening, to demonstrate their point, which had now shifted to how bodies make a difference, several said they could predict my blood type. When I answered, they said, of course, as an ethnographer you are an experimentalist, just like us; theorists have a different blood type.[3]

I am always eagerly asked to identify the relevant blood types if I tell this story among American physicists. They have another somatic theory of mind: Many believe that scientists' minds are distinctive, unlike other humans'. One explained to me, for example, that scientists' minds would be very little affected by "culture," that they were drawn "from out in the tail of the distribution" (drawing the characteristic bell-shaped curve and pointing to the broad lip—not tail—of his bell). Another said that there have been the same proportion of potential scientists in all populations, but that some societies do not encourage or tolerate science. When I mention that in the 1930s psychological anthropologists had a theory that psychological types were equally distributed in all populations with some cultures favoring one sort and other cultures favoring another, they were quite interested. When I add that these ideas are no longer taken seriously, they clearly think that the error is in the anthropologists.

Several months ago I gave two talks at a major high energy physics laboratory in the United States; one, sponsored by a women's group at the lab, was on gender issues in scientific practices and was very well attended by both men and women. At the conclusion, one senior, quite prominent physicist said he was very intrigued by my arguments, which he found compelling. Nonetheless, he was surprised that I had not yet addressed what was, obviously, a crucial issue: the strong correlation between creativity and . . . testosterone. (American men physicists keep their dosimeter badges [which measure one's exposure to radiation] clipped to the inside curve of a pants' pocket, close to their gonads; the Japanese clip their dosimeters onto the center fold of their shirts, near the lower stomach, or *hara*.)

I replied to the senior physicist that, interestingly, many had studied the research on gendered hormones and had found that it all had profound gender biases.[4] He countered that he had read this research in *Science;* I pointed out that *Science* had a history of publishing the very research which had been demonstrated to be heavily laden with gender biases, but always refused to publish the rebuttals to that research. My interlocutor said he was impressed and wanted to read this research, adding that if what I said were true, this would have profound implications for science education. Many others nodded, and later crowded around me asking for references.

I would claim that, so far, heterosexuality is compulsory among high energy physicists; they are also obliged to be married.[5] Since almost all of them are men, they are expected to find suitable wives, women who "understand" why they spend nights at the lab. (I was first declared suitable wife material fifteen years ago; almost all the women high energy physicists are married to physicists.) Everyone says it is not good to spend time on a social life; time should be spent on physics. This terse sexual economy is not unlike the importance of economy in physics: Do not spend time and money on detectors and software where you do not need to. They also say that spending your time and money wisely shows good physics judgment. At every turn American high energy physics labs are a startling juxtaposition of threadbare shabbiness and shiny affluence. At the lab in Japan, the Americans often said the Japanese detectors did not show good physics judgment because everything was "overbuilt." The Americans agreed that the Japanese spent too much money and time and spent it in the wrong places. When I asked if Japanese detectors were sexy, they just laughed.

The American physicists like their machines malleable, but a bit fallible and a little mysterious, responsive to the controlling hands of the knowledgeable physicists. The Japanese like their machines to be predictable, a sustainable resource, an infinite source of reliable data for the ever-hungry physicists. These Japanese and American fantasies about machines are not unlike their fantasies about exotic women and good mothers. Over the last fifteen years, I have spent thirty months at that lab in Japan; I have noticed several liaisons of American men and Japanese women, Japanese men and American women, all of which provokes a great deal of scrutiny and commentary. In fact, the similarities and differences between American and Japanese machines, women, and baseball were ever-present topics of male discourse in the lab. Difference was always ranked.

One morning I climbed onto the detector to talk to some physicists who were inside it, making adjustments. They said they had just been talking about me and had concluded that I could not do my research. Aghast, I asked why not. Well, they explained, you could not find out how we do experiments if you did not come here and spend a lot of time with us, but since you know us, your work is subjective, so it is not research. I asked if there were any alternatives to subjectivity and objectivity; this was judged silly. So in some settings, physicists repeat the usual overdetermined dichotomies of body/mind, emotion/reason, subjective/objective. In other moments, they easily add fiction/fact, words/numbers, women/men, imitative/innovative, the public/scientists. Feminists, postcolonial scholars, and some postmodernists have reminded us that these masochistic slashes sever one part of our bodies from the rest; these cruel dichotomies terrorize us into forgetting that we have worlds of alternatives.

Physicists like their knowledge taxonomical and classificatory: They define bits of matter and energy by their common characteristics and by their distinctions and they arrange these classifications into grids of controlled difference. (The high energy physics example is called SU3; Mendele'ev's Periodic Table of the Elements is an example familiar to anyone who has taken a high school chemistry class.) They also like their knowledge ahistorical: Calendrical, human time slips away but the replicable time of machines and theories can be stored, reserved, accumulated. The world is nothing but basic elements revealed by their signs in detectors.

In characterizing the minds of people in "simple societies," Lévi-Strauss said they engage in *bricolage,* building models that reflect "neither time, nor place, nor circumstance."[6] Foucault described the classical *episteme* as "an exhaustive ordering of the world . . . directed towards the discovery of simple elements and their progressive combination; and at their centre they form a table on which knowledge is displayed in a system contemporary with itself."[7] Lévi-Strauss and Foucault were trying to characterize other minds in other spaces and other times, not the privileged knowledge of contemporary science. None-theless, they aptly described the moral economy of high energy physics, where a common and formulaic lab graffito reads: "186,000mps: it's not only a good idea; it's the law!" We all are law-abiding citizens of nature, but only physicists can read its law books.

Bachigai[8]

Experimental high energy physicists usually do their talks at conferences with the lights off, the "overhead" projector on, and their backs to us, *not,* as etholo-gists might surmise, as a sign of submission, but as an authoritative gesture. They turn away from us to the illuminated facts as a priest might turn to the altar, and they speak to us in that masterful voice of authority and with that rather patron-izing tone of certainty. Often their "transparencies" are handwritten, deliberately, as proof that the enlightened facts we are reading were so recently gleaned that word of their discovery was confirmed only a few moments ago in a telephone call received from the laboratory.

Physicists begin their talks with slides of the laboratory where their research was done and a few more of the research equipment—the detector—they used, while telling us quickly about its design and operation and modification. This part of their talks reminds me of the slides anthropologists use, the ones that attest to the researchers' technical and aesthetic skills and, of course, stand as evi-dence that the speakers really did go somewhere, that they really were *there.* It is only in these introductory pictures that those physicists and anthropologists intimate that they were involved in the production of the news to follow. Those pictures tell an ambiguous story: They tell us that the speaker is an adventurer, a traveler, a discoverer, an eyewitness. They also tell us that their news is pro-duced by their presence and their ingenuity. The subjects in these tales of objectivity are introduced in act I and never reappear in their stories.[9] But they survive: They are there, in control, telling their powerful tales in the dark. Well, I leave the lights on. I write some stories for you, and I am in some of them; I want you to know how I came to learn about these scientists and I want you to understand how the stories some anthropologists of science write might be different from what you expect.[10]

Machines, like Galileo's telescope and the supercollider in Texas, provide the raw material for the stories that scientists tell about nature. Scientists and ma-chines and laboratories provide the not-quite-so-raw material for the stories scientists and anthropologists can tell about making science. So what kind of sto-ries do the machines and scientists and anthropologists tell? Scientists are fond of grand explanatory systems, the sort of authoritative stories Lyotard has called the *"grands récits."*[11] Scientists like their machines to write this way. The easy assumption is that nature coupled with genius authorizes science, so they are entitled to account for everything and reject all other stories too. To borrow (and disrupt) a notion from Hobbes by way of Michel Callon and Bruno Latour, almost all these stories, whether about nature, scientists, or science, are narrative leviathans, producing and reproducing all-encompassing stories of cause and effect through the same rhetorical strategies.[12] They are wandering through those perpetually replicating Cartesian grids, telling stories about huge minds and gargantuan machines with big names, exciting monstrosities that fit nowhere. The erotics of taxonomies, the satisfactions in controlling grids of difference, and the aesthetic pleasures of sameness are fetishized in totemic machines, the only place where theories can become facts.

AMY is the name of both an international collaboration of scientists and their research equipment at KEK, the National Laboratory for High Energy Physics, in Tsukuba Science City, which is located about three hours by public transportation northeast of Tokyo. I have studied them since April 1986. The American group leader chose the name AMY for two reasons: His former next door neighbors' daughter is named Amy, and in his study of Japanese ideographic writing he learned that one possible pronunciation of the characters for beautiful pictures was "ay" and "mee." While he certainly hoped that his group would ultimately gain convincing visual representations of the top quark, he started with the girl's name, moved to a phonetic equivalent in Japanese, and then searched for ideographs with those pronunciations which had meanings he would consider appropriate. He knew that this is the way people make names for machines in physics: Start with a word from the world of ordinary things or commonly known names, then capitalize the letters of that word and turn it into an acronym signifying something from the world of science, hopefully also signifying something from that group's own distinctive hardware and software.

The facility where the AMY group worked and where the AMY detector was situated is called TRISTAN. According to the laboratory director-general:

> Our accelerator plan at KEK was nicknamed as "TRISTAN" after the passionate story of . . . Wagner's opera, with . . . love and dreams for our science research, particularly for hunting quarks in Nippon. The first conception of this idea was about a decade ago, and now our TRISTAN [comes] on stage. An opera is really [the] team work of singers, instrument players, the conductor, the stage manager and many more important people setting the drama behind the scenes. So is the construction of a large accelerator complex such as our TRISTAN. We could only make . . . TRISTAN's initial operation successful, with the excellent cooperative work of our colleagues.[13]

I forgot to tell you that TRISTAN stands for Transposable Ring Intersecting STorage Accelerator in Nippon and that there is no Japanese-language version of the annual report from which I took the director-general's words. The VENUS group said their name meant VErsatile N1hep and Universities Spectrometer, making it a surprisingly double-layered acronym, with N1hep signifying the number one high energy physics lab in Nippon. In the hallway outside the offices of the group members, there was a bulletin board with several snapshots of the VENUS detector's component parts. Running along the top of the bulletin board was a neatly hand-lettered sign in English: VENUS lifts her veil. The SHIP group name is an acronym for their Search for Highly Ionizing Particles. They also called themselves Nikko-maru after the name of the experimental hall where their detector is located (Nikko) and the Japanese word for ship (*maru*). Nikko is a famous mountainous, landlocked resort in Japan; SHIP is a so-called passive detector, meaning that its component solid state track detectors are left in place for many months, removed, and only then analyzed.

Making names in this way shows that the groups know how to make the right sort of puns. Puns are the only form of wordplay I have ever heard among high energy physicists. What is it about puns they find so satisfying and why are other kinds of wordplay so unrecognizable to them? When I am doing fieldwork, physicists occasionally ask why I have no sense of humor: They notice that my laughter at their puns is feigned. It is always a relief to return to anthropology territory and another kind of wordplay where I am reputed to have at least the normal amount of wit. Reader, remember that puns bring together meanings which should be kept apart, a kind of verbal incest. These acronymic couplings physicists make are clever only to those who think that speech and writing, like bodies and minds, ought to be kept apart, that appearances are false and hidden meanings are true. These puns directly contradict what all science and engineering students know should be kept apart.

Why is one message given in those authoritative texts and a contradictory one given in jest, one message given in print and another in speech? Bateson told us that such contradictory messages are double binds: If one message is obeyed, the other must be violated. He told us that such double binds can encode powerful cultural messages about how to think, feel, and act.[14] What a teacher says can be challenged, but it is almost impossible to stop laughing at a good joke. Every laugh is a warning to the students about exactly which borders are never to be crossed. Did you notice that the ordinary meaning of their scientific names is only recognizable in speech and the fact that the name is also an acronym is only apparent in writing by the mark of its capitalized letters? While the scientific meaning of the name is hidden in the written acronym and usually is only meaningful to other scientists in the same speciality, the spoken name itself can be romantic and heroic and it often has allusions to gender or sexuality. Remember the names LASS and SPEAR and PEP at SLAC, the two-mile-long, perfectly straight linear accelerator at Stanford. What has been incestuously conflated in these puns? What is so important, so dangerous, so illicit that it can only be said in jest? Speech and writing, appearance and science, bodies and minds are brought together, all under the name of heroic desire.

Do you remember that TRISTAN is the name of the desire for hunting quarks in Japan? It is not the name of a memory, of nostalgia, of things past. To return to the printed words authorized by the laboratory's director-general about TRISTAN:

There is a famous story about . . . Wagner's idea in composing this opera which is based upon his original musical drama. He wrote in a letter to Franz Liszt, "Because I have never tasted the true bliss of love, I shall raise a monument to that most beautiful of all dreams wherein from b[e]ginning to end this love may for once drink to its fill." It took about ten . . . years of Wagner's work before . . . "TRISTAN und ISOLDE" was first performed at Munich in 1865. . . . Now, we are very glad to publish this TRISTAN construction report on the occasion of the dedication ceremony for TRISTAN on April 7, 1987. Needless to say, our physics program is just about to begin. Taking . . . Wagner's opera, this correspon[d]s to the beginning of . . . Act I when Tristan and Isolde are about to depart to King Mark from a quay. We don't know at present how the highlights of the succeeding acts will develop. We will continue to make our best efforts so as to be able to taste the true bliss of our love, and leave the rest to Heaven.[15]

Why not a condescending name? Why not divine? Why not ironic? Why is the name of all this incest so unabashedly, sincerely heroic? Why do so many physicists around the world love nineteenth-century Romantic European "classical" music, especially opera? Is it the tone of entitlement and authority in music written in the age of European colonialism? Is it only the simple, predictable narrative structure of beginnings, middles, and ends with characters and melodies that are known from the first, the mirror image of our academic articles with their authors and abstracts followed by theories, methods, and data? Is it that the drama is not the point, but only a reassuringly fixed text on which the musicians and actors and academics display their refined capacities for subtle variations within elaborate and precise constraints? Is it that all these players want to have a name *above* the title of their static texts?

What is in a desirable name? The only way that scientists can become immortal is to have equations or equipment named after them, like Maxwell's equations, Lorenz transformations, Feynman diagrams, and Cherenkov counters. Others use the power of discovery to name new particles in ways that invoke a group leader's name or a group's detector. Sam Ting supposedly named a particle "J" because that letter resembled the Chinese character for his name; an experimentalist group at Stanford Linear Accelerator Center (SLAC) named the same particle the Greek letter called *psi* after the shape of the particle's track in their computer imaging system. The conflated ontology of the particle/equation/equipment/image and its heroic maker is affirmed with each utterance, with each inscription. For a moment, repeated wherever there are scientists talking and writing, ephemeral scientists are revived by their immortal ideas/mental tools/machines. These are powerful, heroic, proper names; strangely, it is the progeny that legitimizes its progenitor, the source of the name. The metaphoric trope of romance, of heroism is the only one suited to such authoritative names. The other possibilities—metonymy, synecdoche, and irony—would undermine that passionately, distinctively human authorship by their gestures of reduction, expansion, and reversal. Names like SPEAR and PEP allude to a kind of human potency; SLAC to a certain kind of human anxiety about its loss; VENUS, LASS,

TOPAZ, and AMY point to a certain kind of seductive, dazzling nature about to be revealed in the jungle of computer cables surrounding the eponymous detectors, which in turn encompass the powerful (sometimes bent) accelerated beam of particles. Listing here the "passive" detector, the SHIP at anchor, captained by a woman mining the deep for heavy particles, seems out of place. (By the way, the Japanese word for people, actions, situations, and things out of place is *bachigai*.)

There are some names that tell another story, but they are not punning acronyms. Benki and Tokiwa are names for two magnets at the proton synchrotron (PS), the first research facility at KEK. These are the names of two characters in a famous historical *bunraku* (Japanese puppet theater) play by Chikamatsu, a story about underdogs. Oho is the name of the experimental hall where the AMY group is located; these resident aliens chose the name of the nearest village, rather than names of major sites in Japan like Fuji, Nikko, or even Tsukuba. Instead of identifying themselves with some place all Japanese would recognize as imperial sites, they just used a local, inconsequential place name, knowing that to other foreigners in the international scientific community all the names in the series would be inconsequential. It was a joke about the marginality of the whole place.

Bodies of Evidence

My stories here have not been about some presumed, peripatetic, picaresque, quixotic, and erotic escapades among physicists and their equipment; that is, this has not been some sort of "Fanny in the Lab." Nor are these stories "confessional"; all that you have learned about me is that I was deemed suitable wife material, I once had an unsuccessful pregnancy, I once gained fifty pounds, I once was rather ill, and I have spent two-and-a-half of the last fifteen years in Japan; this does not count as particularly personal information, at least not in the United States. That is, you have learned, so far, nothing of my personal responses to these labels and events, nothing of their consequences, and nothing of my personal relationships with other people. Nor am I necessarily trying to elicit any such responses from you. All of these I take to be characteristic of confessional literature.

I have taken a role in this text, telling about the situations in which I heard these stories, and telling you what was made of me by these physicists, so that you might make something of them. When I first began to study physicists in Japan and the United States during the mid-1970s, I learned that wearing my miniskirts to the lab reduced the physicists' responses to me. Twenty years and fifty pounds later, I found that I was assigned another singular role: *obachan*. This might be translated as auntie; in Japan slight, demure young women become, in time, formidable middle-aged forces. They can be seen everywhere, elbows out, getting seats on the subway, the best vegetables at market, and the best deals at the stock market. They carry large bags in which absolutely anything can be found. *Obachan* are eccentric, endearing, irritating busybodies and will not be ignored. As a fieldworker in my late forties, some of my hosts explained that I was just like an *obachan*.

My point instead is that if I had not attended to all these bodies in the field, the busybody and the bodies that only physicists have, all these erotics of fieldwork, I would have learned much less about these high energy physicists' embodied rationality. These aesthetic pleasures I found in the lab are the same ones the high energy physicists use for problem formulation, research design, and problem solutions, the same ones they use to write, to teach, and to organize a lab. I have tried here to present some stories about how bodies and minds are entwined in labs, stories that may challenge some assumptions about the production of a certain kind of privileged knowledge, a way of knowing that is profoundly gendered and cultural.

Subtext

In case you prefer other modes of discourse about one's "work" than the one I have used in the preceding pages, or if you feel that you still want to know "what really happened" during my fieldwork, here are some other moves I have made.

A. Here is a succinct statement of my research in the traditional, formal style. I have been studying the multinational high energy physics community (especially the Americans and Japanese) since the early 1970s. I have spent about two years at the Stanford Linear Accelerator Center (SLAC) in California; two-and-a-half years at KEK—*Ko-Enerugie butsurigaku Kenkyusho,* the National High Energy Physics Laboratory—at Tsukuba, Japan; six months at Fermi National Accelerator Laboratory in Illinois; and shorter visits to CERN in Switzerland, DESY in Germany, and Saclay in France. I have also visited physics departments at universities throughout the United States and Japan and attended innumerable particle physics colloquia, workshops, and conferences. Altogether I have conducted about five years of research at some of the major national high energy physics laboratories where this community gathers.

Through the anthropological research method called participant-observation, I study the settings and events these physicists construct for themselves and observe the activities, formal and informal, they consider appropriate in those settings. I learn what they believe they need to know in order to act effectively and strategically, whether locally or globally; I then find the patterns in their actions and cosmologies and how all this shifts over time and as the ecology of their community changes. The central questions for my fieldwork are: (1) how knowledge, especially so-called craft or tacit knowledge, is transmitted from one generation to the next in a multinational community that is committed to discovery and in which crucial features of their knowledge are never written; (2) how different styles of research practices emerge and survive; (3) how disputes and factions are formed and maintained; (4) how these practices differ along lines of class, gender, regional and national culture, and national and international political economy; and (5) how national and international political economies are shaped by these physicists and the work they do.

B. You may prefer yet another mode of discourse about this ethnography. My first book on physicists is *Beamtimes and Lifetimes: The World of High Energy*

Physicists (Cambridge, Mass.: Harvard University Press, 1988; paperback 1992). Here is my narrative of its tropes:

Trope/ Culture Theory	Writing/ Topic/ Style	Researcher's Position in Community	Ethnographic Category and Arguments
Metaphor (transfer of meaning from one term to another)	"Realism" surfaces; appearances gazing	Guide	Ecology (including built environment and material culture): 1. Spatial deployment of labs (Bachelard, Yi-Fu Tuan) 2. Lab as massive mnemonic device for determining who people are and what they should be doing 3. Labs create privileged observers AND wandering liaisons culture 4. To control space is to control time, that is, controlling space is an outward (visible) sign of a group's control of beamtime, for example, users get time but no space, hence no power
Metonymy (whole is collection of parts) as culture	"Classification" "natural" array of units; staring	Fieldworker	Social Organization: 1. Funding, designing, executing, analyzing experiments 2. Networks exchanging people and information; all important information is conveyed orally 3. Negotiation by exclusive circle of brokers and jokers 4. Beamtime is a negotiated commodity, a fetishized nexus of social relations
Synecdoche (one stands for all) as culture	"Romance" (nb Northrup Frye); glancing	Marginal Woman albeit useful	Developmental Cycle: 1. Training of a physicist as an emblem of the community's sense of their shared past, present, and future 2. Stages of career as series of exclusionary stories 3. Double-bound picaresque (not bildungsroman) men's lives where losing innocence gains power 4. Time as engendered source of anxiety: insignificance of past, fear of losing time, anxiety about future, fear of obsolescence
Irony (reversal of metaphoric transfer) as culture	"Analytical allegory" re "underlying" patterns and meanings; reflecting	Writing Anthropologist	Cosmology 1. Congruence re cultural constructions of time and space in practice and in knowledge system 2. Times in lab (up/down time, beamtime, detector lifetime, lab

lifetime, career time, lifetime of ideas) classified as replicable (can be accumulated) and ephemeral (slipping away). nb: separating "real" data from "raw" and noise

3. Replicable is desirable; ephemeral is a constant source of anxiety. Replication is both ideal and real; human social world is ephemeral. nb structure of discourse

4. Detectors (material culture) as site and symbol of annihilation and resurrection of time

I was defining culture, then, as situated, deployed, embodied, engaged tropes. The other arguments I was engaged with included: (1) Metaphorically, Kuhn's first component of paradigm is symbolic generalizations (that which is taken for granted, that is, it has not been challenged for decades) and is analogous to Geertz's common sense/local knowledge (what everyone needs to know in order to be taken as a member of the community). (2) Metonymically, Lévi-Strauss sees "primitive mind" as having "classificatory systems of knowledge" (hierarchical, totemic, ahistorical), which, instead, I see as characteristic of high energy physics (HEP). My point is not that HEP are "primitive," but that Lévi-Strauss has fetishized both "primitive" and "science." (3) Synecdochically, Bateson's levels of learning and logical types are taken as meaningful strategic patterns and the HEP community is presented as a discrete, if nomadic culture. (4) Ironically, Foucault's classical episteme is characteristic of HEP and a contemporary knowing male gaze.

C. A fourth mode of discourse about my work is, ironically, from a more declarative tradition:

The first component of a "paradigm," according to Thomas Kuhn, is the "symbolic generalizations" that everyone in a field accepts as given and has not disputed for decades. It is this "ground state," as the physicists would call it, that I have tried to characterize in that book. In Clifford Geertz's language, I described their common sense ("recognizable by the maddening air of certainty with which it is always expressed"). I argued that, just as Evans-Pritchard saw the ecology, means of subsistence, social organization, stages of lives, and knowledge-belief system of the Nuer in Africa as focussed on cattle, the high energy physicists' research equipment called detectors are at the heart of their community, defining what must be and cannot be known, who can and cannot become one of the privileged producers of knowledge, what is debatable, what counts as facts, and noise, and what they see as interesting variations in style.[16] I was particularly concerned with showing how these privileged producers of knowledge are themselves produced and reproduced at each stage of their careers as well as how that very gendered process is similar to how these physicists produce detectors and facts. My recent work can be seen as attending to another part of paradigms, the templates or formulaic modes of thought used in making problems and solutions; I take these templates of craft knowledge to be just as embodied, just as performative, as the "common sense" I described above.

I am studying how Japanese and American physicists decide what new accelerators and new detectors ought to be built during the next ten years and how the ways these kinds of decisions are made change as once-marginalized groups (Japanese men and women scientists, American minorities, including women) are working now to change their international status. The relation of margins and centers is being renegotiated because of major shifts in the political economies that support basic research. "International science" is facing a crisis brought on by the scale of contemporary "big science," shifts in world economies and politics, and demographic and political changes in who can become scientists, do research, and define problems. I believe that these major changes under way in the ecologies in which scientists and engineers work will fundamentally change the practices, organizations and education in science, including high energy physics.

D. Which choreography do you prefer? I like the one with the bodies more or less intact, textually, that is.

NOTES

1. The next four paragraphs are taken from Traweek, "Border Crossings," pp. 429–66.
2. See, for example, Harootunian, *Things Seen and Unseen,* and Field, *"Somehow."*
3. On stomachs and blood types in Japanese body images, see Onuki-Tierny, *The Monkey As Mirror.*
4. See, for example, Longino, *Science As Social Knowledge.*
5. On the idea of compulsory heterosexuality, see Rich, *On Lies, Secrets and Silence.*
6. Lévi-Strauss, *The Savage Mind.*
7. Foucault, *The Order of Things,* p.74.
8. This section is taken from Traweek, "Border Crossings," pp. 429–66.
9. On stories, narrative theory, and rhetoric, see, among a myriad of others, Barthes, *The Responsibility of Forms;* Caplan, *Framed Narratives;* Chambers, *Story and Situation;* Chatman, *Story and Discourse;* Lanham, *A Handlist of Rhetorical Terms;* Trinh, *Woman, Native, Other;* The Personal Narratives Group, ed., *Interpreting Women's Lives;* Polanyi, *Telling the American Story;* Wallis, "Telling Stories: A Fictional Approach to Artist's Writings"; White, *The Content of the Form;* and just about anything by Kenneth Burke. I am especially indebted to Haraway, "Primatology Is Politics by Other Means."
    On narrative and rhetoric in science, see Bazerman, *Written Knowledge* and "Introduction to the Symposium," pp. 3–6; Restivo and Zenzen, "The Mysterious Morphology"; Restivo and Loughlin, "Critical Sociology," pp. 486–508; Restivo, "Multiple Realities," pp. 61–76; Latour and Woolgar, *Laboratory Life;* Knorr-Cetina, *The Manufacture of Knowledge;* Knorr-Cetina and Amann, "Image Dissection," pp. 259–83; Lynch, "Discipline and the Material Form of Images," pp. 37–66; Woolgar, "Discovery and Logic" and "What Is the Analysis," pp. 47–49.
10. There is a large literature on the epistemological stakes in "subject-positioning." Kondo, in her *Crafting Selves,* has compellingly explored these issues in anthropological theory, fieldwork, and writing. I would also recommend Trinh T. Minh-ha's *Woman, Native, Other* and two collections of articles: *Anthropology and the Colonial Encounter,* Talal Assad, ed., and *Traveling Theories Traveling Theorists,* Clifford and Dhareshwar, eds. My current favorite books on these issues in feminist theory are Gloria Anzaldúa's *Borderlands/La Fron-*

tera and Butler's *Gender Trouble.* For suggestions on how these issues might shape science studies, see Haraway, "Situated Knowledges," pp. 575–600.

11. Lyotard, *The Postmodern Condition.*

12. Callon and Latour, "Unscrewing the Big Leviathan."

13. Nishikawa, preface, pp. i–ii. Notice that the name Tristan is not fully capitalized, in the report's title; in this title, the name is not an acronym. The unusual grammatical constructions, spellings, and punctuation are in the original.

14. Bateson, *Steps to an Ecology of Mind* and *Naven.*

15. Nishikawa, preface, note 8.

16. Evans-Pritchard, *The Nuer* and *Witchcraft, Oracles, and Magic.* See also Kelly, *The Nuer Conquest;* Lienhardt, *Divinity and Experience.* For critiques of Evans-Pritchard's ethnographic writing, see Rosaldo, "From the Door of His Tent," in *Writing Culture;* and Geertz, "Slide Show."

Corpologue

HAYDEN WHITE

Bodies and Their Plots

The soul is the prison of the body.
—FOUCAULT

The title of these brief thoughts is adapted from Freud's well-known essay, usually translated into English as "Instincts and Their Vicissitudes." I am going to reflect on bodies and their vicissitudes, but rather more in the spirit of the original German title of Freud's piece than that of the English translation. The German title is "Triebe und Triebschicksale," which literally means: "Drives and Their Fates" but which could be rendered just as well "Instincts and Their Plots." What I propose to outline is a theory of the possible plots in which the stories that we tell—to ourselves, first of all, but also to others, such as our physicians, our lovers, our judges, our therapists, our police, and our oppressors—of bodies can be cast. "Plot" here can be understood as suggesting, first, the place in nature, the grave or as it is euphemistically called, "the final resting place," to which our bodies, *every* body is destined; second, the process of mapping or "emplotting" the trajectory of an entity's development or evolution over the course of its life "story"; and third, the notion of "plot" in the sense of conspiracy or what is called in French "intrigue" involved in imputing a single "history" to congeries of things called by the same name, such as bodies, which may bear only the most contingent relationship to one another.

Our thought about the possibilities for writing a history (or some histories) of the (human) body (or bodies) can profit from brief reflection on Freud's discussion of what the English translation of his essay calls "instincts" and he calls "drives" (*Triebe*). It is obvious that Freud wishes to distinguish between human and generally animal drives, even while maintaining a sense of the similarities or continuities between them—in much the same way that we, in our efforts to theorize a history of the body (or bodies), wish to distinguish between human and animal bodies even while maintaining a sense of the similarities or continuities between them. It is for this reason that Freud eschews any tendency to reify "drives" and construes them less as things than as a kind of relationship. But relationships between what?

Freud calls "drive" a "borderland" concept; he insists that a drive belongs neither to the body nor to the mind, neither to the soma nor to the psyche. It is rather the manifestation of the relationship between these two aspects of human being. Thus, Freud writes, drive is properly understood less as some form of animal "instinct" than as a "psychical *representative* of organic forces." The psyche stands in for or otherwise represents the somatic impulse. This suggests that a drive is a product of the psyche's capacity to re-present organic forces, which is to say, at once *present* them and *transform* them. The psyche's transformations of organic forces constitute their "fates," the "vicissitudes" to which these forces can be subjected. They correspond to what we might call the fundamental plot-structures of the organism's articulation of its needs.

Freud goes on to say that the articulation of "drives" such as love, hate, mastery, self-preservation, and the like may display the effects of a number of different possible "emplotments." And each of these modes of emplotment, we might speculate, would produce a different kind of body—it being understood that by "body" we will mean the totality of somatic effects produced by the psychical representation of an organic force. Thus, for example, a drive may undergo the vicissitude of repression, which is to say, it may be denied and pushed down into the unconscious, there to intensify and find expression finally only as neurotic symptoms. This vicissitude would produce the *mechanical* body, the body recognizable by its tics and parapraxes, obsessional behavior, and incapacity to go into the present. Again, drives may be "sublimated" or disguised and attain expression in a manner more acceptable to society, the censor, or the super-ego than they otherwise would have been. This produces the *serene* body, the body seemingly well organ-ized and at one with the spirit that inhabits it. Or, a drive may be disengaged from its original object of gratification and turned back onto its subject, so that what started out as, say, hatred of another ends up being expressed as hatred of oneself. This produces the *masochistic* body, the body that consists of little more than the sum-total of pain it has inflicted upon itself. And, finally, a drive may be transmuted into its opposite, as when love is transformed into hate or the reverse. This would produce the *divided* body, the body experienced as a site occupied by contending "forces" that continually transmute into their opposites, as in the Jekyll and Hyde syndrome. Thus, a human drive, conceived as a "psychical representation" of an "organic force," can in the process of its articulation undergo a *variety* of kinds of change and produce, not so much a psychic, but rather a physical change in the *body* of the subject.

The important point here is not so much that Freud's theory of "Drives and Their Fates" provides us with a taxonomy of types of psycho-somatism as that his conception of the vicissitudes through which these types are produced provides us with a way of identifying the typical "plots" which histories of bodies are destined to inhabit. Notice that the four fundamental plots to which drives can be subjected are identified by Freud as processes having the structures of (1) repression, (2) sublimation, (3) turning round (upon the subject), and (4) reversal (into an opposite). These four structures, in turn, represent a table of possible relationships between the forms and contents of the drives themselves. Thus, repression and sublimation effect denials of the forms but not the contents of the drives, while turning round upon the subject (transformation of the subject into an object) and reversal into an opposite (transmutation of love into hate) effect changes in the contents but not the forms of the drives. And, indeed, the fourfold classification of the vicissitudes of the drives generates a semantic field that can itself be emplotted quite easily as a Greimasian "semiotic square" or system of oppositions, negations, and implications on the basis of which the distinction between the normal and the abnormal psycho-somatized body can be justified:

normal body

(+)   (-)

sublimation   repression

deformed   **sick**

turning round   reversal into

upon the subject   opposite

monstrous body

This semantic square demonstrates the ways in which the normative and valuative conceptions of both body and psyche are generated by a set of oppositions and negations of what are on the surface presented as simply descriptive terms. Thus, the "normal" body (psyche) can be viewed as that which mediates between the desirable (+) processes of sublimation, on the one side, and the undesirable (-) even if unavoidable processes of repression, on the other. These two processes are comparable inasmuch as each represents a denial of the form of a drive but not its content, but they are opposable in the extent to which one of them, sublimation, is marked as positive (creative, adaptational, etc.) while the other, repression, is marked as negative (disabling, crippling, etc.). It then becomes possible to identify the two remaining strategies—turning round upon the subject and reversal into an opposite—as negations of the primary (deictic) terms (sublimation and repression). Thus, turning round upon the subject can be seen as formally affine with the positive process of sublimation, but having as a "content" its aspect as a "non-repressive" form of behavior. So, too, reversal into an opposite (love into hate) can be seen to be formally affine with repression while having as its "content" a "non-sublimational" effect.

The field of meaning thus constituted allows us, finally, to identify the content of the four kinds of body implied in Freud's classification of the plot-types or trajectories that traverse the soma as psychically represented. Standing against the normal body as its opposite is the monstrous body, which is nothing other than a mediation between the non-repressive and the non-sublimative bodies. The monstrous body would be a product of a process in which the subject had become its own object and whatever affect it had originally endowed the subject with had been transformed into its opposite.

But two other kinds of mediational instrumentalities remain to be named: These are the psycho-somatically "deformed" and "sick" bodies. These distinctions, product of a secondary oppositional structure, feature "forms" and "contents," respectively, as the secrets of their "constitution." The deformed body is a structure mediating between "sublimation" and "turning round upon the subject," both of which have already been unpacked as turning upon a denial of the form (but not the content) of the drive. So, too, the sick body is a product of a mediation between "repression" and "reversal into an opposite," both of which have to do with denial of the content (but not the form) of the drive.

The history of the body—or, indeed, the history of bodies and, beyond that, the histories of bodies—presumes the possibility of identifying a normal body, in which or on which changes and transformations can be traced across different parameters of time and space. Moreover, a history—any history, any kind of history—in order to locate and identify the body whose "story" it would tell, must postulate if only implicitly some kind of anti-body, and anomalous or pseudo-body. This anti-body marks the limit or horizon that the normative body, in the process of its development, evolution, or change, may not cross without ceasing to be a body proper and falling or degenerating into a condition of bodilessness. Everything depends on what the essence of bodilessness is conceived to be—whether bodilessness is thought to be an effect of, say, "spiritualization," or whether, by contrast, it is apprehended as a consequence of a degenerative process, a fall back or dispersal into some originary element, such as *mere* matter or, what amounts to the same thing, matter in general.

The body elevated to or by spirit or, per contra, degenerated into mere matter—these constitute the limits of possibility for the career of *the* body or all bodies, the boundary conditions that mark the line at which bodies cease to be bodies proper and become anti-bodies or better (worse) non-bodies. At least, so it would seem for the main line of the dominant thought about body and bodies in the Western Christian, humanist cultural tradition.

The semantic field called into being, created or invented by this double opposition (or body, on the one side, and both spirit and matter, on the other) implicitly constitutes the (or a) spirit with the function of *organ-ization* without which the body loses its finitude, location in space and time, and perceptibility. Body is matter *organ-ized,* which means (literally) *diversely instrumentalized,* since "organ" (Greek: *organon*) means "that with which one works," work presumed to be directed to a variety of different ends or purposes. The organs of the body, therefore, are presumed to be instruments in the service of different ends and purposes of the (mental) "faculties," on the one side, and the "senses," on the other. The notion of body, then, is no sooner identified as the union, fusion, or merger of spirit with matter than it is at once internally diversified (rendered unlike within itself and among its parts), each part instrumentalized (organ-ized), and each instrument assigned to the service of a mental faculty or physical sense. Whence the hierarchization of the parts of the body, since both the faculties and the senses that these parts serve are deemed more or less "spiritual" (lively) or more or less "material" (inert) in their natures.

The history of the body requires as a condition of its possible realization the preliminary definition of what we must—ironically—call the *corpus* of materials that will serve as the evidence or documentation of the process of development through which the body will be presumed to have passed in the c(o)urse of its articulation. We cannot write a history of the body-in-general, a generic body, because a history cannot, by definition, be about anything in general. A history must be about a specific thing and even better an individual thing, which is to say, an entity whose specificity is manifested in its particular attributes and their organ-ization. So we can't write a history of the body in general or even indeed of a species of body—such as the equine body, the feline body, the canine body, the female body, the male body, the human body, and so on—because species do not have histories except insofar as they undergo transformation through the variegation of their individual members. These members may be said to have "histories" only in the extent to which they escape description in terms of their species attributes alone and in their particular attributes attest to the nonspecificity of the species to which they are thought to belong. Every history is a story of the ways in which the individual (some individual) violates the specificity of species. The individual is a monster, but not all monsters are individuals.

So it is with bodies—or at least so it is with the history of bodies. The monstrous body or, rather, monstrous bodies alone can serve as the subject of any conceivable history of the body. For it is the monstrous that is the norm of all real bodies; the normal representative of a species can have no history since it serves as the ground against which the kind of changes we call "historical" can be measured. The normal—being an abstraction, a positive position derived by a negation of whatever is construed to incarnate negativity (either that or a statistical average of a population of variegated individuals or monsters)—has no history because it cannot change, its sole function being to define abnormal deviation from the norm (as against normal deviation from the norm allowed to those members of the population identified as comprising the normal species attributes).

Whence the rule: The corpus of materials to be treated in the historical investigation of anything whatsoever will be comprised of those documents which have to do with monsters. The history (or histories) of the body (or bodies) will and can only be a history (or histories) of the monstrous body (or bodies). The normal body can have no history. Moreover, the normal body exists as a possible object of investigation, not as a positivity, but only as a double negation, which is to say, a negation of whatever it is that the totality of monstrous bodies is presumed to lack.

So let us try to think of history as inhabited by vast congeries of types of monstrous bodies. A list—composed purely at random or impressionistically by this historian—might contain the following: (MALE): Moses, John the Baptist, Jesus, Nero, Attila, St. Simeon Stylites, Richard III, Luther, Henry VIII, Louis XIV, Robespierre, Napoleon, Byron, Lincoln, Darwin, Wilde, FDR, Michael Jackson, etc. (FEMALE): Deborah, Delilah, Semiramis, Cleopatra, Mary, "Pope Joan," Joan of Arc, St. Teresa of Avila, Marie Antoinette, Marilyn, Madonna, Mother Teresa, etc. You get the idea. I have divided my list into MALE and FEMALE, but surely the gender of the bodies indicated by these names is unimportant, indeed, indeterminable or at best undecidable. To our categories of MALE and FEMALE, we would have to add those of BOTH and NEITHER. In the presence of this list, the taxonomic system begins to come apart. Each of these names summons up a different image of a monstrous body, a body sick, mutilated, deformed, or metamorphosized by discipline or cosmetico-technical means. How are we to approach such bodies?

The approach can only be by way of the imagination. We must augment whatever visual images we may have of these monstrosities by an investigation of how they may have presented themselves to senses other than those of sight. Thus, we must try to imagine, not only how these bodies might have *looked,* but also and above all how they may have *sounded, smelled, felt,* and *tasted.* Think of the *sounds* that might have emanated from these monstrous bodies. Is there a kind of sound identifiable as having its source in the monstrous, as against the normal, body? The stench of the great ascetics, like the supposedly sweet odor of holiness, is a commonplace of the history of religion. Could we imagine a history of bodies as a history of the different ways that bodies smell? The smells of the body must have changed over the course of time and from place to place, along with diet, nutrition, cosmeticism, and the like. Modern techniques of chemical analysis would provide an interesting beginning for this line of inquiry.

And beyond this, of course, we might think of how these bodies may have *tasted.* What kind of liquids did they emit? From which orifices, and in what quantities? These are crucial questions, since the *condition* of the body, the human body, any organism, can be defined in terms of the nature and quantity of the liquids it exudes. Indeed, a whole spate of crucial taboos turns upon superstitions about the nature, quantity, and powers of the bodily fluids. Perhaps it is not so much death as rather the leakage of the body that is the source of ontological anxiety. What would *normal* tears, sweat, urine, faeces, blood, snot, cerumen (earwax) consist of? The body leaks, even when it has not been perforated, punctured, or otherwise penetrated. This is the physico-ontological truth on which the fortunes, not only of the redemptive religions and the medical professions, but also and above all of the cosmetic industry, depend. The care, control, disposal, and cultivation of the body's effusions provide the basis of all "culture."

BIBLIOGRAPHY

Abelove, Henry. "Some Speculations on the History of Sexual Intercourse during the Long Eighteenth Century in England." *Genders* 6 (1989): 125–30.

Abu-Lughod, Lila. "Can There Be a Feminist Ethnography?" *Women and Performance* 5, no. 9 (1990): 7–27.

Adams, H. F. *Advertising and Its Mental Laws*. New York: Macmillan, 1916.

Addison, Joseph, and Richard Steele. *The Spectator*, vol. 1, no. 3. London: Everyman's Library, Dent, 1906.

Adorno, Theodor W. "Perennial Fashion—Jazz." In *Prisms*, translated by Samuel Weber and Shierry Weber. Cambridge: MIT Press, 1981.

d'Alembert, J. le Rond. *La Liberté de la Musique, (1759). In Oeuvres* de d'Alembert, vol. I, p. 520. Manchester: Manchester University Press, 1991.

Anzaldúa, Gloria. *Borderlands/La Frontera: The New Mestiza*. San Francisco: Spinsters/Aunt Lute, 1987.

Appadurai, Arjun. "Disjuncture and Difference in the Global Cultural Economy." Public Culture 2, no. 2 (1990): 1–24.

Arac, Jonathan. *Critical Genealogies: Historical Situations for Postmodern Literary Studies*. New York: Columbia University Press, 1987.

Arico, Denise. "Retorica barocca come comportamento: Buona creanza e civil concersazione." Intersezioni 1 (1981): 338–56.

Assad, Talal, ed. *Anthropology and the Colonial Encounter*. 4th ed. Atlantic Highlands, N.J.: Humanities Press, 1988.

Atkinson, Paul, and Sara Delamont. "Mock-Ups and Cock-Ups: The Stage-Management of Guided Discovery Instruction." *In School Experience: Explorations in the Sociology* of Education, edited by P. Woods and E. Hammersley, 87–108. London: Croom Helm, 1977.

Attali, Jacques. *Noise: The Political Economy of Music*. Translated by Brian Massumi. Minneapolis: University of Minnesota Press, 1985.

Augustine, Saint, Bishop of Hippo. Confessions. Translated by R. S. Pine-Coffin. Harmondsworth: Penguin Classics, 1961.

Auslander, Philip. "Embodiment: The Politics of Postmodern Dance." The Drama Review T120 (Winter 1988): 7–23.

Austen, Jane. Emma. Edited by J. Kinsley. Oxford: Oxford University Press, 1990.

Bacilly, Bénigne de. *A Commentary upon the Art of Proper Singing*. Translated by Austen B. Caswell. New York: Institute of Mediaeval Music, 1968.

Baldwin, James. *Go Tell It on the Mountain*. New York: Dell, 1953.

———. *The Fire Next Time*. New York: Dial, 1963.

Banes, Sally. *Greenwich Village 1963: Avant-Garde Performance and the Effervescent Body*. Durham, N.C.: Duke University Press, 1993.

Barker-Benfield, G. J. *The Horrors of the Half-Known Life: Male Attitudes toward Women and Sexuality in Nineteenth-Century America*. New York: Harper and Row, 1976.

Barron, Stephanie, ed. *"Degenerate Art": The Fate of the Avant-Garde* in Nazi Germany. Los Angeles: Los Angeles County Museum of Art, 1991.

Barthes, Roland. *The Responsibility of Forms: Critical Essays on Music, Art, and* Representation. Translated by Richard Howard. New York: Hill and Wang, 1985.

————. *Camera Lucida: Reflections* on Photography. Translated by Richard Howard. New York: Farrar, Straus and Giroux, 1981.

————. "Lesson in *Writing.*" In *Image*, Music, Text. Translated by Stephen Heath. New York: Hill and Wang, 1977.

————. Empire of Signs. Translated by Richard Howard. New York: Hill and Wang, 1982.

————. "Change in the Object Itself: Mythology Today." In *Image*, Music, Text, 165–69. Translated by Stephen Heath. New York: Hill and Wang, 1977.

————. *Roland Barthes by* Roland Barthes. Translated by Richard Howard. New York: Hill and Wang, 1977.

————. "*Myth Today.*" In Mythologies, 109–157. Translated by Annette Lavers. New York: Noonday, 1972.

Bateson, Gregory. Steps to an Ecology of Mind. New York: Ballantine Books, 1972.

————. *Naven: A Survey of the Problems Suggested by a Composite Picture of the Culture of a New Guinea Tribe Drawn from Three* Points of View. Stanford: Stanford University Press, 1958.

Bateson, Gregory, and Margaret Mead. Balinese Character, a Photographic Analysis. New York: New York Academy of Sciences, 1942.

Baudrillard, Jean. *For a Critique of the Political Economy of the Sign.* Translated by Charles Levin. St. Louis: Telos, 1981.

————. Simulations. Foreign Agents Series. Translated by Paul Foss, Paul Patton, and Philip Beitchman. New York: Semiotext(e), 1983.

Bazerman, Charles. *Written Knowledge: The Genre and Activity of the Experimental Article* in Science. Madison: University of Wisconsin Press, 1988.

————. "Introduction to the Symposium: Rhetoricians on the Rhetoric of Science." *Science, Technology,* and Human Values 14, no. 1 (winter 1989): 3–6.

Beddoes, Thomas. Hygeia: Or Essays moral and medical. Bristol, 1802.

Belo, Jane, ed. Traditional Balinese Culture. New York: Columbia University Press, 1970.

Berry, Jason, Jonathan Foose, and Tad Jones. Up from the Cradle of Jazz: New Orleans Music since World War II. Athens: University of Georgia Press, 1968.

Biagioli, Mario. "Absolutism, the Modern State, and the Development of Scientific Manners." Critical Inquiry, forthcoming.

————. *Galileo Courtier: The Practice of Science in the Culture* of Absolutism. Chicago: University of Chicago Press, 1993.

————. "Scientific Revolution, Social Bricolage, and Etiquette." In The Scientific Revolution in National Context, edited by Roy Porter and Mikulas Teich, 11–54. Cambridge: Cambridge University Press, 1992.

Bianconi, Lorenzo. Music in the Seventeenth Century. Translated by David Bryant. Cambridge: Cambridge University Press, 1982.

Blanchot, Maurice. The Writing of the Disaster. Translated by Ann Smock. Lincoln: University of Nebraska Press, 1986.

Blau, Herbert. The Audience. Baltimore: Johns Hopkins University Press, 1990.

————. *Take* up the Bodies. Urbana: University of Illinois Press, 1982.

Bloch, Ernst, et al. Aesthetics and Politics. London: Verso, 1980.

Boas, Franziska, ed. *The Function of Dance in Human Society: A Seminar on* Primitive Society. New York: Boas School, 1944.

Bourdieu, Pierre. Homo Academicus. Paris: Editions de Minuit, 1984.

Bremer, Fredrika. America of the Fifties: Letters of Fredrika Bremer. Edited by Adolph B. Benson. New York: Oxford University Press, 1924.

Brown, Carolyn. "An Appetite for Motion." Dance Perspectives 34 (1968).

Brown, Michael E. The Production of Society. New York: Rowman and Littlefield, 1986.

————. "History and History's Problem." Social Text 16 (1986): 136–61.

Buckley, Sandra. "Penguin in Bondage." In Technoculture, edited by Constance Penley and Andrew Ross. Minneapolis: University of Minnesota Press, 1991.

Bulwer, John. Chirologia; or the Natural Language of the Hand, and Chironomia; or the Art of Manual Rhetoric. Edited by James W. Cleary. Carbondale: Southern Illinois University Press, 1974.

————. *Philocophus: Or, the Deafe and* Dumbe Mans Friend. London, 1648.

————. *Pathomyotomia, Or a Dissection of the Significative Muscles of the Affec*tions of the Minde. London, 1649.

————. *Anthropometamorphosis: Man Transform'd: Or, the Artificial Changling Historically Pre*sented . . . *with a Vindication of the Regular Beauty and* Honesty of Nature. London, 1653.

Burke, Peter. *The Fabrica*tion of Louis XIV. New Haven: Yale University Press, 1992.

Butler, Judith. "Gender Insubor*dination*." In Inside/Out, edited by Diana Fuss. New York: Rout*ledge, 1991.*

————. *Bodies that Matter: On the Discursive* Limits of "Sex." New York: Rout*ledge, 1993.*

————. *Gender Trouble: Feminism and the Subver*sion of Identity. New York: Routledge, 1990.

Calkins, *Earnest Elmo. The* Advertising Man. Vocational Series. New York: Scribner's, 1922.

Callon, Michel, and Bruno Latour. "Unscrewing the Big Leviathan: How Do Actors Macrostructure Reality and How Do Sociologists Help *Them Do So." In Advances in Social Theory* and Methodology, edited by K. Knorr and A. Ciourel. New York: Routledge and Kegan Paul, 1981.

Calvino, *Italo. If on a winter's* night a traveler. Translated by William Weaver. New York: Harcourt Brace Jovanovich, 1981.

Caplan, *Jay. Framed Narratives: Diderot's Genealogy* of the Beholder. Minneapolis: University of Minnesota Press, 1985.

Carlson, Marvin. "Theatre Audiences and the Reading of Per*formance." In Interpreting the* Theatrical Past. See Postlewait, 1989.

Case, Sue-Ellen. "Tracking *the Vampire." Differences 3, no. 2 (1991): 1–17.*

————. "Toward a Butch-Femme *Aesthetic." In Making a Spectacle: Feminist Essays on Con*temporary Women's Theatre, edited by Lynda Hart, 282–99. Ann Arbor: University of Michigan Press, 1989.

Castiglioni, *Baldesar. The Book* of the Courtier. New York: Anchor, 1959.

Cavell, Stanley. "Music Dis*composed." In Must We* Mean What We Say? Cambridge: Cambridge University Press, 1976.

Certeau, *Michel de. The* Writing of History. Translated by Tom Conely. New York: Columbia University Press, 1988.

Chambers, *Ross. Story and Situation: Narrative Seduction and the* Power of Fiction. Minneapolis: University of Minnesota Press, 1984.

Chartier, Roger. "Social Figuration and Habitus: Read*ing Elias." In C*ultural History, 71–94. Ithaca: Cornell University Press, 1988.

Chat*man, Seymour. Story and Discourse: Narrative Structure in* Fiction and Film. Ithaca: Cornell University Press, 1978.

Clément, *Catherine. Opera, or the Un*doing of Women. Translated by Betsy Wing. Minneapolis: University of Minnesota Press, 1988.

Clif*ford, James. The Predicament of Culture: Twentieth-Century Ethnography, Lit*erature, and Art. Cambridge: Harvard University Press, 1988.

Clifford, James, and Vivek Dhareshwar, *eds.* "Traveling Theories Traveling Theorists." Inscriptions 5 (1989).

Clifford, James, and George E. *Marcus, eds.* Writing Culture: The Poetics and Politics of Ethnography. Berkeley: University of California Press, 1986.

Cohen, Robert. "Why Does Oharu Fain*t? Mizoguchi's* The Life of Oharu and Patriarchal Discourse." *In Reframing Japanese Cinema: Authorship,* Genre, History, edited by Arthur Nolletti, Jr., and David Desser. Bloomington: Indiana University Press, 1992.

————, ed. "Foucauldian Necrologies: 'Gay Politics'? Poli*tically Gay?" T*extual Practice 2 (1988): 87–101.

Collins, *Harry M. Arti*ficial Experts. Cambridge: MIT Press, 1990.

————, ed. "Knowledge and Controversy." *Special issue of Social Stud*ies of Science 11 (1981): 3–158.

————, "The Seven Sexes: A Study in the Sociology of a Phenomenon, or the Replication of Experiments *in Physics." S*ociology 9 (1975): 205–224.

———. "The TEA Set: Tacit Knowledge and Scientific Networks." Science Studies 4 (1974): 165–86.

———. Changing Order: Replication and Induction in Scientific Practice. London: Sage, 1985.

Conquergood, Dwight. "Rethinking Ethnography: Towards a Critical Cultural Politics." Communication Monographs 58 (1991): 179–94.

Cooper, Kenneth, and Julius Zsako, trans. "George Muffat's Observations on the Lully Style of Performance." Musical Quarterly 53 (1967): 220–45.

Copeland, Roger, and Marshall Cohen, eds. What Is Dance? Readings in Theory and Criticism. Oxford: Oxford University Press, 1983.

Couperin, François. L'Art de Toucher le Clavecin. Leipzig: Breitkopf and Härtel, 1933.

Courlander, Harold. Negro Folk Music, U.S.A. New York: Columbia University Press, 1963.

Cowan, Jane. Dance and the Body Politic in Northern Greece. Princeton: Princeton University Press, 1992.

Coward, Rosalind. Female Desires: How They Are Sought, Bought, and Packaged. New York: Grove Press, 1985.

Crichton, Alexander. Inquiry into the Nature and Origins of Mental Derangement, vol. 2. London, 1799.

Dahlhaus, Carl. The Idea of Absolute Music. Translated by Roger Lustig. Chicago: University of Chicago Press, 1989.

d'Andrea, Gisela. "The New German Dance in the Weimar Republic." In Germany in the Twenties: The Artist as Social Critic. New York: Holmes and Meier, 1980.

Darnton, Robert. The Great Cat Massacre and Other Episodes in French Cultural History. New York: Vintage, 1985.

Daston, Lorraine. "Baconian Facts, Academic Civility, and the Prehistory of Objectivity." Annals of Scholarship 8 (1991): 337–63.

Davis, Natalie Zemon. "History's Two Bodies." The American Historical Review 93, no. 1 (Feb. 1988): 1–30.

Delaporte, François. Disease and Civilization: The Cholera in Paris, 1823. Translated by Arthur Goldhammer. Cambridge: MIT Press, 1986.

Dell, Cecily. A Primer for Movement Description Using Effort-Shape Analysis. New York: Dance Notation Bureau, 1970.

Dell'Antonio, Andrew. "The Sensual Sonata: Construction of Desire in Early Baroque Music," forthcoming.

Descartes, Réne. The Passions of the Soul. Translated by Stephen Voss. Indianapolis: Hackett, 1989.

Devereux, George. From Anxiety to Method in Behavioral Sciences. New York: Humanities Press, 1967.

Diamond, Irene, and Lee Quinby. Feminism and Foucault: Reflections on Resistance. Boston: Northeastern University Press, 1988.

Diamond, Stanley. In Search of the Primitive: A Critique of Civilization. New Brunswick, N.J.: Transaction, 1974.

Dictionnaire Encyclopédique des Sciences Medicales. 3rd. series, vol. 67. Paris, 1887.

Dilling, Margaret. "The Familiar and the Foreign: Music as Medium of Exchange in the Seoul Olympic Ceremonies." In Toward One World, 357–77.

Doane, Mary Ann. "Film and the Masquerade: Theorizing the Female Spectator." In Issues in Feminist Film Criticism. See Mulvey, 1990.

Douglass, Frederick. My Bondage and My Freedom. New York: Dover, 1969.

Dower, John. War without Mercy. New York: Pantheon, 1986.

Drewal, Margaret Thompson. Yoruba Ritual: Performers, Play, Agency. Bloomington: Indiana University Press, 1992.

Dreyfuss, Hubert. What Computers Can't Do. New York: Harper and Row, 1979.

Du Bois, W. E. B. The Philadelphia Negro. New York: Schocken, 1967.

Duncan, Isadora. Mitt Liv. Translated by Märta Lindqvist. Stockholm: Alfabeta, 1986.

Durrell, Lawrence. The Alexandria Quartet. New York: E. P. Dutton, 1961.

Eaton, S. How to Advertise a Bank.

———. *How to Make* Advertisement Pay.

Eichberg, Henning, et al. *Massenspiele: NS Thingspiel, Arbeiterweihespiel und olympisches* Zeremoniell. Stuttgart-Bad Cannstatt: Fromann-Holzboog, 1977.

———. "The Nazi Thingspiel: Theater for the Masses in Fascism and Proletarian *Culture.*" New German Critique 11 (1977): 133–50.

Engel, *Johan Jacob. Idées sur le geste et l'*action théâtrale. Geneva: Slatkine Reprints, 1990.

Engström, Albert. *August St*rindberg och Jag. Stockholm: Bonniers, 1923.

Evans-Pritchard, E. E. *The Nuer: A Description of the Modes of Livelihood and Political Institutions of a* Nilotic People. New York: Oxford University Press, 1978.

———. *Witchcraft, Oracles, and Magic* among the Azande. London: Clarendon Press, 1976.

Farenga, Vincent. "Periphrasis on the Origin *of* Rhetoric." MLN 94: 1033–55.

Fergusson, Erna. *Dancing Gods: Indian Ceremonials of New Mexico* and Arizona. Albuquerque: University of New Mexico Press, 1966.

Feyerabend, *Paul K.* Against Method. London: Verso, 1975.

Field, Norma. "Somehow: The Postmodern as At*mosphere.*" *In Postmode*rnism and Japan, edited by Masao Miyoshi and H. D. Harootunian. Durham, N.C.: Duke University Press, 1989.

Forte, Allen. *The Structure* of Atonal Music. New Haven: Yale University Press, 1973.

Foster, *Susan Leigh. Reading Dancing: Bodies and Subjects in Contemporary* American Dance. Berkeley: University of California Press, 1986.

Foucault, Michel. *The Histo*ry of Sexuality, vol 1. Translated by Robert Hurley. New York: Pantheon, 1978.

———. *Discipline and Punish: The Bir*th of the Prison. Translated by Alan Sheridan. New York: Pantheon, 1977.

———. *Madness and Civilization: A History of Insanity in th*e Age of Reason. Translated by Richard Howard. New York: Panthe*on, 1965.*

———. *The Order of Things: An Archaeology of the* Human Sciences. New York: Vintage, 1973.

Franko, Mark. *Dance As Text: Ideologies of t*he Baroque Body. New York: Cambridge University Press, 1993.

Fraser, Nancy. "Foucault's Body Language: A Post-Humanist Politica*l Rhe*toric?" Salmagundi 61 (1983): 55–70.

Freneuse, *Seigneur de. Comparaison de la musique italienne et de la musique française. In Source Readings* in Music. History, 489–507. See Strunk, 1950.

Freud, Sigmund. "Instincts and Their Vissi*citudes.*" *In On* Metapsychology, edited by Angela Richards and translated by James Strachey, vol. 11, 105–138. Harmonsworth: Pelican, 1984.

Galison, Peter. *How* Experiments End. Chicago: University of Chicago Press, 1988.

Gammand, Lorraine, and Margaret M*arshment, eds. The Female Gaze: Women As Viewers of* Popular Culture. Seattle: Real Comet, 1989.

Garafola, Lynn. *Diaghilev's* Ballets Russes. New York: Oxford University Press, 1989.

Gautier, *Théophile. Histoire de l'Art Dra*matique en France. 6 vols. Paris, 1858–1859.

Gay, Peter. *Weimar Culture: The Outs*ider As Insider. New York: Harper and Row, 1968.

Geertz, Clifford. "Slide Show: Evans-Pritchard's African Transpa*ren*cies." *In his Works and Lives: The Anthropol*ogist as Author. Stanford: Stanford University Press, 1988.

Giedion, Siegfried. *Mechaniza*tion Takes Command. New York: Oxford University Press, 1948.

Goebbels, *Joseph. Die Tagebücher von Joseph Goebbels: Sämt*liche Fragmente. Munich: K. G. Saur, 1987.

Goffman, *Erving. Gender* Advertisements. New York: Harper and Row, 1979.

Goldstein, *Jan. Console and Classify: The French Psychiatric Profession in th*e Nineteenth Century. Cambridge: Cambridge University Press, 1987.

Gooday, Graham. Paper on the laboratory-based training practices of late nineteenth-century English physicists. In the scientific journal Technology and Culture, forthcoming.

Gooding, David, et al., eds. The Uses of Experiment. Cambridge: Cambridge University Press, 1989.

Goody, Jack. The Domestication of the Savage Mind. New York: Cambridge University Press, 1977.

Greenblatt, Stephen. Shakespearean Negotiations. Berkeley: University of California Press, 1988.

Haraway, Donna. "The Promises of Monsters: A Regenerative Politics for Inappropriate/d Others." In Cultural Studies Now and in the Future, edited by Lawrence Grossberg, Cary Nelson, and Paula A. Treichler. New York: Routledge, 1991.

———. "Situated Knowledges: The Science Question in Feminism and the Privilege of the Partial Perspective." Feminist Studies 14, no. 3 (fall 1988): 575–600.

———. "Primatology Is Politics by Other Means." In Feminist Approaches to Science, edited by Ruth Bleier. New York: Pergamon, 1986.

———. "A Manifesto for Cyborgs: Science, Technology, and Socialist Feminism in the 1980s." Socialist Review 8, no. 2 (March-April 1985): 64–107.

Harootunian, H. D. Things Seen and Unseen: Discourse and Ideology in Tokugawa Nativism. Chicago: University of Chicago Press, 1988.

Hayes, Roland. Angel Mo' and Her Son. Boston: Little, Brown, 1942.

Hermand, Jost, and Frank Trommler. Die Kultur der Weimarer Republik. Munich: Nymphenburger Verlagslandlung, 1978.

Hilton, Wendy. "A Dance for Kings: The Seventeenth-Century French Courante." Early Music 5 (1977): 161–72.

Hirschbach, Frank, et al. Germany in the Twenties: The Artist as Social Critic. New York: Holmes and Meier, 1980.

"The Historical Ethnography of Scientific Rituals." Special issue of Social Epistemology 6, no. 4 (October-December 1992).

Hjärne, Boo. "Isadora Duncan." RidaℲ 3, no. 6 (1906).

Hobsbawm, Eric J. Nations and Nationalism Since 1780. Wiles Lectures. New York: Cambridge University Press, 1990.

Hudson, Richard. Passacaglio and Ciaccona: From Guitar Music to Italian Keyboard Variations in the Seventeenth Century. Ann Arbor: UMI Research Press, 1981.

Huizer, Genit, and Bruce Mannheim, eds. The Politics of Anthropology: From Colonialism and Sexism toward a View from Below. The Hague: Mouton Publishers, 1979.

Hume, David. "My Own Life." Appended to The History of England, vol. 1, part 5. Boston: Aldine Books, n.d.

Hunter, John. A Treatise on the Venereal Disease. London, 1766.

Huyssen, Andreas. After the Great Divide: Modernism, Mass Culture, Postmodernism. Bloomington: Indiana University Press, 1986.

Inglis, Fred. Media Theory. Cambridge, Mass.: Blackwell, 1990.

"Interview with Yvonne Rainer." Camera Obscura no. 1 (1976): 76–96.

Irigaray, Luce. Speculum of the Other Woman. Translated by Catherine Porter. Ithaca: Cornell University Press, 1985.

Isherwood, Christopher. Music in the Service of the King. Ithaca: Cornell University Press, 1973.

Jameson, Fredric. "Periodizing the Sixties." In The Sixties without Apology, edited by Sayers et al. Minnesota: University of Minnesota Press, 1984.

Jameson, Horatio. The American domestick medicine; or medical admonisher: containing some account of anatomy, the senses, diseases, casualties; a dispensatory, and glossary . . . designed for the use of families. Baltimore: F. Lucas, 1817.

John of Salisbury. Policratus. Translated by William Dalglish in "The Origin of the Hocket," Journal of the American Musicological Society 31 (1978): 3–20.

Johnson, Mark. The Body in the Mind: The Bodily Basis of Meaning, Imagination, and Reason. Chicago: University of Chicago Press, 1987.

Kaeppler, Adrienne. "Method and Theory in Analyzing Dance Structure with an Analysis of Tongan Dance." Ethnomusicology 16, no. 2 (1972): 173–217.

Kantorowicz, Ernst. *The King's Two Bodies*. Princeton: Princeton University Press, 1957.

Kapferer, Bruce. *Legends of People, Myths of State: Violence, Intolerance, and Political Culture in Sri Lanka and Australia*. Washington: Smithsonian Institution Press, 1988.

Kealiinohomoku, Joann. "Theory and Methods for an Anthropological Study of Dance." Ph.D. diss., Indiana University, 1976.

Kelly, Raymond. *The Nuer Conquest: The Structure and Development of an Expansionist System*. Ann Arbor: University of Michigan Press, 1985.

Kepler, Johann. *Ad Vitellionem paralipomena. . . .* Brussels: Culture and Civilization, 1968.

Kivy, Peter. *The Corded Shell: Reflections on Musical Expression*. Princeton: Princeton University Press, 1980.

Kiyoshi, Ezaki. *Shajo jinbutsu satsuei nyumon*. Tokyo: Kodaisha, 1938.

Knorr-Cetina, Karin. *The Manufacture of Knowledge: An Essay on the Constructivist and Contextual Nature of Science*. Oxford: Pergamon, 1981.

Knorr-Cetina, Karin, and Klaus Amann. "Image Dissection in Natural Scientific Inquiry." *Science, Technology* and *Human Values* 15, no. 3 (summer 1990): 259–83.

———. "What Is the Analysis of Scientific Rhetoric for? A Comment on the Possible Convergence between Rhetorical Analysis and Social Studies of Science." *Science, Technology* and *Human Values* 14, no. 1 (winter 1989): 47–49.

Koegler, Horst. "In the Shadow of the Swastika: Dance in Germany, 1927–1936." *Dance Perspectives* 57 (spring 1974).

———. "Mary Wigman ist im September in Berlin *gestorben*." Theater Heute 14, no. 11 (November 1973): 1–4.

———. "Tanz in den *Abgrund*." In *Ballet: Chronik und Bilanz des* Ballettjahres, 39–51. Velber bei Hannover: Friedrich, 1973.

———. "Tanz in die dreissiger Jahre." In *Ballet: Chronik und Bilanz des* Ballettjahres, 39–51. Velber bei Hannover: Friedrich, 1972.

Kondo, Dorinne. *Crafting Selves: Power, Gender, and Discourses of Identity in a Japanese Workplace*. Chicago: University of Chicago Press, 1990.

Kramer, Lawrence. "Culture and Musical Hermeneutics: The *Salome* Complex." *Cambridge Opera Journal* 2 (1990): 269–94.

Kuhn, Annette. *The Power of the Image: Essays on Representation and Sexuality*. London: Routledge and Kegan Paul, 1985.

Kuhn, Thomas. "Second Thoughts on Paradigms." In *The Essential Tension*, 293–319. Chicago: University of Chicago Press, 1977.

———. "The Function of Measurement in Modern Physical *Science*." In *The Essential Tension*, 178–224. See Kuhn, 1977.

Kurath, Gertrude Prokosch. *Half a Century of Dance Research: Essays by Gertrude Prokosch Kurath*. Flagstaff, Ariz.: Cross–Cultural Resources, 1970.

Kurath, Gertrude Prokosch, with Antonio Garcia. *Music and Dance of the Tewa Pueblos*. Santa Fe: Museum of New Mexico, 1970.

Laban, Rudolf von. *The Mastery of Movement*, 2d ed. London: MacDonald and Evans, 1960.

———. *Choreutics*. Edited by Lisa Ullmann. London: MacDonald and Evans, 1966.

———. *Modern Educational Dance*. London: MacDonald and Evans, 1948.

———. *A Life for Dance: Reminiscences*. Translated by Lisa Ullmann. New York: Theatre Arts Books, 1975.

Lang, Paul Henry. *George Frideric Handel*. New York: Norton, 1966.

Lanham, Richard A. *A Handlist of Rhetorical Terms: A Guide for Students of English Literature*. Berkeley: University of California Press, 1969.

Laqueur, Thomas. "Orgasm, Generation, and the Politics of Reproductive Biology." *Representations* 14 (1986): 1–41.

Laqueur, Walter. *Weimar: A Cultural History*. New York: Putnam's, 1974.

Larousse, Pierre. *Grande dictionnaire universel du XIXe siecle: français, historique, geographique. . . ,* vol. 14. Paris: Administration de Grand dictionnaire universel, 1875.

Latour, Bruno. *Science in Action*. Cambridge: Harvard University Press, 1987.

Latour, Bruno, and Steve Woolgar. Laboratory Life: The Social Construction of Scientific Facts. Beverly Hills, Calif.: Sage, 1979.

Lauretis, Teresa de. "Sexual Indifference and Lesbian Representation." In Performing Feminisms: Feminist Critical Theory and Theatre, edited by Sue-Ellen Case, 17–39. Baltimore: Johns Hopkins University Press, 1990.

Le Cerf de la Viéville, Jean Laurent. Comparison de la musique italienne et de la musique français. Paris: 1705. Partial translation in Oliver Strunk, Source Readings in Music History.

Leenhardt, Maurice. Do Kamo: Person and Myth in Melanesia. Mythology Series. New York: Arno, 1978.

Lellemand, C. F. Des Pertes Séminales Involuntaires, vol. 3. Paris, 1838–1842.

Leppert, Richard. The Sight of Sound: Music, Representation, and the History of the Body. Berkeley: University of California Press, 1993.

Lévi-Strauss, Claude. The Savage Mind. London: Weidenfeld and Nicolson, 1966.

Levine, Lawrence. Black Culture and Black Consciousness. New York: Oxford University Press, 1977.

Lienhardt, Godfrey. Divinity and Experience: The Religion of the Dinka. London: Oxford University Press, 1961.

Lipsitz, George. Time Passages: Collective Memory and American Popular Culture. Minneapolis: University of Minnesota Press, 1990.

———. Class and Culture in Cold War America: "A Rainbow at Midnight." South Hadley, Mass.: Bergin and Garvey, 1982.

Little, Meredith Ellis. "Recent Research in European Dance, 1400–1800." Early Music 14 (1986): 4–14.

———. "The Contribution of Dance Steps to Musical Analysis and Performance: La Bourgogne." Journal of the American Musicological Society 28 (1975): 112–24.

———. "Dance under Louis XIV and XV: Some Implications for the Musician." Early Music 3 (1975): 331–340.

Lomax, Alan. The Land Where the Blues Began. New York: Pantheon, 1993.

Longino, Helen. Science As Social Knowledge: Values and Objectivity in Scientific Inquiry. Princeton: Princeton University Press, 1990.

Loraux, Nicole. "Therefore, Socrates Is Immortal." In Zone 4: Fragments for a History of the Human Body, Part Two.

Luxon, Thomas. "The Place of Displacement: The Self's Other in Paul, Genesis, and Reformation Typology." Unpublished ms.

Lynch, Michael. Art and Artifact in Laboratory Science. London: Routledge, 1985.

———. "Discipline and the Material Form of Images: An Analysis of Scientific Visibility." Social Studies of Science 15: 37–66.

Lyotard, Jean-François. The Postmodern Condition: A Report on Knowledge. Minneapolis: University of Minnesota Press, 1984.

MacAloon, John J. Brides of Victory: Gender and Nationalism in Olympic Ritual, forthcoming.

———. "Olympic Games and the Theory of Spectacle in Complex Societies." In Rite, Drama, Festival, Spectacle: Rehearsals toward a Theory of Cultural Performances, edited by John MacAloon, 241–80. Philadelphia: Institute for the Study of Human Issues, 1984.

Maletic, Vera. Body, Space, Expression: The Development of Rudolf Laban's Movement and Dance Concepts. New York: Mouton de Gruyter, 1987.

Malinowski, Bronislaw. A Diary in the Strict Sense of the Term. London: Routledge, 1967.

———. Argonauts of the Western Pacific. New York: E. P. Dutton, 1961.

Manning, Susan. Ecstasy and the Demon: Feminism and Nationalism in the Dances of Mary Wigman. Berkeley: University of California Press, 1993.

Marchand, Roland. Advertising the American Dream: Making Way for Modernity, 1920–1940. Berkeley: University of California Press, 1985.

Marin, Louis. Portrait of the King. Translated by Martha M. Houle. Minneapolis: University of Minnesota Press, 1988.

Marshall, Paule. Praise Song for the Widow. New York: E. P. Dutton, 1984.

Martin, John. *Introduction to Dance.* New York: Norton, 1939.

Martin, Randy. *Performance as Political Act: The Embodied Self.* Westport, Conn.: Greenwood Press, 1990.

Mather, Betty Bang. *Interpretation of French Music from 1675–1775 for Woodwind and Other Performers.* New York: McGinnis and Marx, 1973.

Mattheson, Johann. *Der vollkommene Capellmeister.* Translated by Ernest Harriss. Ann Arbor: UMI Research Press, 1981.

Mauss, Marcel. "Techniques of the Body." *Economy and Society* 2, no. 1 (Feb. 1973): 70–87.

McClary, Susan. "Narrative Agendas in 'Absolute' Music: Identity and Difference in Brahms' Third *Symphony.*" In *Musicology and Difference: Gender and Sexuality in Music Scholarship,* edited by Ruth Solie, 326–44. Berkeley: University of California Press, 1993.

———. *Georges Bizet: Carmen.* Cambridge Opera Handbooks. Cambridge: Cambridge University Press, 1992.

———. *Feminine Endings: Music, Gender,* and Sexuality. Minneapolis: University of Minnesota Press, 1991.

McClary, Susan, and Robert Walser. "Start Making Sense: Musicology Wrestles with Rock." In *On Record: Rock, Pop, and the Written Word,* edited by Simon Frith and Andrew Goodwin. New York: Pantheon, 1990.

Mead, Margaret, and Frances Cooke MacGregor. *Growth and Culture: A Photographic Study of Balinese Childhood.* New York: Putnam, 1951.

Mellors, Wilfrid. *François Couperin and the French Classical Tradition.* New York: Dover, 1968.

Meyer, Morris. "I Dream of Jeannie: Transsexual Striptease As Scientific Display." *The Drama Review* 35 (1991): 25–42.

Miller, Daniel. *Material Culture and Mass Consumption.* Cambridge, Mass.: Blackwell, 1987.

Mizoguchi, Kenji, director. *The Life of Oharu.* Saikaku ichidai onna, 1952.

Moi, Toril. *Sexual/Textual Politics: Feminist Literary Theory.* London: Routledge, 1988.

Montaigne, Michel de. *Journal de voyage en Italie par la Suisse et L'Allemagne en 1580 et 1581.* Edited by M. Rat, Garnier. Paris, n.d.

———. *Complete Works: Essays, Travel Journal, Letters.* Translated by Donald M. Frame. Stanford, Calif.: Stanford University Press, 1957.

Mørk, Ebbe. "Husk Mig for Min Dunst Ikke for Mine Elskere." *Politikken,* October 12, 1969.

Moss, Suzan. "Spinning through the Weltanschauung: The Effects of the Nazi Regime on the German Modern Dance." Ph.D. diss., New York University, 1988.

Muller, Albert. *Ueber unwillkurliche Samenverluste.* Rorschach: Louis Huber Verlag, 1869.

Müller, Hedwig. "Dokumentation: 3. Deutscher Tänzerkongress, München 1930." *Tanzdrama* 13 (1990): 17–29.

———. *Mary Wigman: Leben und Werk der grossen Tänzerin.* Berlin: Quadriga, 1986.

———. "Wigman and National Socialism." *Ballet Review* 15, no. 1 (Spring 1987): 65–73.

Müller, Hedwig, and Norbert Servos. "From Isadora Duncan to Leni Riefenstahl." *Ballett International* 5:4 (April 1982): 14–23.

Mulvey, Laura. "Visual Pleasure and Narrative Cinema." In *Issues in Feminist Film Criticism,* edited by Patricia Erens. Bloomington: Indiana University Press, 1990.

Myerhoff, Barbara. *Number Our Days.* New York: Simon and Schuster, 1978.

Ness, Sally Ann. *Body, Movement, and Culture: Kinesthetic and Visual Symbolism in a Philippine Community.* Philadelphia: University of Pennsylvania Press, 1992.

New York Nation, May 30, 1867.

Nietzsche, Friedrich. *The Birth of Tragedy, and the Case of Wagner.* Translated by Walter Kaufmann. New York, Vintage, 1967.

Nishikawa, Tetsuji. *Preface to Tristan Electron-Positron Colliding Beam Project.* Tristan Project Group, KEK report 86–14. Japan: National Laboratory for High Energy Physics, 1987.

Novack, Cynthia. *Sharing the Dance: Contact Improvisation and American Culture*. Madison, Wis.: University of Wisconsin Press, 1990.

Okamoto, Ippei. "Heiki no Heitaro." In Ippei Zenshu, vol. 13. Tokyo: Senshinska, 1930.

Oliver, A. R. *The Encyclopaedists as Critics of Music*. New York: Columbia University Press, 1947.

Onuki-Tierny, Emiko. *The Monkey As Mirror: Symbolic Transformations in Japanese History and Ritual*. Princeton: Princeton University Press, 1987.

Ortner, Sherry. "Theory in Anthropology Since the Sixties." *Comparative Studies in Society and History* 26 (1984): 126–66.

———. "The Virgin and the State." *Feminist Studies* 4, no. 3 (1978): 19–35.

Outram, Dorinda. *The Body in the French Revolution: Sex, Class and Political Culture*. New Haven, Conn.: Yale University Press, 1989.

Page, Christopher. *The Owl and the Nightingale: Musical Life and Ideas in France, 1100–1300*. Berkeley: University of California Press, 1991.

Parrish, Lydia. *Slave Songs of the Georgia Sea Islands*. Hatboro, Pa.: Folklore Associates, 1965.

Payne, Daniel. *Recollections of Seventy Years*. New York: Arno, 1968.

Peiss, Kathy. "Making Faces: The Cosmetics Industry and the Cultural Construction of Gender, 1890–1930." *Genders* 7 (March 1990): 143–69.

The Personal Narratives Group, eds. *Interpreting Women's Lives: Feminist Theory and Personal Narratives*. Bloomington: Indiana University Press, 1989.

Phelan, Peggy. *Unmarked: The Politics of Performance*. New York: Routledge, 1993.

Piacenza, Domenica da. *De arte saltandi et choreas ducendi: De la arte di ballare et danzare [1416]*.

Plato. Timaeus. Translated by Francis Cornford. New York: Bobbs Merrill, 1959.

———. *The Republic*. In *The Collected Dialogues of Plato*. Edited by Edith Hamilton and Huntington Cairus. New York: Pantheon, 1966.

Polanyi, Livia. *Telling the American Story: A Structural and Cultural Analysis of Conversational Storytelling*. Cambridge: MIT Press, 1987.

Polanyi, Michael. *Personal Knowledge*. London: Routledge, 1958.

Postlewait, Thomas. "Autobiography and Theatre History." In *Interpreting the Theatrical Past: Essays in the Historiography of Performance*, edited by Thomas Postlewait, 248–72. Iowa City: University of Iowa Press, 1989.

Preston-Dunlop, Valerie. "Laban and the Nazis." *Dance Theatre Journal* 6, no. 2 (May 1989): 155–68.

Radcliffe-Brown, A. R. *The Adaman Islanders*. Cambridge: Cambridge University Press, 1933.

Ralph, Richard. *The Life and Works of John Weaver: An Account of His Life, Writing and Theatrical Productions, with an Annotated Reprint of His Complete Publications*. New York: Dance Horizons, 1985.

Rameau, Jean-Philippe. *Démonstration du principe de l'harmonie*. Paris, 1750.

Restivo, Sal. "Multiple Realities, Scientific Objectivity, and the Sociology of Knowledge." *Reflections* 1, no. 1 (Summer 1980): 61–76.

Restivo, Sal, and Julia Loughlin. "Critical Sociology of Science and Scientific Validity." *Knowledge: Creation, Diffusion, Utilization* 8, no. 3 (March 1987): 486–508.

Restivo, Sal, and Michael Zenzen. "The Mysterious Morphology of Immiscible Liquids." *Social Science Information* (1982).

Rice, Anne. *Cry to Heaven*. New York: Pinnacle, 1982.

Rich, Adrienne. *On Lies, Secrets and Silence*. New York: Norton, 1979.

Rilke, Rainer Maria. *The Selected Poetry of Rainer Maria Rilke*. Translated by Stephen Mitchel. New York: Vintage, 1989.

Roach, Joseph. "Power's Body: The Inscription of Morality as Style." In *Interpreting the Theatrical Past: Essays in the Historiography of Performance*, edited by Thomas Postlewait and Bruce A. McConachie. Iowa City: University of Iowa Press, 1989.

———. "Theatre History and the Ideology of the Aesthetic." *Theatre Journal* 41, no. 2 (May 1989): 155–68.

Robertson, Jennifer. "The Politics of Androgyny in Japan: Sexuality and Subversion in the Theater and Beyond." American Ethnologist 19, no. 3 (August 1992): 1–24.

Robeson, Paul. "I Want to Be African." In Paul Robeson: Tributes, 55–59. New York: The Paul Robeson Archives, 1976.

Rosaldo, Renato. "From the Door of His Tent: The Fieldworker and the Inquisitor." In Writing Culture: The Poetics and Politics of Ethnography, edited by James Clifford and George Marcus. Berkeley: University of California Press, 1986.

Rosand, Ellen. Opera in Seventeenth-Century Venice: The Creation of a Genre. Berkeley: University of California Press, 1989.

Rothenbuhler, Eric. "Values and Symbols in Orientations to the Olympics." Critical Studies in Mass Communication 6, no. 2 (1989): 138–57.

———. "The Living Room Celebration of the Olympic Games." Journal of Communication 38, no. 4 (1988): 61–81.

Rousseau, Jean-Jacques. "Le Luxe, Le Commerce et Les Arts." In (Oeuvres Complètes, edited by Bernard Gagnebin and Marcel Raymond, vol. 3, 516–24. Bibliothèque de la Pléiade, vol. 11, no. 153. Paris: Gallimard, 1959.

Russell, John. "Wannabe Black? The Imaging of African-Americans in Contemporary Japan." Unpublished.

Sahlins, Marshall. "China Modernizing, or Vice-Versa." In Toward One World, beyond All Boundaries: The Seoul Olympic Anniversary Conference, edited by Koh Byong-ik, vol. 1, 78–96. Seoul, 1990.

Savigliano, Marta. Tango and the Political Economy of Passion. Boulder, Col.: Westview, 1994.

Saxon, Lyle, Edward Dreyer, and Robert Tallant. Gumbo Ya-Ya: A Collection of Louisiana Folk Tales. Gretna, La.: Pelican, 1988.

Scarry, Elaine. The Body in Pain: The Making and Unmaking of the World. New York: Oxford University Press, 1985.

Schaffer, Simon. "Self Evidence." Critical Inquiry 18 (1992): 327–62.

———. "Glass Works: Newton's Prisms and the Uses of Experiment." In The Uses of Experiment, 67–104. See Gooding, 1989.

Schechner, Richard. Between Theater and Anthropology. Philadelphia: University of Pennsylvania Press, 1985.

Schrader, Bärbel, and Jürgen Schebera. The "Golden" Twenties: Art and Literature in the Weimar Republic. New Haven: Yale University Press, 1988.

Schudson, Michael. Advertising, the Uneasy Persuasion: Its Dubious Impact on American Society. New York: Basic, 1984.

Secondat, Charles-Louis de, Baron Montesquieu. Persian Letters. Translated by C. J. Betts. Harmondsworth: Penguin, 1973.

Servos, Norbert. "Pathos and Propaganda? On the Mass Choreography of Fascism." Ballett International 13, no. 1 (January 1990): 62–66.

———. Pina Bausch Wuppertal Dance Theater. Cologne: Ballett-Bühnen Verlag, 1984.

———. "Whether to Resist or Conform: Ausdruckstanz Then and Now?" Ballett International 10, no. 1 (January 1987): 18–21.

Shapin, Steven. "A Scholar and Gentleman: The Problematic Identity of the Scientific Practitioner in Early Modern England." History of Science 29 (September 1991): 279–327.

———. "The House of Experiment in Seventeenth-Century England." Isis 79, no. 296 (1988): 373–405.

Shapin, Steven, and Simon Schaffer. Leviathan and the Air-Pump. Princeton: Princeton University Press, 1985.

Shorter, Edward. The Making of the Modern Family. New York: Basic, 1977.

Silverberg, Miriam. "Remembering Pearl Harbor, Forgetting Charlie Chaplin, and the Case of the Disappearing Western Woman." Positions 1, no. 1 (spring 1993): 24–76.

———. "Constructing the Japanese Ethnography of Modernity." The Journal of Asian Studies 51, no. 1 (February 1992): 30–54.

———. "Constructing a New Cultural History of *Modern Japan*." Boundary 2. Special issue on "Japan in the World," vol. 18, no. 3 (fall 1991): 61–89.

———. "The Modern Girl as *Militant*." In *Recreating Japanese Women*, 1600–1945, edited by Gail Bernstein, 239–66. Berkeley: University of California Press, 1991.

———. *Changing Song: The Marxist Manifestos of Nakano Shigeharu*. Princeton: Princeton University Press, 1990.

Smith, Michael. *The Mardi Gras Indians* of New Orleans. New Orleans: Pelican, 1994.

Snell, Robert. *Théophile Gautier: A Romantic Critic of the Visual Arts*. New York: Oxford University Press, 1982.

Sontag, Susan. "Fascinating Fascism." *New York* Review of Books (February 6, 1975): 23–30.

Sorell, Walter. *The Mary Wigman Book*. Middletown, Conn.: Wesleyan University Press, 1975.

Spencer, Paul, ed. *Society* and the Dance. Cambridge: Cambridge University Press, 1985.

Stearns, Marshall. *The Story of Jazz*. London: Oxford University Press, 1970.

Spivak, Gayatri Chakravorty. *In Other Worlds: Essays in Cultural Politics*. New York: Routledge, 1988.

Stevens, Wallace. "Thirteen Ways of Looking at a *Blackbird*." In *The Palm at the End of the Mind: Selected* Poems and a Play. Edited by Holly Stevens. New York: Vintage, 1972.

Stokes, Geoffrey, Ken Tucker, and Ed Ward. *Rock of Ages: The Rolling Stone History* of Rock and Roll. New York: Rolling Stone, 1986.

Strunk, Oliver. *Source Readings* in Music History. New York: Norton, 1950.

Stuckey, Sterling. " 'Ironic Tenacity': Frederick Douglass' Seizure of the *Dialectic*." In *Frederick Douglass: New Literary and Historical Essays*, edited by Eric Sundquist, 23–32. New York: Cambridge University Press, 1991.

———. *Slave Culture: Nationalist Theory and the Foundations of Black America*. New York: Oxford University Press, 1987.

Sweet, Jill D. *Dances of the Tewa Pueblo Indians*. Santa Fe, N.M.: School of American Research, 1985.

Taketoshi, Yamamoto. *Kokoku no Shakaishi*. Tokyo: Hosei Daigaku Shuppanska, 1984.

———, ed. *Mannensha Kokoku Nenpan*. Reprint. 18 vols. Tokyo: Ochanomizu Hobo, 1984.

Tany, Thomas. *TheaurauJohn His Aurora in Trandagorum in Salem Gloria, Or the discussive of the Law and Gospell betwixt the Jew and the Gentile in Salem Resurrectionem*. London, 1655.

Taruskin, Richard. "The Pastness of the Present and Presence of the Past." In *Authenticity* and Early Music, edited by Nicholas Kenyon, 137–207. Oxford: Oxford University Press, 1988.

Taylor, John Tinnon. *Early Opposition to the English Novel*. New York: Columbia University Press, 1943.

Thomas, Gary. "Was George Frideric Handel Gay? On Closet Questions and Cultural *Politics*." In *Queering the Pitch: The New Gay and Lesbian Musicology*. Edited by Philip Brett, Elizabeth Wood, and Gary Thomas. New York: Routledge, 1994.

Thomas, Helen, ed. *Dance, Gender and Culture*. London: Macmillan, 1993.

Tissot, S. A. *A Treatise on the Curse of Onan*. London: B. Thomas, 1766.

Traweek, Sharon. "Border Crossings: Narrative Strategies in Science Studies and among Physicists in Tsukuba Science City, Japan." In *Science As Practice* and Culture, edited by Andrew Pickering, 429–66. Chicago: University of Chicago Press, 1992.

———. *Beamtimes* and Lifetimes. Cambridge: Harvard University Press, 1988.

Trinh, T. Minh-ha. *Women, Native, Other: Writing Postcoloniality* and Feminism. Bloomington: Indiana University Press, 1989.

Tyler, Stephen A. "Post-Modern Ethnography: From Document of the Occult to Occult *Document*." In *Writing Culture: The Poetics and Politics* of Ethnography. Edited by James Clifford and George Marcus. Berkeley: University of California Press, 1986.

Ulmer, Gregory L. "The Object of Post-*Criticism*." In *The Anti-Aesthetic: Essays on Post-modern Culture*. Edited by Hal Foster. Seattle: Bay Press, 1983.

Vail, June. "Issues of Style: Four Modes of Journalistic Dance Criticism." In *Looking at Dance: Critics* on Criticism, edited by Susan Lee and Lynne Anne Blum. Pittsburgh: University of Pittsburgh Press, 1993.

Venette, Nicholas. *Conjugal Love or the Pleasures of* the Marriage Bed. London, 1750.

Wallace, Michele. *Invisibility Blues: F*rom Pop to Theory. London, Verso, 1991.

Wallis, Brian. "Telling Stories: A Fictional Approach to Artists' *Writings. In Blasted Allegories: An Anthology of Contem*porary Artists, edited by Brian Wallis. Cambridge: MIT Press, 1987.

Walser, Robert. *Running with the Devil: Power, Gender, and Madness in H*eavy Metal Music. Middletown, Conn: Wesleyan University Press, 1993.

Weaver, John. *The Life and Works of* John Weaver, ed. Richard Ralph. New York: Dance Horizons, 1985.

Weintraub, Karl. "Autobiography and Historical *Consciousness." C*ritical Inquiry 1, no. 4 (1975): 821–48.

Whigham, Frank. *Ambition and Privilege: The Social Tropes of Elizabethan* Courtesy Theory. Berkeley: University of California Press, 1984.

White, Hayden. *The Content of the Form: Narrative Discourse and Historical* Representation. Baltimore: Johns Hopkins University Press, 1987.

Wigman, Mary. *Deut*sche Tanzkunst. Dresden: Carl Reissner, 1935.

———. *The Language of* Dance. Middletown, Conn.: Wesleyan University Press, 1966.

Willett, John. *Art and Politics in t*he Weimar Period. New York: Pantheon, 1978.

Williams, Raymond. *The Politics of Modernism: Against the New* Conformists. Edited by Tony Pinkney. London: V*erso, 1993.*

———. *The Socio*logy of Culture. New York: Schocken, 1982.

———. *The* Long Revolution. London: Cox and Wyman, 1961.

Wittgenstein, Ludwig. *Philosophical In*vestigations. Oxford: Blackwell, 1953.

Wittig, Monique. The Lesbian Body. Translated by David Le Vay. London: Peter Owen, 1975.

Woolf, Virginia. *Ogonblick av Liv* (Moments of Being). Translated by Harriet Alfons. Stockholm: Alba, 1977.

Woolgar, Steve. "Discovery and Logic in a *Scientific Text." In Advances in Social Theory and Methodology: Toward an Integration of Micro- and* Macro-Sociologies, edited by K. Knorr and A. Ciourel. New York: Routledge and Kegan Paul, 1981.

———. "What Is the Analysis of Scientific Rhetoric for? A Comment on the Possible Convergence between Rhetorical Analysis and Social Studies *of Science." Scied by Nicholas* Kenyon, 137–207. Oxford: Oxford University Press, 1988.

Taylor, John Tinnon. Early Opposition to the English Novel. New York: Columbia University erican Shakers—Person, Time, Space, and Dance-Ritual." Ph.D. diss., Columbia University, 1983.

Zarlino, Gioseffo. *Istitutio*ni harmoniche. Venice, 1573.

Zizek, Slavoj. *The Sublime Obj*ect of Ideology. London: Verso, 1989.

NOTES ON CONTRIBUTORS

Mario Biagioli teaches history of science in the Department of History at the University of California, Los Angeles, and is co-director of its Center for Cultural Studies of Science. He has written about the history of early modern science, science at court, Nazi science, and science museums, and is the author of *Galileo, Courtier: The Practice of Science in the Culture of Absolutism* (1993).

Sue-Ellen Case, professor of English at the University of California, Riverside, is the author of *Feminism and Theatre* (1988) and the editor of several anthologies of performance theory and criticism. She is currently at work on a new book titled *Performing Lesbian in the Age of Technology*. Her meditations for this volume follow her articles "The Butch-Femme Aesthetic" and "Tracking the Vampire."

Susan Leigh Foster, choreographer, dancer, and writer, is professor and chair of the Department of Dance at the University of California, Riverside. Her book *Reading Dancing: Bodies and Subjects in Contemporary American Dance* (1986) received the De La Torre Bueno prize for scholarship on dance. She is currently completing work on *Storying Bodies: The Choreography of Narrative and Gender in the French Action Ballet*.

Stephen Greenblatt is professor of English at the University of California, Berkeley. His books include *Renaissance Self-Fashioning: From More to Shakespeare* (1980), *Shakespearean Negotiations: The Circulation of Social Energy in Renaissance England* (1988), *Learning to Curse: Essays in Early Modern Culture* (1990), and *Marvelous Possessions: The Wonder of the New World* (1991). He is a founder and editor of the journal *Representations*, and he is currently at work as the general editor of the *Norton Shakespeare*.

Lena Hammergren is research fellow and director of the Dance Studies Division within Theatre and Film Studies at Stockholm University. She is the author of *Form och Mening i Dansen* (*Form and Meaning in Dance*) (1991), a study of Mary Wigman and Birgit Akesson. Her current work concerns twentieth-century dance in relation to Swedish body politics.

Thomas W. Laqueur is professor of history at the University of California, Berkeley, and director of The Doreen B. Townsend Center for the Humanities. He is the author of *Religion and Respectability: Sunday Schools and the Working Class Culture, 1780-1850* (1976) and *Making Sex: Body and Gender from the Greeks to Freud* (1990), and co-editor of *The Making of the Modern Body: Sexuality and Society in the Nineteenth Century* (1987).

John J. MacAloon is professor of social sciences at the University of Chicago. His anthropological and historical research focuses on performance theory, intercultural relations, and political cultures of sport. His books include *This Great Symbol: Pierre de Coubertin and the Origins of the Modern Olympic Games* (1981), *The Olympics and Intercultural Exchange in the World System* (1988), and the forthcoming *Brides of Victory: Gender and Nationalism in Olympic Ritual*.

Susan A. Manning is the author of *Ecstasy and the Demon: Feminism and Nationalism in the Dances of Mary Wigman* (1993). Her current research concerns the formation of a national identity for American dance at mid-century. She is associate professor in the departments of English and Theater and an affiliate of the interdisciplinary Ph.D. program in theater and drama at Northwestern University.

Randy Martin, associate professor of sociology at the Pratt Institute and a dancer, is the author of *Performance as Political Act: The Embodied Self* (1990) and *Socialist Ensembles: Theater and State in Cuba and Nicaragua* (1994), and co-editor of the forthcoming *New Studies in the Politics and Culture of U.S. Communism*.

Susan McClary, professor of musicology at McGill University, has published critical essays on music, ranging from Monteverdi to Madonna. Her most recent books include *Feminine Endings: Music, Gender, and Sexuality* (1991) and *Georges Bizet: Carmen* (1992). She has written and produced a music-theater piece titled "Susanna Does the Elders" (1987), and she recently delivered the Ernest Bloch Lectures at the University of California, Berkeley.

Cynthia J. Novack, associate professor of dance at Wesleyan University, is an anthropologist and dancer/choreographer. Her publications include the ethnography *Sharing the Dance: Contact Improvisation and American Culture* (1990) and articles in *Women and Performance*, *The Drama Review*, and several anthologies of writing about dance, anthropology, and cultural criticism. She is currently working on a collection of writings about choreography and improvisation based on the work of the Richard Bull Dance Theatre.

Peggy Phelan is the author of *Unmarked: The Politics of Performance* (1993), and co-editor of *Acting Out: Feminist Performances* (1993). She is chair of the Department of Performance Studies, Tisch School of the Arts, New York University.

Joseph Roach, professor of English at Tulane University, has written previously on the history of performance, gesture, and expression, including *The Player's Passion: Studies in the Science of Acting* (1985), which has recently been republished in paper by the University of Michigan Press. He co-edited *Critical Theory and Performance* (1992) and is associate editor of *Theatre Journal*, *Theatre History Studies*, and *Text and Performance Quarterly*.

Miriam Silverberg teaches modern Japanese history at the University of California, Los Angeles. She is the author of *Changing Song: The Marxist Manifestos of Nakano Shigeharu* (1990) and essays such as "The Modern Girl as Militant" in Gail Bernstein, ed., *Recreating Japanese Women, 1600-1945* (1991), and "Constructing a New Cultural History of Modern Japan" in Masao Miyoshi and H.D. Harootunian, eds., *Japan in the World* (1993). She is currently writing *The Japanese Culture of Modernity*.

P. Sterling Stuckey is professor of history at the University of California, Riverside. He is the author of *Slave Culture: Nationalist Theory and the Foundations of Black America* (1987) and *Going through the Storm: The Influence of African American Art in History* (1994). He is currently working on two book projects: a study of Herman Melville's *Benito Cereno* for Cambridge University Press and an extended treatment of the Ring Shout during and following slavery.

Sharon Traweek is professor of history at UCLA and director of the Center for the Cultural Study of Science and Technology. She is the author of *Beamtimes and Lifetimes: The World of High Energy Physicists*.

Hayden White is University Professor at the University of California and professor of history of consciousness at the University of California, Santa Cruz. He is the author of *Metahistory: The Historical Imagination in Nineteenth-Century Europe* (1973), *Tropics of Discourse: Essays in Cultural Criticism* (1978), and *The Content of the Form: Narrative Discourse and Historical Representation* (1987).

INDEX